T0367525

CAPITALISM

CAPITALISM
A MODERN ECONOMIC HISTORY

Edmund Clingan

iUniverse

CAPITALISM
A MODERN ECONOMIC HISTORY

iUniverse books may be ordered through booksellers or by contacting:

iUniverse
1663 Liberty Drive
Bloomington, IN 47403
www.iuniverse.com
1-800-Authors (1-800-288-4677)

ISBN: 978-1-4917-7214-0 (sc)
ISBN: 978-1-4917-7213-3 (e)

Library of Congress Control Number: 2015911262

Print information available on the last page.

iUniverse rev. date: 07/22/2015

CONTENTS

PREFACE

I began teaching this course at Queensborough Community College in 2007 on the eve of the financial crisis. I had been publishing work in German history, especially in the era of the Depression, and was starting work on the impact of economic wealth on international power. That book eventually became *Twilight's Last Gleaming*. As I researched that book, it became clear to me that very few people understood economic history. I knew that economic history had shriveled in my own discipline and was scorned in economics. As I guided that first class in 2007, I taught that the historical record suggested huge problems ahead for the global economy. I would like to think that the class benefited and perhaps profited from my warnings, which were vindicated within a year. In the classes that have followed, I have consistently had problems getting the students to read and comprehend the textbook. There are a few good textbooks on economic history, but their prose is too dense and their assumptions of prior knowledge too broad. I have produced a book that uses plain words, assumes no prior knowledge of history or economics, and omits mathematical equations.

Like most children, economic and financial matters mystified me though I knew they were important. I was riveted by John Kenneth Galbraith's series for the BBC, *The*

Age of Uncertainty. It was a clear and humorous explanation of economic ideas and their consequences and probably remains the single biggest influence on my approach to the subject. Years later, as a graduate student at the University of Wisconsin-Madison, I had the privilege of hearing Galbraith speak. Here was an economic vision both easy to grasp and with high predictive ability.

I was moved to write *Twilight's Last Gleaming* in the years when the U.S. economy was stagnating and public figures on television, newspapers, and magazines could not explain why. During my research, I came to understand the enormous role of energy in economic history. This was the missing piece of the puzzle. During my childhood, there had been two "energy crises," but close examination had revealed to me that these were not true problems of supply and demand and of course the oil price crashed in the 1980s. But in 2005, the rapid growth of global oil production ceased and since then has only grown by a small amount. These are matters of public record but are not referred to by the popular publications. Omission and misinformation became common, leading to mistaken and tragic economic policies and a frustration when an economic rebound never came. Understanding real economic history became more important than ever. Even the excellent Paul Krugman seems to have a historical knowledge limited mostly to the last century and to the United States.

This book on global economic history begins with the sometimes brutal parameters laid out by prehistoric geography. It also has a chapter on the ancient economies. This serves mainly as a contrast to the history of capitalism that takes up the rest of the volume. It gives the reader a sense of what genuine noncapitalist and precapitalist economies looked like. There is also a chapter on Communist economic history for much the same reason. It tries to envision what a noncapitalist economy would look like in the present day and what problems it would encounter. Communism ended up as an inefficient form of state capitalism. Capitalism has been around for six hundred years and is not so easy to shake. Whether you love it or hate it, you will come away wiser about capitalism's nature.

A complete scholarly apparatus would make this book unwieldy. I have only provided some key citations in the text to the sources I relied on most heavily. A brief guide to further reading at the end of the book allows readers to take the next step into deeper considerations of the problems raised in this book.

As with my previous textbooks *An Introduction to Modern Western Civilization* and *Century of Revolution: A World History, 1770–1870*, I pledge that any profit made on this book will be donated to the Queensborough Community College Fund.

Chapter 1

CREATED UNEQUAL

INTRODUCTION AND DEFINITIONS

Defining Economics

One of the fundamental problems in economics, and therefore in economic history, is defining terms. There are a host of terms used without common agreement. That is why this book can be "a modern economic history" but cannot pretend to be "*the* modern economic history." My task is simpler because many economic ideas floating around out there are proved wrong by history. John Kenneth Galbraith remarked that a sense of history is what divides good economics from bad economics.

Just finding agreement on a definition of "economics" proves impossible. In 1970 the *American Heritage Dictionary* defined it as "the science that deals with the production,

1

distribution, and consumption of commodities." (1970, 413) The oil crisis of the 1970s, however, shook old certainties and some economics textbooks by the end of that decade incorporated scarcity as a fundamental part of the definition. Paul Samuelson, the author of the leading textbook for decades, defined economics as "the study of how societies choose to employ scarce resources that could have alternative uses in order to produce various commodities and distribute them for consumption, now or in the future, among various persons and groups in society." (Samuelson, 3) You should notice that he had abandoned any pretense to science. In the 1980s and 1990s, economics diverged increasingly from historical study and, one might say, the real world. On the one hand, many economists grew to love intricate models with complex mathematical equations having questionable assumptions or leaving out messy factors that would shake the model. On the other hand, many saw economics as a branch of another "soft science," psychology. Gary Becker defined economics as the study of human choice behavior: "All of economics whether represented through articulation or empirically through mathematical means is essentially an analysis of the behavior choices of human beings." (Becker 4–5) Paul Krugman in 1996 gave a definition of "The study of the phenomena emerging from the interactions among intelligent, self-interested individuals."

Since 2007, there has been another sharp turn. At the beginning of that year, George Akerlof gave the Presidential Address to the conference of the American Economics Association and called for a return to reality and empirical studies. At the same time, the global economy began its worst crisis since the Great Depression, an event that many scholars had said was impossible. Just four years earlier, Robert Lucas of the University of Chicago in *his* Presidential Address to the

AEA had said "the central problem of depression-prevention has been solved." Through the crisis, many economists have repeatedly made erroneous and even fraudulent statements and predictions. Thirty years of wrongheaded thinking will not go away quietly.

Neither side has a deep awareness of history. At best they will refer to the late 1800s but no further back. For the most part, then, this book can skirt many of these contentious issues and build a case simply from historical examples. I will start with a different definition of economics.

David Ricardo (died 1823) devised the traditional threefold division of the economy among land (belonging to the landlord), capital (investment money and tools owned by the investor/shop owner), and labor (belonging to the worker). As Ricardo saw it, the first two are in scarce supply while the third is plentiful, so wages would always be barely above survival level. This "iron law of wages" has long been disproved. Karl Marx (died 1883), swallowing Ricardo's assumptions, felt that ending the private ownership of land and capital was the necessary prerequisite to freeing the worker and ensuring his proper pay. This error goes a long way to explaining why communism does not work. Ricardo's assumptions describe many societies in many stages of history but did not accurately describe his own society. Let us define economics as the study of the relationship between labor and capital. Labor means human labor. Capital is anything with a value. This removes Ricardo's artificial distinction. It is also a step to the understanding that in medieval Europe, relative to labor, capital was not scarce, *it was plentiful*. It has continued to be plentiful in a growing area of the world down to the present day. Things of little value, such as sand and crude oil, have become very valuable as silicon chips and gasoline. Without this relationship, capitalism would not work, for it depends on a constant search to make labor more efficient and productive. In the last one hundred years, one part of capital, *energy*, has become so valuable that it forms its own special category. The staggering growth of energy production has enabled the massive and unprecedented growth of global economies and population. Any threat to energy supplies convulses the global economy.

To repeat: **economics is the study of the relationship between labor and capital**.

A warning about economic determinism

This book emphasizes the growth, development, and impact of the economy in history. This will reveal many insights that often are hidden by the year-to-year changes in politics and culture. This does not mean that politics, culture, thought, art, religion, and social structures are not important. Many students get so caught up in the new discovery of the power of economic history that they come to believe that everything depends on the economy. This is called **economic determinism**. In short, the economy determines everything. **This is not true**. Economic determinists are perpetually surprised when something upsets their carefully constructed models. Economic determinists who get their hands on some power are usually dangerous because they ignore the real existing lives of men and women for some theory of how things should be. Trying to prove theories can cost the lives of millions. Russian Communists believed that it was "scientifically impossible" that nationalism could tear the Soviet Union to pieces.

So: economic determinism does not work and it can be dangerous.

Understanding economic history and how it fits into the broader tapestry of history and human experience is enormously enriching and will give the reader understanding that most do not have. I am not saying that you are guaranteed to be a successful investor and make millions, but economic history does give you an advantage.

Measurements

Statistical analysis is the lifeblood of economic history. Today we compile measurements on all aspects and sectors of the economy around the world. How fast are prices rising? How many people are looking for work? These numbers affect billions around the world. But what economic changes cause prices to rise? What causes mass unemployment? These are more subtle questions.

In today's world, there are three economies always operating at the same time. There is one's **personal economy**. You and all the individuals around the world are economic actors and indeed there is a branch of economics called **microeconomics** just to study this. You have an **income** from your job or an allowance from your family, or perhaps you have no income at all. You have **assets**: all the things you own. It is an interesting exercise to list all the things you own, put a value on them, and sum them for your total assets. But there are things called **invisible assets**: your education is an asset, so is your health. Hardest for the individual to calculate is **personal profit**. At the end of the year, are you richer or poorer than you were at the beginning? Think carefully. You may have spent a lot of money or taken out a student loan to go to college. The value of your listed assets may have dwindled. But have they? One recent study puts the value of the Bachelor's degree at $500,000 for a lifetime. Your income, assets, and personal profit do not always move in the same direction.

The second level is the **corporate economy**. These days, corporations most commonly refer to businesses, but the word originally referred to any body of people. Corporations also measure their wealth by income (also called revenue, usually from their sales), assets, and profit (also called "earnings"). Of course, sometimes corporate bodies suffer losses (or "negative earnings" if you really want to avoid that painful word).

The third level is the **national economy**. This is the sum of all the individuals and corporate bodies within the borders of a nation. This is the level we will look at most commonly throughout the book. It is very hard to measure precisely a nation of millions, much less hundreds of millions. The most common economic measurement, the national equivalent of income, is **Gross Domestic Product (GDP)**. The speed of growth of production or GDP is the number most watched by economists, journalists, governments, and politicians. How fast did it grow last year? Or (horrors) did it shrink and doom people to lower wages and lost jobs? Economists and statisticians estimate the value of all the economic activity. **Production** can be of goods or services. Various **factors** (such as labor, energy, money, and raw materials) make up production. (Cameron, 12) What should be counted and how it should be valued often result in controversies. For example, in 2014 Italy decided to include the value of drug deals and prostitution in its GDP. We commonly speak of **per capita GDP**. This number means "per person" or the GDP divided among the number of people. This is a very rough way of measuring wealth. If GDP grows at the same rate as the population, people are not getting richer on average. **Productivity** is different from production. It is a ratio of the production over the input of factors. "Labor productivity," the most common meaning, indicates how much product was made for each worker. "Land productivity" means how much farm product was made for each acre or other land unit. "Energy productivity" means how much product was made for each energy unit.

The GDP number is adjusted by **price inflation**, for if prices rose faster than the measured growth, the GDP shrank "in real terms." Whenever we say "**real**," we mean "adjusted for inflation." "**Nominal**" means "not adjusted for inflation." A nation also has assets, but these are almost never measured and compiled. There are too many, they are constantly moving back and forth to other countries, and the total of invisible assets is huge. Finally, there is the national equivalent of profit and loss. In narrow terms, this is the "**trade balance**." In broader terms, to account for the flow of investments, software, and other harder-to-measure goods, we have the **current account balance**. This should mean "is value flowing into or out of the country?" In practice, it is vaguer. All the world balances added together should equal zero, but they do not. If a country's assets grow at a faster rate than the trade deficit, one can run a deficit forever and simply keep converting those assets into money to pay the bills. The United States has run a trade deficit for most of the last forty-five years, sometimes substantial deficits, and some have predicted bankruptcy and national ruin for nearly that long. They are falsely equating a national economy with a corporate or personal economy.

These three economies work together but prosperity at one level does not guarantee prosperity for all. We will see cases where national economy is clearly growing, but most people's personal economies are not. The economy of the United States has grown without a doubt since 1970. But pay for the ordinary man or woman has fallen in that time. How can this be? Where did the wealth go? This brings up the issue of **income distribution** and **equality** and **inequality**. National wealth has never been equally distributed. Many societies, such as China for most of its history, are profoundly unequal with huge and harmful consequences for their economies. In the United States, wealth at the very top has grown enormously. Not just the famous 1 percent, but even more the .01%. The six heirs to the Wal-Mart fortune have $90 billion, which is more money than the eighty million poorest Americans *put together*. (Bivens)

As we go through economic history, we will regularly check on the interplay of the three economies and the level of inequality.

A question of source material

History is based on the study of written records, and economic history focuses on measurements and statistics of economic activity. In the ancient world (history before the year 500), these records are fundamentally nonexistent. We can try to guess from some descriptions and we have some archeological records, but we never know if we are getting a complete picture. This has led to sharp disagreements about ancient economic history. I will give a brief overview in Chapter 2, but whether capitalism was even possible in the ancient world is an irresolvable debate.

We have access to more records from the medieval world (the years between 500 and 1500). We have scattered local records that we can analyze to establish a fairly clear view of the economy of some villages. In some cases, we can even follow the village over time and see if it was prospering or suffering and how this compares to general views of a region or country in the same period. In the early modern period (1500 to 1750), we have incomplete national records, but we can make educated guesses within certain parameters. We have fairly detailed records of some corporate bodies and we have a fairly good sense of wages and prices. After 1750, our records are increasingly diverse for an ever more widespread area of the world. Accordingly, as the book goes on, you will see more numbers being used to describe historical trends.

Now that we have defined some of our basic terms, we can begin our quest to understand how and why the economic world developed and how we fit into this world.

WHY EURASIA?

People live around the world: in the Americas, in Asia, Australia, Europe and Africa. Yet in most economic development from the beginning of history, the vast landmass of Eurasia always led and set the pace. Africa, linked to Eurasia by the Sinai peninsula, lagged somewhat behind. The Americas and Australia were left in the dust with the latter not advancing beyond a Paleolithic culture when the Europeans showed up in the eighteenth century and destroyed the native culture. The people outside Eurasia were just as clever as anyone else and adapted well to their unique environments. Nature dealt them a bum hand and never gave them a chance to catch up.

The physiologist Jared Diamond in his Pulitzer prize-winning book *Guns, Germs, and Steel*, gives an excellent summary to explain how Eurasia got ahead. Australia is today one of the world's great food producers, and the continent is not far away from New Guinea, which established farming thousands of years ago. But, as Diamond explains, that agriculture is in the highlands. Crops would have to adapt first to the swampy lowlands, then somehow cross the barrier of the Australian desert to reach the quality farmland. Plants are sensitive to the seasons, temperature, and the angle of the sun and can move horizontally (east-west) much faster than vertically (north-south). The fertile southeastern Australian plains lie two thousand miles south of the New Guinea highlands. (Diamond, 315–16)

Diamond's principle of verticality also explains why the Americas got a late start on plant domestication. There are perhaps 200,000 wild plant species. Humans eat a few thousand of these but have domesticated just a few hundred. Twelve species make up 80 percent of the modern world's annual harvest. These consist of cereals (wheat, rice, corn, barley, sorghum), a pulse (the soybean), roots (potato, manioc, sweet potato), sugar sources (cane, beet) and one fruit (banana). (132) Of the fifty-six grass species with seeds ten times the median size (thus not requiring tremendous labor to grow and harvest), thirty-two occur in West Asia, North Africa, and Mediterranean zone of Europe. (139) Corn developed in Mexico, but took several thousand years to become a major food, and even longer to spread north and south. Mesoamerica did not have settled villages until around 1500 BC and cities by 400 BC. It had only two small domesticated animals: the turkey and the dog. It had no pack animals. In the area of what is today the eastern United States, farming did not become important until about 200 BC, and it was not until around AD 900 that Mexican corn had adapted to shorter summers. Around 1100, beans arrived from Mexico. (109) This caused a cultural flowering in the Mississippi and Ohio River valleys. Cities appeared here seven thousand years after the first city in western Asia. The Andes highlands developed an economy centered on crops and llamas and guinea pigs, but the hot lowlands of Central America stopped the spread of this package. (187)

The Americas were also handicapped on animal domestication, especially of large animals. Eurasia had seventy-two animals that are terrestrial, herbivorous or omnivorous, and weigh on average over a hundred pounds. They domesticated thirteen of them. The Americas had only twenty-four and domesticated only one, the llama, in the Andes. (162) The late start handicapped them in all other technology. They had not developed iron technology when Columbus showed up in 1492. Eurasia had developed it 2,500 years before.

Why not Africa? It lacked a natural breadbasket because this vast continent hugs almost four thousand miles north and south of the equator. The chief food producing regions of the world are between 35° and 55° north and south latitudes. Around the equator, heavy warm rains leach the soil of vital nutrients and leave it poor in quality. Equatorial forests provide the shade and protections for their own soil, but when people cut down the trees, the crops are naked to the merciless sun and rain. Africa's verticality also hurt the spread of crops. Sorghum and African yams adapted to the Sahel and tropics with their warm temperatures, summer rains, and relatively constant day lengths. These tropical plants could not spread south of the Fish River. Climate and disease (especially sleeping sickness) stopped the spread of animals: horse, sheep, cattle, goats. Ethiopia received the Middle Eastern package of domesticated plants and animals, but it could not spread to the hotter south. Parts of southern Africa are good farmland today but had to wait until crops from similar climes four thousand miles or more away were planted. (186–87) Africa also had the spectacular bad luck that it had fifty-one animal candidates for domestication and did not domesticate any of them. Again, this is in no way the fault of the people of Africa. As will be mentioned shortly, most animals cannot be domesticated. African zebras resemble horses but are not domesticated. American bighorn sheep resemble Asian sheep but are not domesticated.

THE NATURAL ECONOMY

This is the economy where human labor is closest to nature: hunting and gathering animals and plants. For tens of thousands of years, people refined their hunting tools. They invented better needles that could sew skins for clothes, tents, or skin boats. Humans spread out to more remote areas, including Australia by fifty thousand years ago, northern Eurasia by thirty-five thousand years ago, and the Americas fifteen thousand years ago. Most peasant farmers and herders are not necessarily better off than hunters and gatherers. To quote Jared Diamond, farming does not automatically mean "less physical work, more comfort, freedom from starvation, and longer expected lifetime." (104) Farming often means more work. Many first farmers were smaller, less nourished, suffered from more serious diseases, and died at a younger age. A number of hunter-gathering societies rejected farming. Deserts and grassland prairie that required iron tools for farming separated California hunters from Arizona farmers. The Khoi herders south of the Fish River could not adopt equatorial plants that were not suited for the temperate zone.

There is a grey zone between gathering and farming. Hunters have been seen clearing, planting, weeding, and harvesting without settling. The Apache Indians farmed in summer and hunted in winter. Some areas are so rich in resources that hunter-gatherers settled down as in the Pacific northwest which has a rich fish environment. We do not have any written records but we note a pattern in prehistoric Japan, coastal Peru and the east coast of the Mediterranean Sea: all settled and took up farming later. (106) Farming does not necessarily mean settled. An early pattern where there was an abundance of land was to plant until the soil was exhausted, then move the entire village. People needed to satisfy their hunger and meet specific needs for protein, fat, salt, sweet fruits, and simply good taste.

Advances could be gradual and piecemeal. Food production in southwestern Europe (present-day Spain and Portugal) started with sheep and only gradually took in crops. Japan had a slow transition. Southern Sweden adopted farming around 3000 BC for three hundred years, then went back to hunting-gathering for four hundred years. (109)

You may ask: if agriculture does not mean an easier and better life than hunting and gathering, why do it at all? There are a number of reasons. Not that many big game animals can live in a particular area, so that sharply limits the number of people in an area. A band of hunters and gatherers likely killed its young and old members or left them to die on a regular basis. Conditions would have worsened if the hunters wiped out all the big animals in an area, as frequently happened. A shift to full-time farming would have been necessary to the band's survival. It must have seemed easier at first: in the hills of the Fertile Crescent (present-day Iraq and Syria), wild stands of wheat could be easily harvested, yielding calories up to fifty times greater than the work expended to harvest them. Many of the first plants cultivated in the Fertile Crescent were self-pollinating. But farming increased population density and made it impossible to return to hunting and gathering. Farming was not a permanent cure to the problem of population pressure. We know that there were regular occasions where the crops failed and again the youngest and oldest were sacrificed. Close contact with animals and stirring up soils also increased diseases. With their greater numbers, farmers could violently push hunters off of the land. Diseases could also thin out the already low density of hunters while farmers had greater immunity. This happened in Indonesia, tropical southeast Asia, most of subequatorial Africa, and probably parts of Europe. In historical times, we have seen it occur in Australia and the western United States. (110–12)

Somewhere in here the free market was born and died. A fair trade was made. The next time two hunters planned a trade, they thought of ways to cheat the other. Fights broke out and some judging authority had to be "paid" to regulate the situation.

BEGINNINGS OF AGRICULTURE

Plant and animal domestication go together. Farmers grow plants to feed the animals and use animal manure to fertilize the soil. Tame dogs protect the flocks, cats attack varmints that would eat the plants. Although we have no written records, it seems likely that the move to farming changed the way people thought. Domestication fosters a longer-term view because farmers need to plan the breeding of plants and animals.

The earliest wave of plant domestication around 10,000 BC involved crops that did not need much modification. Villagers ground them into meal or flour and baked or brewed them into various forms. Around 4000 BC came the first fruit and nut trees: olives, figs, dates, grapes, for example. They would not yield food for at least three years and reached full maturity after about ten years. This required a settled village life. Other fruit trees, such as apples, pears, plums, and cherries required knowledge of tree grafting and took until around 400 BC. (124)

Domesticatable animals such as the wild ox, goat, sheep, and dog are widely distributed across Europe and Asia. They provided meat, milk, cheese, butter, skins for clothes and tent coverings, and leather for shields and armor. By 2500 BC, the big animals that could be domesticated were domesticated. (165)

Many animals have been tamed, not domesticated: they are captured in the wild, not bred in captivity. Diamond summarizes the factors that allow for domestication. Raising domesticated carnivores takes an enormous amount of resources. You want your animal to grow quickly and not all animals do that. Some animals refuse to breed in captivity. Others are aggressive and dangerous. Some panic so easily that they will kill themselves or escape any pen. Others lack a dominance structure and will not accept human guidance or will attack animals not of their herd. This eliminates most animals from consideration and explains why no large animals native to sub-Saharan Africa were domesticated. (169–73)

Technology Arising from Domestication

Domestication of plants was the starting point for technological development because it spun off other technologies. This is why the lag in the development of farming put other areas behind the civilizations of Eurasia.

At first, farmers would use slash-and-burn agriculture: burn down the trees to fertilize the soil, farm it until the land was exhausted, and then move on. By 9000 BC in the Middle East, there were small villages of some twenty-five houses. First they used a digging stick, then the hoe, and finally the plow, which could dig more deeply, churn up and oxygenate soil. Farmers prized sharp-edged stone axes to clear fields. Trade could carry axes of better rock hundreds of miles from their origin.

Pottery developed because grain storage was essential for the non-growing season. Clay vessels are more durable than skins or leather. Some areas used pottery by 25,000 BC. One has to find the right kind of clay, mix it with key ingredients such as chopped straw, and then fire it. It needs a hot oven of 450°C (842°F) to change it to keep its shape wet or dry. At 1400°C (2552°F), it undergoes another change: silica becomes glassy and pottery even more rigid. By 6000 BC, southwest Asia had pottery kilns that could maintain a temperature of 1000°C (1832°F). People discovered sun-baked mud and created the brick by 3000 BC.

Domesticated flax yielded linen, sheep yielded wool. Devices spun these fibrous materials into thread, then wove the thread into cloth or linen. The first evidence of weaving by hand is twenty-five thousand years old from Central Europe. Nine thousand years ago there were weaving machines. Sailors applied cloth to make the sailboat.

Estimates of world population are imprecise and based on fragmentary documents but it seems the world contained perhaps four million people in 10,000 BC, five million in 5000 BC, fourteen million in 3000 BC; twenty-seven million in 2000 BC, fifty million in 1000 BC, and one hundred million in 500 BC. (McEvedy and Jones, 344) A food surplus allowed for a division of labor and the emergence of a group of people who did not engage in food production. The surplus could be traded to outside groups for goods. The first city was Çatal Hüyük, Turkey (6000-5600 BC), which grew rich on the obsidian trade. After processing, this volcanic glassy rock has an edge as sharp as a modern surgeon's scalpel.

Early Areas of Farming

In addition to the areas of South America and Mesoamerica mentioned above, it seems certain that farming developed independently in southwest Asia and the Yellow River valley of

China. From these centers, farming spread to Egypt, Europe, the Indus River valley, and southeast Asia. It is not clear whether farming developed independently in West Africa and New Guinea or whether it was brought in from another center.

In southwest Asia (modern Iran and Iraq), farming started in the foothills of the Zagros mountains where the wild ancestors of wheat and barley grew on rainy slopes. This started more than ten thousand years ago. It was only after about three thousand years that the farmers moved down to the floodplain of the Tigris and Euphrates Rivers. The yearly floods provided fresh rich soil. The disadvantages were intense heat, lack of adequate rain, and the floodwater from the rivers. Farmers developed heat-resistant strains of wheat and barley and dug elaborate irrigation trenches to control the flood water. Although these cultures were still prehistoric, we imagine that it must have taken considerable leadership and organization to control the floods. From the start of written records, private property was recognized and respected. (Neal and Williamson I, 26) Over time, a problem developed. Irrigation over hundreds of years gradually concentrated salt deposits and reduced the fertility of the soil. The center of population and power in Mesopotamia (Greek for "the land between the rivers") was near the Persian Gulf (Sumer) in 3000 BC, moved north to Babylon by 1500 BC, and had moved further north to Assyria by 700 BC. The Egyptians did not use irrigation on the Nile River, so this never became a problem.

Farming began in the Indus River valley, which is mainly located in present-day Pakistan, about a thousand years after southwest Asia. The distance is not great and there is evidence of sea trade between the two from the dawn of history, so historians suspect there was no independent origin in the Indus. It developed cities and writing several hundred years after Mesopotamia. This civilization covered a larger area than either Mesopotamian or Egyptian civilizations because India is enormously fertile. More than half of the land in the modern republic of India is arable (farmable) as opposed to 19 percent in the United States. To the east of the Indus is desert, and then gradually thick, summer monsoon-fed jungle appears with its center in the Ganges River. The Himalayan mountains to the north of the Ganges create a "rain-shadow" effect. As the hills and mountains force the moist air of the Indian Ocean upward, it cools and must release rain. Only iron-equipped humans could deal with this jungle. After 1000 BC oxen-drawn iron plows came to the Ganges. In rain-rich Bengal, rice would become the main crop. Once the Ganges was planted, similar agriculture grew in similar river climates: the Brahmaputra that flows through India and Bangladesh, the Salween (Burma), and the Mekong (Laos/Thailand/Cambodia) between 100 BC and AD 500.

Farming also spread from southwest Asia to Anatolia (modern Turkey), which also has vast fertile areas. From Anatolia, it crossed to Europe by 7000 BC. It took more than three thousand years for farming to spread north and west into Europe. With a mainly horizontal alignment, it should have spread more quickly, but Europe, like the Ganges, had vast forests that limited settlement until iron technology developed. The first cities of Europe were in Greece and Crete after 2000 BC where they farmed the light, shallow soil with frequent plowing and a **two-field system** (that means that each piece of land could only be planted every other year).

Yellow River Agriculture

The Yellow River (or Huang He), like the Tigris River, is wild and difficult to tame. It has changed course several times throughout history. Like the Mesopotamians, the Chinese seem to have started farming the fertile soil above the river valley, then moved down onto the floodplain. The Yellow River deposits far more soil than the Tigris, Euphrates, Nile or Indus. Unlike southern Mesopotamia, enough rain falls that it does not require irrigation, just flood control ditches. The area was also cooler than Iraq and lies above the critical 35° north latitude. It became a center to grow wheat and millet.

The intense development of the Yangzi River basin would not occur until after about AD 250. It was humid and warm, a very different environment from the Yellow River. There was no danger of silting and river shifts because the mountain sediment deposited in lakes. There was more danger of disease, notably malaria and dengue fever, as well as parasites. The different ecology meant that the Yangzi became a rice growing center, rather than the wheat and millet of the north.

CONCLUSION

Modern economic life is profoundly shaped by economic developments dating back ten thousand years that were in turn created by geography and nature. The relative scarcity of domesticatable plants and big animals put the Americas at a severe disadvantage from which it never recovered. Australia continued to have a hunting-gathering economy until the arrival of the Europeans. Africa south of the Sahara desert was only a step or two behind Eurasia. But capitalism did not develop in any of these areas in ancient times and that is what we will examine in the next chapter.

TIMELINE

10,000 BC	First wave of domestication of plants and animals in southwestern Asia
8000 BC	Farming in Indus River valley
7000 BC	Farming in Europe
6000 BC	First city Çatal Hüyük Farming in northeast Africa
5000 BC	Farming in western Africa
3500 BC	Farming in Mesoamerica, Andes, and Amazon regions
3000 BC	Brick for building material Cities in Mesopotamia
2600 BC	Cities in Egypt and Indus River
2500 BC	Cities in Yellow River valley
1900 BC	Cities in Crete
200 BC	Cities in Mesoamerica and South America
AD 250	Intensive development of Yangzi River valley began
AD 1000	Cities in West Africa and North America

KEY TERMS

economic determinism

income

assets

profit

Gross Domestic Product (GDP)

price inflation

current account balance

inequality

two-field system

Chapter 2

ANCIENT ECONOMIES

Why am I including a chapter called "Ancient Economies" in a book titled *Modern Economic History*? Capitalism is today so all-encompassing that most people do not know what a pre-capitalist or non-capitalist system looks like. It is complicated by the lack of source material that I mentioned in the last chapter. The chapter will focus almost entirely on the Middle East and the Mediterranean because our economic records from the rest of the world cannot even be called "fragmentary." I assume that China and the Indus/Ganges river areas were at roughly the same level of economic development. This was certainly true for coins, the most durable economic record.

The Debate of the "Primitivists" and the "Modernizers"

No one can deny that the modern economy is radically different from earlier economies. The ancient economy hardly grew at all measured by per capita GDP in real terms. After moving from the natural economy to the farming economy, the lives of the average man and woman were little-changed despite huge technological advances. This should be a clue that technology is overrated. Taken by itself, it does not change that much, only changes the forms. Life expectancy at birth hardly changed from the average of twenty-five years. This is misleading because so many died before their fifth birthday. If you got past that, you could easily live into your forties if you were a man. Women faced the formidable challenge of childbirth: the average woman needed to bear around five children just to maintain the population; bearing six to nine children was common and each took an enormous physical toll on the mother. Some people have always lived into their seventies. People's height and weight shrank relative to their hunting and gathering ancestors and did not recover.

The "modernizers" believe that ancient economies differed only in scale, not in substance from modern economies. Populations were much smaller and certain economies of scale were therefore impossible. Ships were much smaller and carried less. Volume of trade was much smaller, which limited the division of labor, which in turn limited productivity. Modernizers emphasize how many capitalist features existed in the ancient world and try to see if there were critical turning points missed where antiquity failed to break through into capitalism.

The "primitivists" believe that antiquity was structurally different and could never have evolved into capitalism without the massive structural breakdown that marked the end of the ancient world between the years 400 and 700. Writers as different as Adam Smith and Karl Marx wrote in terms of qualitatively different stages culminating in Smith's "state of commerce" or Marx's "capitalist stage." Early writers of this group believed erroneously that the economy mainly rested on self-sufficient households growing and making all they needed. When it was shown that much of the ancient world had circulating money, commercial manufacturing, and relatively large volumes of long-distance trade, the "modernizers" seemed to have won the debate. (Scheidel and von Reden, 253)

In his 1973 book *The Ancient Economy*, Moses Finley said that considerations of status and civic ideology governed economic decision-making, not supply and demand. Elite values that determined status constrained economic development. How can one have a successful business selling certain goods when those goods are constantly offered as gifts? From top to bottom, "status" was a more useful category of analysis than "class." A person's occupation and/or income determines their class. People who make more money are considered "upper class," those who make less are "lower class," and so on. Some occupations are respected and even if the incomes of their members are low, people generally consider those members to be of a higher class. But how can we account for the phenomenon of the ancient world where some people willingly became slaves so they could be in the household of a prominent family? In modern class terms, slave would be the bottom occupation but an important slave had a higher status than many free men in the ancient world. This is completely alien to our expectations.

Finley went to say that this world of status

> 1) inhibited the growth of markets for land, labor and capital, and therefore of technology and trade; 2) encouraged the social marginalization of trading and banking; 3) reinforced the primacy of the political over the economic because people

rose politically by giving away or selling at a cost below market certain goods, especially food. Furthermore, it 4) favored coercive exploitation and redistribution over market exchange and 5) expanded chattel slavery and predatory imperialism.... 6) Subsistence farmers and elite rentiers only worked for self-sufficiency not to accumulate wealth that could have been used for investment. 7) Most market exchange was local and small scale; 8) agricultural rents and taxes rather than trade or investment generated most upper-class wealth.

Finley's final point was that ancient cities were parasites upon the farm economy, which produced most of the wealth. (Scheidel and von Reden, 2)

Forty years of research has only deepened the debate. Finley was clearly right that while there was trade that encompassed Europe, Asia, North Africa and East Africa, it did not resemble even the interdependent markets of the late Middle Ages. There was nothing resembling a state economic policy nor was "economics" a subject of study for the ancients. There is a book of the ancient Greek philosopher Aristotle's lectures titled *Economics*, but it actually has nothing to do with the topic. Aristotle did devote some of his lectures on *Ethics* to money, exchange, and the just price.

The Meaning of Money

On the other hand, Finley clearly underestimated the volume of market exchange, even in a world of gifts. He also downplayed the role of money. Almost all societies have developed some kind of means of payment. Money, even if it is not denominated, exists in a generally recognized system of payments. Money can be used to pay a debt, buy a good or service or be a gift to another person or a god. Western civilization prefers precious metals, Pacific islanders prefer shells of various kinds that they prized and used extensively for decorative purposes in both secular and religious contexts. Money also serves as a store of value and must be stable over a long interval.

Certain societies use money in very different ways. Early European explorers saw the exchange of unusual items such as salt, pieces of cloth, cowrie shells, pieces of wood, feathers, and human skulls, and called them "money." In the 1920s, even as many of these cultures were being overwhelmed, scholars began to delve into what was really happening. A study of the Lele people of the Congolese basin revealed that their cloth "money" could only be used to purchase a few high quality goods and then only if the buyer was unrelated to the seller. Cloth paid for certain social rituals: entrance to religious cult groups, fees to ritual healers, marriage dues, rewards for giving birth and reporting would-be seducers, fines for adultery, compensation for fighting within the village, fulfillment of blood debts, and tribute to chiefs. Ritual gifts were given in cloth. If a person did not have enough cloths to make payments, kinsmen would make loans or gifts. The entire function of this "money" was to increase prestige and promote village harmony. The village elders held most of the cloths and used them to control the younger members of the village. (Williams, 208–10)

In many economies now, buying and selling are the primary ways of acquiring and distributing commodities, and money pays for labor. In other societies, the creation and maintenance of social relationships through gift-giving and ritually conditioned exchanges and payments have been more important. How much did this hold true in the precapitalist world? How much money was "social" and how much "commercial" in the modern way we would understand? It is extremely hard to tell. That money served a very different function may explain what we would consider "odd" behavior in the ancient world.

ANCIENT MANUFACTURING AND TECHNOLOGY

In the modern world, we have faith in technology. Even if the human race gets into trouble, there will be some kind of invention to rescue it. As Arthur C. Clarke put it "Sufficiently advanced technology is indistinguishable from magic." The actual history of technology is far more complicated. Successful inventions must fit into a particular time and culture. Not every invention brings an economic advantage to all situations. Because Mesoamericans lacked pack animals, wheeled vehicles offered no advantage. In Tokugawa Japan, wheeled vehicles were banned as a way for the rulers to maintain control. Existing interests can crush superior technology. Betamax was a better video recorder, WordPerfect a better word processor than Microsoft's products. The "Qwerty" keyboard has survived several shifts of technology despite being designed to avoid the collision of metal typewriter keys. Entrenched powers have prevented technological advance. Some technologies provide social value and prestige: the Apple Corporation has not invented most of the consumer technologies that it is known for but has marketed them cleverly so that a certain color of earphones indicates the prestige of an Apple product. People have been killed for their brand of sneaker. Finally, a technology's advantage should be easy to see. In the ancient world, steam technology was invented several times but never adopted because its advantages could not be seen or there was fear that it would throw people out of work. A Roman emperor rejected steam-driven door openers because it would take away jobs. A later ruler accepted a steam-driven device to lift his chair because it would seem like magic to the unsophisticated. Steam power would have to wait 1,700 years. The bicycle had to be invented twice. How many technologies are languishing today because the time is not right? (Diamond, 247–49)

Simple Machines

A machine magnifies or transmits human or animal effort. Simple machines developed in prehistory included the wheel, the screw, the lever, the inclined plane, the wedge (which is a double inclined plane), and the pulley. Complex machines would grow from the simple ones. The wheel would be used to harness water power after 200 BC, while the potter's wheel would make superior ceramics and by 500 BC was being used as a lathe to cut moldings and grooves. Wells require pulleys. The technology of the screw was used to press wine after 1000 BC and raise water after 700 BC.

Writing

Writing is another form of technology. As knowledge became more specialized and complicated, it became necessary to preserve it in written form. By 3400 BC, trade was so complex that people needed writing to prevent theft and accounting mistakes. Most writing began as pictures representing things and gradually the pictures became simplified and combined to indicate new words. Egypt acquired writing from the Sumerians by 3000 BC. It spread to the Indus River civilization by 2300 BC, and to southern Europe by 2000 BC. China and Mesoamerica seem to have developed writing independently.

A standardized, phonetic **alphabet** likely existed by 1200 BC after a series of experiments cleared up the ambiguities of picture-signs.

Metal Technology

Copper was the first industrial metal used extensively: it is soft, attractive, and widely available. Copper-smelting requires a temperature of 1983° F and an atmosphere rich in carbon and poor in oxygen. This temperature was not achieved until pottery-making became common, so one sees how plant domestication, food storage, and pottery led to other technologies. As early as 4000 BC, the Middle East area was using copper. Copper reached India by 3000 BC, southern Europe by 2500 BC, southern Russia by 2000 BC, northern Europe by 1950 BC, Britain by 1900 BC, and Scandinavia by 1500 BC. Native copper working developed or spread in the Adena culture of the Ohio River valley around 700 BC and southern Colombia by 325 BC.

Coppersmiths quickly learned which other elements strengthened or weakened copper. A 10 percent tin mix would create bronze, which has a lower melting point. Unlike copper, bronze could be used in a variety of large tools and weapons. Tin sources are rare, and it required extensive trade routes over thousands of miles to bring tin to civilization. The earliest bronze artifacts come from the Middle East, Southeast Asia, and Central Europe around 3000 to 2500 BC. China with good tin supplies also developed fine bronze works before 2000 BC. Bronze artifacts made their way along trade routes so that even northern Europe had bronze weapons before 2000 BC; that means before they were smelting copper. In the Americas, it seems that the Incas of Peru developed bronze around AD 1400.

THE ARCHAIC ECONOMY

By 2000 BC, about a thousand years after the beginning of history, the cities of Mesopotamia formed the core of a trading system that extended from the Aegean islands to Afghanistan and the Indus valley. We have records of precious metal weights being used as early as 2300 BC. Mesopotamians valued land purchases in both grain and silver. New Kingdom Egypt had scales that were accurate to 1 percent. Mesopotamian law codes outlined fines in weights of silver. Both grain and silver set the value of labor and other things. Kings and temples seemed to hoard gold and silver in Mesopotamia and Egypt. Gold and silver were useful as money because they did not suffer short-term decay or fluctuate from year to year like the grain supply. Thus, they were a reliable store of value. Merchant-moneylenders were common. Interest rates were high, but clearly there was some credit system. Governments put out law codes that guaranteed contracts and ensured honest weights and measures. (Neal and Williamson, I, 28)

By 700 BC, there was even more sophistication. Eurasia was adopting iron. Iron is more plentiful than copper, but it requires a temperature of 2800° F to melt. The secret was to use lesser heat to soften it, then hammer it to produce "wrought iron." This rusted quickly and did not hold an edge well. Mixing the iron with hot charcoal and carbon monoxide gas "steels" the iron. When worked properly, it has twice the strength of bronze. Later would come "quenching" the hot iron in cold water, which makes it hard but brittle unless tempered. Around the fourth century BC, ironmasters figured out the next step: reheat the iron to about 1260° F and allow it to cool. (Raymond 62–63) Iron had a major impact on agriculture, war, and industry. In agriculture, peasants could use cheap iron axes to clear land, iron plows to prepare land, and iron scythes to harvest crops. Iron axes cleared the forests of the Ganges valley and central Europe. By 500 BC, the Chinese were burning carbon fuel to create a carbon-monoxide rich atmosphere; this lowers the melting point of iron to 2070° F and creates brittle iron with a 4.5% carbon content. You then stir it (puddling) in the open air to reduce the carbon content. Ancient Romans discovered the melting, but never the puddling, so they threw away cast iron. Puddling was not developed in the West until 1784. (74–78) South Asia developed another method after 600 BC: ironmasters put pieces of wrought iron into tiny containers with pieces of wood and leaves and heated them in a charcoal pit. The iron melts and absorbs the carbon uniformly. This **wootz steel** was the highest quality of its time. It would later diffuse in the Islamic world as "Damascus steel," be forgotten, and then be reinvented by the eighteenth-century British as "Sheffield steel." (78–80)

Regrettably, we have almost no historical sources of any kind from the southern and eastern Asian civilizations, so our best examples are from the Middle East, especially the Assyrian empire. As mentioned in the last chapter, the center of power in Mesopotamia had moved to the north. Assyrian cities had to import food and now used different metals of exchange: copper, tin, and silver. The government collected taxes in cloth, cattle, or other goods. While there may not have been an overall government approach to the economy, the Assyrian empire did have some policies. It fixed prices to prevent unreasonable sales. It carefully assessed economic resources for military purposes. The government would extend interest-free loans to peasants during hard times to save them from those charging excessive interest.

THE GREEK ECONOMY AND MOVE TO CASH CROPS

Greece had always been on the edge of the advanced economies. Farming was difficult because the Greek rivers turn wild when the mountain snow melts in the spring. To make matters worse, Greeks early in their history cut down many of their forests and suffered severe soil erosion. Greece had no tin, a little silver, and limestone and marble for building. The Greeks had to find creative solutions. The first was to focus on **cash crops**. These are crops that are grown for profit, rather than consumption. The Greeks planted olives to make olive oil and grapes to make wine. This allowed them to produce five times more energy calories from the land than they would have with grain. (Neal and Williamson, I, 63, 94) They would trade the products directly or indirectly for the needed food from Egypt, Sicily, and the Black Sea shore. The second solution was **colonization**. From 750 BC to 550 BC, the Greeks colonized areas of the Mediterranean and Black Seas. The Greeks built trade routes to present-day Spain and France. Their trade reached all the way to Britain for tin.

Increased trade led to a specialized Greek society: landowners specialized in cash crops, merchants specialized in overseas trade. Local retailers, shipowners, and traders were involved in commerce. A new urban lower class of craftsmen, artisans and sailors evolved. The desire for profit drove all of them. We see evidence of some loans, investments in trading ventures, and a couple of banks accepting deposits for reinvestment. More people lived in Greece in 300 BC than in the year 1900. (I, 49)

The Greeks' great rivals in trade were the Carthaginians of North Africa, who put out their own colonies in the western

Mediterranean. We have never found ancient Mediterranean coins in western Africa, but there were some caravan routes established in ancient times going to the bend of the Niger River. Carthaginian or Phoenician ships also ventured out into the Atlantic and went down the west African coast. We do not know how far they got, but there was an unconfirmed story of a sailor going all the way around Africa.

DEFINING CAPITALISM

Yet for all this technological advance and growing sophistication, there was no appreciable growth in wealth. The gains in efficiency were all swallowed by increased population. The Greeks ate no better than the Egyptians two thousand years before; they did not live longer, nor were they taller or more robust. All of these societies had a surplus of labor and a shortage of capital. There was no incentive to make labor more efficient and hence, no drive towards capitalism. This is called the **Malthusian trap** after the nineteenth-century British writer Thomas Malthus who stated that in the long run, population exceeds food supply and thus suffers periodic collapses.

Many people have different definitions of capitalism. Some identify it with a free market, but there has never been a free market, just one subject to degrees of manipulation by various interests. Capitalism has nothing to do with free trade and indeed has thrived at times when trade was highly regulated. It has nothing to do with democracy; it was dominant three hundred years before democracy began in the West. It was also dominant hundreds of years before industrialism, so Marx is wrong to identify the rise of the factory as the dawn of a new economic age. Lately, "institutional" economists have identified capitalism with respect for private property. They have tried to tailor this definition to England. But in truth, England did not respect private property much more than other nations. Writing laws to steal land does not make justice. One could ask the English smallholder forced out by enclosure, or the Irish or the Scots, how well the English landowners of Parliament respected their property rights.

I will offer three general definitions. Capitalism is:

1. An economic system where the person who puts the money into an enterprise receives a share of the profit, rather than the people directly involved in the enterprise.
2. An economic system where individuals or groups of individuals place capital at risk with an expectation of receiving back a profit commensurate with the risk.
3. An economic system where production is primarily for profit rather than consumption.

Capitalism rises and grows when there is a relative shortage of labor compared to capital. Even though the labor supply has grown dramatically in the last thousand years, the supply and value of resources have grown even faster allowing capitalism to spread to a larger part of the world. We will see in the next three chapters that Western European capitalism manifested itself in a number of institutions and practices that formed the structure of a new economic system that was fully functioning by about 1450. The ancient world had some of these capitalistic institutions without ever breaking through to a full capitalist system. We will examine how the ancient system fell short and ultimately collapsed.

Coinage

The kingdom of Lydia was on the western Anatolian coast. The area was a source of electrum, a natural alloy of gold and silver. Between 650 BC and 625 BC, Lydia minted a coin with a lion's head as a medium of exchange for goods. There was no "face value" on the coin; perhaps it was first weighed for value as metal tokens had been. Silver coins replaced electrum after around 550 BC. Lydia also minted a few gold coins. At that time, coinage spread to Greece. Soon, counterfeiting appeared; it is reported that in Greece around 540 BC, a counterfeiter passed off fake gold coins.

At almost exactly the same time as Lydia, China developed bronze coinage: "spade money" and "knife money." The First Emperor (d. 210 BC) built a series of roads, unified weights and measures, and standardized coinage by issuing the copper *cash* with a hole in the middle and the inscription "half-ounce." Around 118 BC, the Han Emperor Wu introduced the "five grain" bronze coin that lasted until AD 621. This coinage system featuring a hole in the middle spread through Asia and reached Japan in AD 708, Vietnam in 970, and Korea in 996. It lasted into the twentieth century. (Williams, 136)

The Persian empire conquered Lydia after 550 BC and adopted common weights and measures and coinage. It built royal roads including an all-weather road from Sardis to Susa that stretched 1,677 miles with 111 post stations. The King's messengers could manage it in a week (ten miles an hour on constantly fresh horses). Merchants on donkeys needed three months (eighteen miles a day). The Persians were the first to use the horse efficiently for communication and transport in their empire. They built a canal to link the Nile River with the Red Sea and developed ports. They encouraged voyages of exploration. There was some credit banking. Most or all of the cities were **monetized**, meaning that most payments for goods, services, and taxes were made in coins, not other goods and services. The King's peace helped economic growth. The government took in more in taxes than it spent (a budget surplus). The gold and silver simply piled up uselessly in the palace at Susa, hurting the economy and lowering wages. (Neal and Williamson, I, 30, 39) Persia conquered as far as the Indus River and it seems that silver coinage came to northern India around 500 BC.

THE CLASSICAL EURASIAN SYSTEM

Alexander and After

In just seven years, **Alexander the Great** (336–323 BC) overthrew the Persian empire and brought a Greek army to the Indus River. He introduced coinage in Egypt. It helped cement a trade area that extended from the Ganges well into Central Asia back to the Mediterranean and up into northern Europe. In Denmark, we have found a carved elephant made in India dating from this era. When Alexander's troops looted the Persian capitals, they found stupendous amounts of silver collected for decades in the basements of the palaces. If there was ever a moment for the ancient world to break through into capitalism, this would have been it, with the release of all this stored money. Alexander's armies created a cosmopolitan Greek civilization in the eastern Mediterranean that would persist in some form for almost two thousand years. These **Hellenistic** ("Greek-like") kingdoms used the released Persian gold and silver to improve roads and harbors and build bridges. State and private banks spread. Greek goods went to India, Arabia, and sub-Saharan Africa. Surplus wheat came from Egypt,

Sicily, and Crimea in southern Russia. Feeding kingdoms remained a problem but the trade in pickled, salted, and dried fish grew to help relieve hunger. Alexander had tried to assure communications by planting new colonies and founding new cities with his army veterans.

Much later in the book we will see how Japan developed capitalism in the nineteenth century largely independent of the West. However, the Japanese did have the western capitalist model to observe. It may be that the Hellenistic world failed to break into capitalism because it had no model and the imbalance between capital and labor was not so extreme or prolonged as to force a path to capitalism as happened in western Europe.

There was little trade in manufactured goods until the Roman empire. Individual craftsmen made most goods. There were some small-scale operations of an owner and a few slaves. Royal and city governments became involved in manufacturing as a state enterprise. Most trade over the sea was in merchant ships that were long, narrow, and speedy, with a small crew. They were able to carry 250 tons. This created jobs for sailors, shipbuilders, dockworkers, accountants, and teamsters. It also created opportunities for pirates who were always a threat in the Mediterranean.

The Machinery of Capitalism and Its Failures

In chapter 4 and 5 we will discuss the building blocks of capitalism that created the world's first fully functioning capitalist system by the end of the middle ages in western Europe. In this section I want to preview those building blocks, survey what the ancient world succeeded in, and then its drawbacks and failures that explain why capitalism did not develop in the ancient world despite undeniable capitalistic aspects.

Money

By 200 BC coins were circulating in China, northern India, southwest Asia, Egypt, and the Mediterranean basin. There was a common coinage among most of the Hellenistic kingdoms, so one could expect a coin to be accepted from northern Greece to the Indus River. Only Egypt stuck to its own standard. Evidence from Athens suggests that a considerable amount of money was needed for wealthy citizens to support the fleet and to pay for festivals. (Scheidel, Morris, and Saller, 377) The western Mediterranean Sea and then western Europe were brought into the money economy and adopted the inventions and techniques developed to the southeast. Imposing money taxes forced the western Mediterranean countryside into the money economy. In the east, increased long-distance trade probably promoted urban growth and enlarged the size of the monetary economy. However, many parts of Egypt and western Asia remained demonetized as the main coin was too heavy for daily use. Only the capitals and army garrisons had coins circulating briskly. (Scheidel, Morris, and Saller, 417–18)

Richard Saller suggests that GDP per capita and productivity grew in this area up to 25 percent from about 200 BC to AD 70 and then slipped back. That is only 0.1% per year growth. That was still 50 percent to 100 percent higher than the average growth rate in Greece for the previous six hundred years, which would be a cumulative 35 per cent increase. (Scheidel, Morris, and Saller, 5–6) Economic historians use $350 in international dollars of the year 1990 as a baseline of **subsistence**. Below that level, many people are not able to sustain their lives. If we assume that Greece started out at subsistence level, then at the peak of the classical world around AD 100, the per capita GDP was only $600 in current terms. In a separate study, Dennis Kehoe estimated the equivalent of $530 to $600. (Kehoe in Scheidel, Morris and Saller, 546–47) All of these figures would put the ancient Roman empire among the very poorest of today's countries. That despite a period of Roman peace, the technological advances of the ancient world, the roads, running water, and trade networks. At the same time population likely doubled. (Cameron, 39)

Greeks and many others hoarded money. We still dig up vast hoards. Some of the silver liberated from Persia was just buried in another form. The ancient Greek philosopher Aristotle, who was one of Alexander's teachers, saw money as simply a guarantee against future problems. There were no "investment opportunities" or productive functions for money as an alternative to hoarding. This is not unknown in modern times. The U.S. stopped minting silver coins in 1965 and within a few years, almost all had disappeared. Look in your change. If you have a lot of pennies, you probably have one made before 1965, but you have probably never received a silver American coin.

Paul Millett has suggested that labor and investment are tied together. You need to have a significant pool of unattached labor requiring wages; without this pool there cannot be a significant market in investment for establishing productive enterprises. Much of the labor in classical Greece and Rome consisted of slaves hired out by masters. Once a credit system arrived with markets in labor and investment, hoarding disappeared. (Meikle in Scheidel and von Reden, 242)

Banking

This was almost nonexistent. Millett said there were no more than eight lending institutions in Athens using the most liberal definition. (242–3) Most loans were for necessities such as ransom, fines, burials, food, tax payments and public service, rather than business investments. (Osborne in Scheidel and von Reden, 121) Most liquid capital that was borrowed came from family relations, patrons, or clients. Personal relations, not business relations, were the paramount consideration in making a loan. Records from Babylon during the Persian Empire suggest that banking was much like pawnbroking, where the banker took security for a loan. 20 percent interest per year was a standard rate, though most loans were for terms of six months or less with no interest. Indian bankers of the fifth century charged interest varying from 15 percent to 240 percent a year. The Roman empire made loans for specific purposes such as encouraging Italians to leave and buy land elsewhere.

Bankers were often foreign-born residents, which increased the local population's dislike of them. They often used slaves as their agents. Temples became quasi-banks because they received valuable offerings and collected rents from extensive landholdings. They provided loans at interest to the local cities. Most of the time, the temple effectively removed money from circulation. (Scheidel, Morris, and Saller, 358) In an emergency, the authorities could melt down gold and silver statues and strip the ivory to pay for war. Of course, it was a disaster when outsiders sacked and looted a temple as the Phocians did to Delphi in 356 BC and the Romans did to Jerusalem in AD 70.

Overseas Trade

The ships were generally small and independently operated. Most carried about sixty to eighty tons though some gigantic grain transporters could carry 375 tons. (Scheidel, Morris, and Saller 585) Trade was a small portion of economy because production was more or less the same everywhere, transport costs were high, and therefore only luxury goods were in circulation and the markets for common goods other than food were insufficient. Trade grew in the Mediterranean and reached a high point from 200 BC to AD 200, based on the number of shipwrecks we have found on the sea bottom. After AD 200, the volume declined and would not recover until the 1500s. (Scheidel, Morris, and Saller, 572) The status of traders was fairly low, and successful merchants, even in port cities, preferred to buy land with their profits rather than build up their trading businesses. There were maritime loans made to finance voyages, but this was not a sustained business. (587) Even when one considers Rome's enormous grain trade, investment in ships was less than 1 percent of total capital assets of the richest group of Romans.

A city such as Athens was only interested in developing import trade, not export trade. There was no concept of a city budget or a trade balance. A substantial amount of trade was nonmarket and noncommodified. People exchanged gifts, especially patrons and clients. They were not necessarily of an equal value or exchanged at the same time. Civil wars were fought over social issues and could result in huge redistribution of wealth.

Joint-Stock Companies

Free peasant proprietors producing at or near subsistence level made most things in the Greek world. There were small numbers of craftsmen producing in workshops. Textiles, which would be so important later in the history of capitalism, were overwhelmingly produced by women in their homes. (338) Contracted wage labor only worked in large-scale city building programs, such as fifth-century BC Athens, which attracted craftsmen from abroad. Casual harvest labor also paid wages. The Roman empire had partnerships of merchants who collected taxes and supplied goods to the state, but there was no business with large numbers of investors or that tried to pull in small investors.

Accounting

Evidence of any kind for ancient accounting is very scarce, except for some Egyptian papyri. A third-century Alexandrian magnate had estates whose account books have survived. He seemed to be able to evaluate profitability in cash terms and run his estate in a highly centralized, efficient, resource-sharing and cash-conscious manner. (Scheidel and von Reden, 166–67) The records refer frequently to accounts being kept. The Hellenistic world definitely had single-entry bookkeeping. (Neal and Williamson, I, 58) But there is no sign of vital accounting tools such as double-entry bookkeeping or an accounting of debits and credits to be settled on a day of reckoning. Mathematics was cumbersome. Only south Asia had the vital mathematical and accounting concept of zero after AD 300.

THE MATURE ANCIENT SYSTEM

The ancient Roman Empire was likely at about the same level of wealth and development as the other major civilizations of Eurasia, including the Sasanid Empire of Persia, the Han Dynasty of China, and the Gupta Dynasty of South Asia. The complex overland route between China and India developed. The economic influence of these civilizations reached deeply into uncivilized areas. Mediterranean-area coins were found down the coast of east Africa all the way to Natal in exchange for ivory, palm oil, tortoise shell, slaves, spices, and incense. In the fifth century, Indian culture interacted with cultures in southeastern Asia and spread as far as Bali. There were land and sea trading links between south and east Asia as Indian cloth traded for spices from the islands. Rome paid a ransom in 410 that included three thousand pounds of Indian pepper to make a barbarian horde leave. We know of one Roman mission of about the year 170 that reached China. There may have been others.

Internal peace and a single currency spurred Roman growth and likely did the same for the major Asian states. Roman power destroyed the pirates of the Mediterranean and made the sea safe for commerce. At their heights, the Roman Empire and Han China seem to have had about the same population of sixty million. Expansion brought the benefits of civilization such as city life, fine pottery, wine drinking, wide use of olive oil, glass vessels, window glass, and artistic bronze ware to new and far-flung areas. Certain areas came to specialize in what they produced efficiently, which would have increased wealth.

Trade System

The ancient trade network extended into Scandinavia, Germany, Poland, and the north coast of the Black Sea. The Romans took advantage of the annual monsoon to trade with India. There is a description of trade with the Malay peninsula. Egyptians, Greeks, and Syrians resided permanently in India, trading gold for pepper. Silk from China also came through India since the Persians (who were often at war with Rome) forbade goods bound for the empire from crossing their land. All of the Roman coins scattered throughout Asia, Africa, and barbarian Europe suggest that Rome was running a trade deficit as it sent out gold and silver for eastern grain and luxuries.

Investment and Manufacturing

Italian industry reached its peak in the first century with the low cost of slave labor and a concentration of capital in the Emperor's hands. However businessmen often bought land with their profits rather than maintaining or expanding an enterprise. There was little incentive to improve slave agriculture. Because it was cheaper to produce many goods locally rather than to import because of expensive transport, inefficient industries persisted. There was no mass market. Manufacturing was done on a small scale: "factories" actually combined a workroom, a retail shop and living quarters. Only a very few factories for making tile, brick, glass and pottery employed hundreds.

The rare stories we have of Roman investment and development usually had bad endings. For example, around the year 50, there was a huge government effort to drain Lake Fucinius near Rome and then give the land to those who helped finance the project. But the project cost far more than that land's value and the drainage soon fell into disrepair. (Scheidel and von Reden, 264)

COLLAPSE OF THE ANCIENT SYSTEM

At one time, historians wrote as if the fall of the ancient civilizations in Europe and Asia was like turning off a light. One moment their economies were running well, the next they collapsed. We now accept that it was a very long process of perhaps four hundred years. There are odd parallels between the Roman Empire and Han China but both seemed to hit their economic high point around 170 and then started to decline. William Jongman has argued that as population grew, productivity and per person wealth fell. (Scheidel, Morris, and Saller, 595) On top of that, inequality seemed to grow so that the ancient economies not only fell into the old Malthusian trap but also saw their domestic markets collapsing as fewer people could afford to buy goods beyond subsistence. The annual minimum income of the knightly class was at least a hundred times that of the ordinary Roman. (600) After 450, the Gupta empire that dominated the northern part of the Indian subcontinent fragmented and collapsed. The rise of Islam around 650 dealt the final blow to the traditional trade relations of the ancient world. There has also been a long-time belief that productivity growth was hampered by slaves who had no incentive to work harder. Slavery would also prevent the formation of a large class of consumers that could sustain a domestic manufacturing market. (Neal and Williamson, I, 63) Others have challenged this, and it seems clear there are not enough data or documents to prove the case either way.

China

The burden of taxes on the peasantry grew increasingly oppressive, and there were two major revolts in 184. Professional armies commanded by wealthy landowning generals replaced a peasant draft army. This soon led to civil wars as the generals tried to take control. Peasants fled the fighting in the areas where taxes were still collected. The census showed only 16 million where once there had been 60 million. This does not mean that three-fourths of the people had died, but many had moved out of the government's control. Barbarian bands roamed deeply, and in 316 the Xiongnu sacked the capital of Loyang and killed thirty thousand people. The north fell into the hands of the Mongolian Toba people. There was a new rush south to the Yangzi River to get away from the barbarians. Three hundred years of violence and mayhem followed.

Rome

The reign of the emperor **Marcus Aurelius** (161–180) was often seen as the high point of the Roman Empire but also the beginning of the long decline of the ancient world. Wars against barbarians and Persians took up most of his attention. Worse, an epidemic of smallpox spread through the empire and emptied entire districts, especially in the core. Problems recurred: 1) a two-front war against the Persians and barbarians strained the army and the treasury; 2) the Empire lacked the money to pay for wars, building programs, and a growing administration; 3) areas of war had left devastated cities and fields. 4) There was a growing gap between the rich and the poor in cities and between the cities and the countryside.

The third century saw repeated civil wars as army generals tried to win and hold power as emperor. Corruption grew as military commanders, soldiers and imperial agents demanded food, livestock, and labor. Inhabitants sought safety and many deserted their farms. Richer landlords took advantage to claim deserted farms and increase their own holdings. Those farmers who had remained felt compelled to look to large landowners on villas for protection from barbarians, bandits, or the demands of imperial officials. The great landlords were able to field small armies of their own. Small landlords turned over their lands and were forbidden to leave, thus becoming **serfs**. A law of 322 reduced **sharecroppers** (farmers who paid crops to rent land and tools) to serfdom. Estates became quasi-legal units, free from the jurisdiction of the cities with local lords administering justice.

It may be that the Romans invented debasement and manipulation of coinage. There was a bronze coinage used for local transactions, probably no more than 5-10% of total coin stock. After 200, *denarius* coins were only 60 percent of the silver content of two hundred years earlier. By the 250s, the *denarius* was only 2 percent silver. The mines were exhausted of gold and silver. Roman technology could mine about 650 feet below the water table. (Scheidel, Morris, and Saller, 567) But it could not go deeper because of flooding. The windmill had not yet been invented. The waterwheel was coming into use in the third and fourth centuries. Oxen remained the main source of animal power, not horses. What the Romans needed was a steam engine to pump the water out. Alan Bresson says the only thing preventing Roman steam engines was a lack of coal in the Mediterranean area, but the engine never even got to that point. (Neal and Williamson, I, 69) William Jongman points out that British coal production under Roman rule increased ninefold, so there was a theoretical source of coal but bringing it to the precious metal mines was prohibitively expensive. (83) There had been uses of steam power, as seen earlier, but the Romans lacked the incentive to make labor go further and build a capitalist system.

Emperor **Diocletian** (284–305) attempted to fix wages and prices but his edict was unenforceable. Diocletian had divided the poorer, embattled western part of the empire from the East. Emperor **Constantine** (306–337) moved the capital east to Constantinople in the richer, Hellenistic part of the Roman empire. After he died, civil wars resumed. Barbarians pressed harder and they began to break through after 378. Mainly Germanic tribes streamed into the west and took over. Commerce became dangerous as pirates spread again. Wars devastated the industries of Gaul and the Rhineland. Cities made less money and the destruction in the country made it harder to feed the cities. In 476, the empire in the West officially ended. From 535 until 570 wars between the Germans and eastern Romans (Byzantines) greatly damaged Italy.

South Asia

The **caste** system began to harden: there were several thousand castes based on profession, religion, race, and where one lived. This fragmented society and set rigid rules; those who would not obey became outcastes, the lowest category. We have no population records from this area to compare with Rome or China, but the archeological record does not indicate a significant loss of population. The estimated population in 200 was forty-one million, somewhat below those of Rome and Han China. In 400, it was forty-seven million, probably comparable to Rome and above China. By 600 and 800, it was fifty-three million and sixty-four million respectively. (McEvedy and Jones, 183) Both of these figures would be substantially above those of China and western Europe. This created a certain continuity in southern Asian history but also ensured that it would not be the originating area of capitalism. Labor would remain the cheapest commodity. Meanwhile, the fall of the Western empire, the rise of Islam, and the decline of Mediterranean trade had effectively cut off the dense populations of North Africa and the east from the rich resources of Western and Central Europe.

CONCLUSION

The ancient economy was not capitalist nor did it ever come close to breaking through to capitalism. Labor remained plentiful and the cheapest commodity. Both the "modernizers" and the "primitivists" make valuable explanations. There were capitalistic aspects in the ancient world but they were smaller and scarcer than the modern world. It is also true that the desire for dignity and higher social status shaped the economy. Consumers received significant goods, especially food, as free gifts. Few solicited investment and few invested. Slavery distorted the labor market and most production was for consumption.

TIMELINE

4000 BC	Copper smelting developed
3400 BC	Writing invented
3000 BC	Bronze technology
625 BC	Coinage developed in China and Lydia
500 BC	Iron smelting in Europe and Asia
336–323 BC	Alexander the Great
200 BC	Water wheel invented
AD 170	Roman mission reached China
AD 240	Han dynasty in China collapsed
AD 300	South Asia developed mathematical concept of zero
AD 450–500	Gupta dynasty of southern Asia fragmented and fell
AD 476	End of Roman Empire in West
AD 535–70	Devastating Italian wars

KEY TERMS

"Primitivists" and "Modernizers"
wootz steel
cash crops
Malthusian trap
cash
sharecroppers

Chapter 3

PRE-CONDITIONS OF CAPITALISM

Western Europe after the fall of Rome was a unique society for a number of reasons. Never before had a society with a heritage of civilization and a high level of social organization been based in the countryside. Also unique was that there was a shortage of labor and a surplus of resources. It had good soil, forests, mountains, navigable rivers, seas, and rainfall. In every previous world society, labor had always been the cheapest commodity so that there was no incentive to increase labor efficiency and productivity because that would lead to mass unemployment. Slaves were common in these civilizations. Now labor was very valuable and there was a need for a capital-intensive system.

At the same time there were two other dynamic cultures that could have developed capitalism: China under the Song and early Ming dynasties and the Islamic area that stretched from Spain to southern Asia. In the year 1000, Europe had thirty-six million people, China sixty-six million, and the

Indian subcontinent seventy-nine million. Unlike China and Europe, India had no eight-hundred-year population dip. There were too many people. Alan Macfarlane suggests that the concentration of rice-growing over wheat-growing in East, South and Southeast Asia creates long-term economic problems. It reduces the demand for animals, reduces the need for grinding machinery, reduces the size of holdings, increases the demand for human labor and thus population, and increases inequality thus inhibiting the development of a domestic market. (Macfarlane, xx) The caloric yield per acre of rice is greater than wheat, corn, and oats, but it has less protein. India, for all its fertility, lacked a natural breadbasket of high productivity because all of its land is below 35° N of latitude. The monsoons partly compensate for this, but they are unpredictable, erratic, and destructive. The states of India would not pioneer capitalism.

Why Europe?

China lost perhaps three-fourths of its population from wars and refugees fleeing to the Yangzi valley and to Korea. Yet capitalism did not start there; it simply fell back into a Malthusian cycle. Western Europe perhaps lost more than three-fourths of its population starting with the plague at the time of Marcus Aurelius, the collapse of the Western Empire, the Italian Wars of the sixth century, the plague of Justinian, the Muslim invasion, and the crisis of the ninth century. The extreme example is Rome itself, whose population fell from one million or 750,000 to twenty thousand by 800; that's a 97 percent or 98 percent decline. Markets collapsed. England seems to have reverted materially to pre-Roman status. At the same time, the tighter integration of Ireland and the zone between the Rhine and Elbe Rivers perhaps increased the value of capital substantially. There was greater economic activity in Scandinavia and Eastern Europe than there had been in Roman days.

THE CARAVAN ECONOMY AND ISLAM

The Desert Environment

Breadbaskets between 35° and 55° constitute one kind of world. The deserts of 30° latitude were another world and a formidable barrier. They slowed the spread of Mesoamerican culture to the north. The major deserts in the Old World were the Sahara, the Syro-Arabian Desert where Syria, Iraq, and Jordan meet, the Great Indian east of the Indus River, the Taklamakin in western China, and the Gobi between China and Mongolia.

The Domestication of the Camel

Camel caravans appeared in the time of the ancient Assyrian and Babylonian empires. The camel ("the ship of the desert") needs less water and eats more kinds of shrubs than goats or sheep. The "**North Arabian saddle**" was invented between 500 BC and AD 200. This allowed riders a firm seat and allowed camels to carry up to five hundred pounds. Camels, horses, mules, and donkeys could travel faster cross-country than carts. This trade abandoned the wheel as enough camels were bred sometime before AD 500. The further one got from the Arabian breeding center, the less the impact of the camel and the less displacement there was of wheeled vehicles. Two-humped Bactrian camels crossbred with others and created a better animal. Large numbers of camel breeds followed, specializing in different traits. One man could handle six camels. Camels would travel twenty miles in six hours, then forage. (McNeill)

The Origins of Islam

Islam did not originate in the desert but rather the wetter area of southwestern Arabia. **Muhammad** (c.570–632) was a merchant in the caravan trade. Islam therefore honored merchants. In 610, Muhammad had a religious experience and called for religious reform in Arabia and submitting to God. He urged the Arabs to put aside the tribal ties that divided them and to be part of one religious community. He attacked undue wealth and social inequality. Islam prohibits **usury**, which it defines as the lending of money at any rate of interest. By the time he died, Muhammad had united Arabia. Over the next eighty years, the Arabs would roam west conquering Spain and east taking Persia. Regular pay and battlefield booty attracted tribesmen.

Caravans and Islam

Islamic traders pushed across the Sahara desert to west-central Africa and after 900 entered China looking for silk. Camel caravans now could penetrate isolated regions and remote oases; for many isolated peoples, the contact with modern society was a shock. Islam made it a religious act to endow caravan supply posts with food and fodder. This cut transport costs enormously. Costs fell to 3 percent in one journey over fifteen hundred miles. Experienced camel-drivers knew where to find water in the worst desert. Even bulk staples such as food were transported several hundred miles, not just luxury goods such as silk, gems, spices, and incense. Beyond the world of Islam, it was cheaper to ship or to use carts. From about 630 to 1300, the caravan and Islam supported each other. Religious rewards made transport costs cheaper while the caravan introduced Islam to new areas. (McNeill) Even the non-Islamic nomads of Eurasia came to appreciate caravans while they used horses rather than camels.

The Muslims built huge and beautiful cities including Cordoba in Spain, Cairo in Egypt, and Baghdad in Mesopotamia. They created a vast currency zone united by the dirhem and dinar, the gold and silver coins. There was a labor shortage, perhaps a severe labor shortage, in the Islamic world relative to the resources. It could draw on some of the richest provinces of the former Roman and Persian empires while the caravans allowed access to new areas at lower costs. However, the constant wars created vast numbers of slaves, and the slave market was replenished by transshipments of slaves from areas of eastern Europe and western Africa not controlled by the Muslims.

Islamic Finance

With usury banned, the Muslims developed a wide variety of business techniques to move money and make profit without quite violating the ban. They developed the **bill of exchange** in the eighth century, which started as a kind of IOU that could be traded for goods by merchants. This meant merchants would not have to carry large amounts of coin, gold, or silver that might attract thieves. Muslims also developed the joint-stock company by the eleventh century with the Karimi network in the Arabian Sea. Investors pooled money together and then took respective shares of profits. Today Islamic deposit bankers have deposits technically buying shares of the bank and then splitting a pool of profit minus an agreed-upon management fee; they have gained profit at interest (American credit unions operate in a similar way). There were also "sleeping partnerships": the investor joined with the merchant and they "split" the profit in such a way as to provide a rate of return. Many financial terms derive from Arabic including check, coffer, and zero.

Why did not the Islamic World Pioneer Capitalism?

It seems clear from the above description that the Islamic world was generally richer than the western world. The great Islamic cites built mosques, palaces, libraries, schools, and hospitals at a time when northern European towns consisted of wooden huts surrounding a sheltering castle. The flow of slaves dragged down the economy and sent gold and silver to Europe and sub-Saharan Africa.. There was also a steady decline in the status of middle-class and upper-class women in the Islamic world. While western women were not legally equal in the Middle Ages, they did have some property rights and at times could wield considerable amounts of power. The grinding discrimination robbed Islam of the labor and talent of half of the upper-class population. The Arab caliphates disintegrated after the tenth and eleventh centuries. Less sophisticated groups became dominant. Turks from central Asia conquered Baghdad in 1055 and gradually seized control of the Muslim heartland. Berbers from the North African mountains took over Morocco in 1056, then spread into parts of Algeria and Spain. Finally, the Mongols in 1258 destroyed Baghdad. Also, the usury prohibition hindered economic development as it would in West Europe. I have listed above some of the clever ways to get around the ban on interest. There were significant but shrinking numbers of non-Muslims who were not bound by this and finally there were unscrupulous Muslims who simply ignored religious rules. However, there was a large and growing pool of men with sufficient piety who observed the rule. But they were under no obligation to give away their money for free. Vast amounts of potential investment funds were withheld or used to buy land or goods. On occasion, lenders secured approval for what was close to a loan at interest from secular and Islamic authorities. The interest rate was close to 20 percent, which shows the shortage of investment funds.

THE OPENING OF THE SILK ROAD

The new Islamic caravan routes interacted with the existing Silk Road. Han China established this five thousand mile overland route in the first century when it seized control of the Tarim basin. China had obtained large Ferghana horses from the west around 100 BC. When the Han Empire collapsed in 240, the Sogdians of the Samarkand region took control. (Neal and Williamson, I, 103) By 589, China had recovered from the Han collapse. Buddhism spread to China via the overland route and by the sea route to India. Buddhism reached Japan in 538 and integrated that land into the wider economy, making China the center, not the end, of the distribution line. The **Sui Dynasty** (c.581–618) was short-lived but did build the Grand Canal to connect the Yellow and Yangzi Rivers. The years between 550 and 600 mark the peak of Byzantine coins in China. The Silk Road saw trade in other luxury goods such as glass bowls from Persia, precious and semiprecious stones, metalwork, rugs, and spices. Merchants, monks, missionaries, pilgrims, soldiers, scholars, artisans, horse trainers, and entertainers all traveled the road.

T'ang China (618–907)

The new regime tried to make peasant landholding more equal and give them better conditions. This aided grain and livestock productivity and expanded the market for a time although inequality soon returned. The rice-growing lower Yangzi valley became the economic center. There were post-stations every ten miles to speed communication. In the 650s, China conquered Samarkand and increased its Silk Road profit. It began a merit-based civil service to improve government efficiency. The official census of 754 recorded fifty-three million persons, almost the same as Han China at its peak. Trade introduced tea from southeast Asia in the eighth century. The popularity of tea drinking allowed a dense population to grow without the threat of water-borne diseases. Commerce brought the chair from the West. China was using coal by the fourth century. It invented the wheelbarrow, a simple technology that made transporting goods much easier. It also expanded its earlier inventions of paper and porcelain. In the eighth century, overseas trade with India and the Middle East exploded as China used larger, more watertight vessels. The trade with India also brought the number zero. The city of Guangzhou became the center of this trade.

China lost perhaps three-fourths of its population after the Han Empire fell, yet capitalism did not start there. In the first place, there was not as much of a real population loss as it appears from the census. At the end of the Han and in subsequent years, many simply evaded the government's attention by fleeing to the south or to Korea. As order was restored, they returned or simply reported their family's presence to the census authorities. There was never a prolonged period where capital outstripped labor. There is the rise of rice growing which was more important in the T'ang than it had been in the Han and thus lessened the demand for animal power and grinding machinery while increasing inequality. As late as the eighth century, three-quarters of the Chinese people lived in the north where wheat and millet were the chief crops. By 1300, three-quarters lived in the south. (Maddison 1998, 14) Superior plows reduced the need for animal power even further. The farmers' livestock were mostly scavengers such as pigs and poultry who had to find their own food. Pigs also have greater dietary efficiency: they convert one-fifth of what they eat into food fit for human consumption while cattle only convert one-twentieth. (Crosby, 173) Technological advance slowed and even reversed itself: glassmaking faded in Asia while growing in Europe; this proved important because of spectacles and the need for lenses to conduct many scientific experiments. (Macfarlane, xxvi) For the first half of its life, the T'ang used silk, not coins, to pay for its armies and government in central Asia. (Neal and Williamson, I, 109) As Angus Maddison stated "There is little convincing evidence for believing that China was on the brink of developing a mechanised industry." (Maddison 1998, 14)

A Muslim army defeated the Chinese in 751 near today's Kazakhstan/Kirgyzstan border. The area became a buffer zone as Chinese control over central Asia ended. The T'ang had to regroup in a weakened and less centralized form. T'ang came to an end in 907 when power fell into the hands of foreign generals.

CHINA'S GOLDEN AGE

In 960, a Chinese general seized power and established the **Song Dynasty** (960–1279). It governed a smaller area than the T'ang dynasty had. From 1100 to 1140, a Mongol/Chinese mix of people conquered the northern part and set up the Chin dynasty. However, the "**Southern Song**" held the Yangzi valley, which was the wealthy core, and soon became richer with a bigger budget and larger bureaucracy than Song had seen. The government bureaucracy guided farm development and improvement. (Maddison 1998, 13)

Population and Agriculture

The population in the south may have tripled from the eighth to the eleventh centuries and perhaps exceeded a hundred million. The yield from seed was 10:1 as opposed to 4:1 in Europe. Champa rice from southeast Asia grew in two-thirds the time it had taken before. This made it possible to get two crops of rice a year. Later on, a few areas with rich soil were able to get three crops of rice a year. Farmers in some warm areas planted cotton. Because the land was in such short supply (only 10 percent can be farmed as opposed to 25 percent in Europe), no land was left unplanted (fallow) after 1000. The need for farmland destroyed the forests. Chinese farmers used extensive labor, human waste as fertilizer, and irrigation. They also developed new tools that would much later be independently developed in European farming such as the seed drill and the horse hoe. Cash crops included fruits, cotton, silk, and sugar cane. (Neal and Williamson, I, 128–29)

Printing and Manufacturing

Printing started in the ninth century. China developed movable type by 1030, although the type was rarely used because of the large number of characters. Illustrated agricultural handbooks became very popular and spread farming knowledge. Large commercial cities such as Hangzhou prospered. In the Song years, Chinese ironmasters combined the water wheel with the bellows to create a **blast furnace** that could truly melt iron. The wood from the devastated forests fed the furnaces. Government-run spinning and weaving mills produced cheap, durable, and comfortable cotton clothing for consumption, not profit. Angus Maddison estimated that China enjoyed a 33 percent rise in real per capita income from 960 to 1280; this would be about a tenth of one percent per year. (Maddison 1998, 14) That is about the same as the Mediterranean world during the rise of Rome.

The Chinese understood magnetic polarity at least back to the third century. The first attested use of the compass was in 1119. But the overseas trade was at first in the hands of Arabs and Persians while Koreans dominated the trade with Japan. There were thousands of foreigners in the commercial cities of Guangzhou, Yangzhou and Quanzhou. By the late Song, Chinese merchants dominated the trade with Korea and Japan and were venturing down to southeast Asia. Song porcelains are found as far away as Zanzibar off the coast of East Africa.

Money, Credit and Banking

If Maddison is correct about per capita income and the population doubled, then the overall economy grew considerably. China needed much more money to support this rapid growth. T'ang had minted at most 310,000 strings of copper cash a year. By the eleventh century, the Song government was minting six times as much. Copper ran short, so it developed paper money as early as 811. By southern Song, China had established a system of credit, banking, and investment. The bureaucracy and "degree holders" who earned money from land, trade, and teaching formed the elite. Urban merchants and manufacturers deferred to the bureaucracy and gentry. China lacked balance unlike Western Europe, where nobles and religious authorities formed countervailing forces to the state. The Chinese state was very good at intensifying agriculture but not so good at other things. Because of high overland transport costs, China was not a national market, but rather a series of semiclosed regional economies. (Maddison 1998, 25) Great inequality of income limited the craft market to government, court officials, and aristocrats. The Chinese used iron for weapons and decorative art, not for tools. One should also note that, like the Muslim areas, there was a steady decline in the status of upper-class and middle-class women, symbolized by the rise of "foot binding" that broke the arch and deformed the toes of women and left them hardly able to walk.

THE RISE OF THE MONGOLS

The nomadic group to the north gradually conquered the Chinese area from 1205 to 1279. There was much destruction at this time: the Yellow River changed its course in 1194 causing massive flooding. The Grand Canal ceased to function. The Mongols razed many cities. The takeover of Southern Song had taken the longest and been the most difficult before **Kubilai Khan** (1260–1294) completed the conquest. The Mongols adopted Chinese ways of rule, but many Chinese were hostile. The Mongols therefore welcomed foreigners to help in their government. This created a cosmopolitan system that stretched from the Pacific to the Black Sea as the Mongols subjugated many of the Turkic peoples of central and western Asia and conquered Persia. The Mongols introduced sorghum to the Chinese farming system. (Maddison 1998, 13)

The century from 1240 to 1340 saw expanded contact with Europe along the Silk Road because the Mongols controlled the entire way and their Khanates cooperated to make transport costs remarkably low. (Neal and Williamson, I, 114) Gunpowder, paper money, printing, porcelain, textiles, playing cards, medicines, art motifs, and the compass all flowed west. Building on the growing Chinese presence at sea, Kubilai tried unsuccessfully to conquer Japan twice and Java once. His envoys traveled as far as southern India and Sri Lanka demanding tribute and ten states of southern Asia complied. The most famous merchant of the time was the Venetian **Marco Polo**, who stayed in the East from 1275 to 1295. Going the other way, a Nestorian monk named Rabban Sauma born in Beijing traveled to Europe in 1287.

THE MING DYNASTY

Famine and plague and renewed flooding of the Yellow River struck China in the 1320s. The Mongol rule weakened, and revolts began. By 1368, the Mongols were pushed out of China and the Ming Dynasty was established. After Tamerlane died in 1405, central Asia fragmented and the unity of the Silk Road was broken. The Persians won their independence in 1469.

Under the Mongols, the Arabs had strengthened their sea trade with China with regular trading voyages between Hormuz (in the Persian Gulf) and Quanzhou. The Ming immediately renewed the Mongols' tributary arrangements, including payments from Japan, Vietnam, Cambodia, Tibet and Korea. From 1405 to 1433, the Ming Emperor Yongle sent out seven maritime voyages under the Muslim eunuch **Zhang He** that traveled to Aden and Hormuz. Chinese communities were growing in southeast Asia. Yongle paid for this, the move of the capital from Nanjing to an expanded Beijing, and the rebuilding of the Grand Canal by printing paper money which ended up losing 99.9% of its value. The Chinese money reverted to a silver-based system, sharply limiting the capacity for economic growth. Voyages were tremendously expensive and did not seem to yield much except spectacle.

This only explains part of the reason why the Ming rulers turned their backs on the sea. Why did they not go further? To the Chinese, there was little of interest beyond the trading coast of East Africa. Southern Africa was less developed and there was no knowledge of West Africa. Traveling thousands of miles more to western Europe promised little advantage. The Ming had no goal to strive for except getting more tributaries. Bureaucrats who had a long-standing rivalry with eunuchs later destroyed the records of the voyages. There was possibly a backlash against all foreigners after the Mongol experience. I think this is the key moment where we see that China had not developed capitalism that would have put Europe at a disadvantage. Traders and capitalists, working with the Portuguese government, were at the forefront of European exploration of Africa and, as we shall see, despite great expense and disappointments, they could turn their focus on the goods and trade of southern and southeastern Asia that promised much profit.

AGE OF THE CRUSADES

This brings us back to western Europe. The people of this area had abundant resources and the technical skill while having a prolonged period of reduced labor force. Population estimates are very difficult but it seems fair to say that the western European area that had been under Roman control did not regain its population level of the year 200 until nine hundred years later. This is where capitalism gained its impetus: for hundreds of years the Europeans needed to figure out how to get the most of their limited labor force. When they enslaved people, it was to sell them to the Muslim world to raise gold and silver, which were also in short supply. So slavery was not used as a solution to the labor shortage.

Better Nutrition

The West had no way to take advantage of this as long as fear and uncertainty kept the trade routes effectively closed and it lacked hard money (gold and silver). The attacks of the Muslims and Vikings made trade in the Mediterranean and North Seas and the English Channel almost impossible. Population began to rise from the tenth to the thirteenth centuries with new settlements and larger towns and cities. There was a slow transition from a **two-field system** to a **three-field system** in Europe away from the Mediterranean: one field was left fallow (the farmer would plow it and remove weeds regularly but would not plant any crop), he would plant one field with winter grain (wheat, rye, or barley), and would plant the third with another crop, often oats or legumes (protein-rich peas, lentils or broad beans). This change alone increased production by a third with less plowing of fallow. Land was so plentiful that they did not need the desperate measures of the Chinese. Farm productivity grew by about 50 percent. (Cameron, 51) As legumes became a staple of the spring planting, the diet for peasants was richer in protein than for the lower class of the old Roman Empire. This made for taller, heavier, healthier, and stronger peasants. Women had a better chance of surviving childbirth. Peasants had the energy to clear brush and light woods, then began to nibble at the edges of the great European forests. They built huge numbers of bridges across Europe's streams and rivers, connecting many of the towns and villages. This brought down the cost of land transport.

Horseshoes had been virtually unknown and inept harnessing cut off air from the horse's lungs. Farmers invented the modern rigid horse collar that rests on the horse's shoulders. This increases the work performed by the horse by three or fourfold and became common by 1000. The horse is also faster than an ox. Earlier farmers had avoided the horse as a farm animal because it needed to eat hay from a meadow and expensive grain. Now the three-field system could provide the needed oats. Nailed horseshoes came into use along with better ways of harnessing horses in tandem instead of side-by-side.

Pointing toward Capitalism

By the eleventh century, the Europeans had subdued the Vikings and driven the Muslims from Sardinia, Corsica, and Sicily. Flanders in the north and Italy in the south began to flourish as trade centers. During the eleventh century, Jews played a vital role in trade, lending money to kings, nobles, and merchants. Jews in large numbers began to live in Europe away from the Mediterranean. Around the year 1000, Jewish merchants in the Mediterranean were trading salt, wine, grain, cloth, and slaves. The Jews lacked a wasteful military class and were either banned from land ownership or feared that Christian expulsion orders could confiscate their land at a moment's notice. (Lopez, 61) The Church's prohibition on usury increasingly hampered Christian businesses just as Islamic rules hampered the Muslims. Christian rules did not bind Jews, who were also well-positioned to trade in the Mediterranean basin from Spain and Italy to the eastern coast.

When Western Europe launched **Crusades** (religious wars primarily aimed at the Muslims) after 1096, anti-Semitism rose considerably. Heightened religious fervor labeled Jews as heathens almost as bad as the Muslims. The men of the new middle class, deeply in debt to Jewish moneylenders, would take advantage to wipe out their debts violently. This Christian middle class also took over a great deal of merchant activity from the Jews. By 1100, Jews were becoming ghettoized and were prohibited from most professions. The regular contact with the Islamic world brought a flood of financial innovations and goods including sugar cane, silk, rice, paper, and cotton. (Braudel II, 556)

TIMELINE

AD 100	Silk Road linked west and China by land
AD 300	Camel caravans began in Asian deserts
AD 610–632	Beginnings of Islam with Muhammad
AD 618–907	T'ang Dynasty in China
AD 960–1279	Song Dynasty in China
1055	Turks conquered Baghdad
1056	Berbers conquered Morocco
1096	European Crusades began
1260–1294	Kubilai Khan; Mongols at height of power
1279	Mongols conquered China
1368	Ming dynasty drove Mongols out of China
1405	Death of Tamerlane; central Asian authority fragmented
1405–1433	Voyages of Zhang He

KEY TERMS

"North Arabian saddle"
usury
blast furnace
Kubilai Khan
Marco Polo
Zhang He
three-field system

Chapter 4

THE MACHINERY OF CAPITALISM

EUROPEAN COINAGE, AFRICAN GOLD

The Early Middle Ages

Barbarians had minted expensive gold coins but only for gifts, exchange, and tribute. They had not used it as real money. After the fall of the Roman Empire, its gold coins were hoarded, buried, or continued to flow to the east until they disappeared by 700. Each year, 5 percent of the gold in circulation is lost because of wear. (Kindleberger 1993, 24) Coins are important in a modern economy because they allow for more and easier trades. For perhaps 150 years from 500 until 650, there was no silver minting outside Italy, but then silver coins were struck in England and Frisia and then elsewhere. Where did the silver come from? We do not know for sure but the source dried up within a hundred years. For quite a while, western Europe had to get its precious metal from the outside. Much of it came from the Muslim world in exchange for slaves who were taken in eastern Europe. There was no central control of minting. Abbeys, cities, and individuals all minted coins alongside kings. Counterfeit coins were so common that merchants carried kits to detect fake silver and bit into gold coins to make sure they were not made of soft lead.

New Silver Sources

The Romans had neither possessed the technology nor the desire to invent the technology that would deepen their precious metal mines. The old mines in Spain and Cyprus were lost or forgotten. The Frankish Emperor **Charlemagne** (d.814) revived silver mining and coinage when he conquered Bohemia with its rich mineral resources. His father had created a money system where a pound of silver would be divided into 240 silver pennies. Silver flowed from German and Czech mines unknown in ancient times. By the tenth century, miners bored into the Harz mountains at a rate of eight inches a day. Coinage was still regional: the further east you went, the rarer coins became. Charlemagne's silver coins circulated only in Scandinavia and in his empire. In the Mediterranean, Muslim and Byzantine gold coins ruled.

African Gold Kingdoms

The Arabian camel was introduced into the Sahara after the year 0 and transformed the desert into a trading region. Between the desert and the forest zone of the African coast was the savannah agricultural belt that had been farmed for thousands of years. It had poor soil and unpredictable rainfall. By the Middle Ages Arabo-Berber merchants had organized trade along four main routes. West Africa had a series of large kingdoms that grew rich trading gold and slaves from the coast to North Africa in exchange for salt from Sahara mines.

Gold and salt had exactly the same value per pound in the West African trade. (Kindleberger 1993, 24) It is estimated that they dug out 500,000 ounces of gold each year from the packed earth that contained gold nuggets and dust. The location of the gold mines was a secret, but they were roughly at the extreme western end of the Niger River tributaries and later to the east by the Black Volta River.

Ghana, which is located in present-day Mali (not present-day Ghana), was the first of these West African kingdoms that grew rich on this trade sometime before 800. It did not control the mines but no gold could flow for salt without its agreement. With trade came Islam from the north, and many converted. The Ghanaian rulers remained pagans but employed Muslim advisers. Around 1200, Berber Muslims attacked Ghana. These attacks triggered internal revolts and the kingdom collapsed.

Power shifted east to the Kingdom of **Mali**, which dominated the region from about 1250 to 1450. The ruling class and the merchant cities were mostly Muslim. The most famous merchant city was Timbuktu, which was founded in 1087. Mali reached its height under **Mansa Musa** (1312–1337). This king made a pilgrimage to Mecca in 1324 and spent so much gold in Egypt that prices fell for the next twenty years. As the gold supply began to dry up and new mines opened further to the east, power shifted again in that direction and the **Songhai Empire** (1468–1591) rose and captured Timbuktu. It was centered at Gao, just east of the bend of the Niger. In 1591, the Moroccans marched twelve hundred miles south across the Sahara desert, overthrew Songhai, but could not keep it because it was so far away. Songhai's collapse led to chaos in West Africa and encouraged the slave trade.

Coins in Europe

By 1100, silver coins had replaced barter or payments in kind throughout most of Europe. New silver mines opened in the 1160s from England to Italy, swelling the silver supply. Gold coins appeared, especially after 1252 when Genoa and Florence minted large numbers of coins from African gold. Northern and Eastern Europe's coinage was more centralized, though the west was starting to get control of minting. The Holy Roman Empire that dominated central Europe, for example, had five hundred mints coining seventy currencies. (Neal and Williamson, I, 254) Coins circulated briskly and stimulated commerce. Trade within Europe tended to be with coins, but trade with Asia was largely by precious metal. In 1204, the Venetians sacked Constantinople, the capital of the Byzantine Empire. This had the effect of establishing the Florentine florin as the unofficial common currency of the Mediterranean basin.

BANKING: THIRTEENTH-CENTURY GROWTH AND PROBLEMS

The banking system also grew in the thirteenth century: **pawnbrokers** who would lend money in exchange for holding collateral; **deposit bankers** who protected money and kept accounts in Venice and Genoa as early as the twelfth century; and **merchant bankers** who fostered investment in commercial ventures. (*Cambridge Economic History* V, 300) The pioneers in this field were the **Knights Templar**, a crusading order that became fabulously wealthy by setting up banking centers in Paris, Jerusalem, and other major cities. A crusader could deposit his plunder with the Templars in Jerusalem, receive a letter of credit, and draw upon his loot in France. The

Templars modeled this transfer system on the Muslim system they had observed that allowed people to transfer their money long distances. The Templars advanced credit to merchants and governments.

Bankers had problems in their relations with the state because kings and nobles would often borrow money for wars and then repudiate the debt, ruining the bank. King Philip the Fair of France charged the Templars with witchcraft, stole their money, and burned their leaders alive. Deposit bankers gave favored customers overdraft privileges. Jews and Lombards (people of northern Italy) formed banking communities, especially in pawnbroking. The first Lombards were reported in the Netherlands in 1127. Governments taxed Lombards and Jews heavily, persecuted them, and expelled them periodically. "Lombard Street" became another name for banking.

THE MEDIEVAL ECONOMY

Manorialism is a word used to describe the organization of farms in medieval Europe. It is the economic counterpart of **feudalism**, which describes the political organization. A **manor** was an agricultural estate in a particular locality that was under the control of a single lord. Sometimes the manor contained two or more villages, sometimes villages were divided into two or more manors. Village and manor often coincided. Some manors had been created by strongmen during the chaos of the ninth and tenth centuries. Kings and great lords had granted some. The Catholic church controlled many manors.

At no time in the history of medieval Europe did manors produce a majority of farm crops nor did they employ the majority of farm workers. There was a core with many manors between the Loire and Rhine Rivers. In England around 1300,

25 percent of the production came from manors, 50 percent came from rented land, and another 25 percent came from free landowners. (Neal and Williamson, I, 232–33) By 1280, serfdom had ended in the Paris region. (Braudel, II, 257) Thus it is highly misleading to generalize about a "manorialist" (or worse, a "feudal") stage of production, as if everyone were locked into this system.

Lords and Serfs

Knights with only one manor might live on it themselves; others with more than one had stewards or bailiffs run affairs and collect the lord's revenues. **Serfs** had to pay fees and perform services for the lord, they could not leave the land without the lord's permission, and they were subject to the lord's courts. The lord served as judge, jury, and occasional executioner. Between one-third and one-half of the arable land was reserved for the lord and known as the *demesne*. Serfs had to farm the lord's land as well as their own. This could take up to three days a week. The serfs had to pay fees for pasturing cows, fishing in streams, sending their pigs into the forest, or gathering wood. Aside from all this, the peasant was supposed to pay a tithe (one-tenth of all produce) to the parish church. The lords often held monopolies over flour mills and ovens, forcing the peasants to pay yet another fee if they wanted to grind their wheat into flour or bake bread. In the harvest season, the lord got to sell his produce first and thus at a higher price.

Technological Advances

Europe made greater use of water wheels (which had elaborate systems of gearing) for grinding grain, sawing wood, fulling wool, making paper, mashing hops for beer, hammering metal, or operating forges. (Landes, 46) England had six thousand water wheels by the late eleventh century. In the north where water could freeze, windmills became important in the twelfth century. (Neal and Williamson, I, 242–46) Holland and Flanders used these to pump out water from their low-lying areas and then kept the water out with dikes. This increased the size of their farmland considerably. The spinning wheel and wheelbarrow appeared. Foot-operated treadles operated lathes and looms. The magnetic compass came from China. Around 1280, the first eyeglasses appeared. These could double the career of a skilled worker. David Landes suggests that making precision lenses paved the way for precision tool making. (Landes, 46–47) Alan Macfarlane states that "glass made a new science and technology possible by providing the new instruments" such as microscopes and barometers. (Macfarlane, xxvi) Around 1300 came the first weight-driven mechanical clocks. These were the most complex mechanisms ever invented in the world up to that time. They introduced greater punctuality and began to tie workers to "the clock." With their animals and technology, the Western Europeans were learning how to make their scarce labor go further and find substitutes for human energy.

Sea Trade

Overland trade costs four to six times that of water transport. Though water trade was very desirable, it was very difficult to get an accurate reading of market conditions hundreds of miles away, and it was hard to enforce contracts. After 1000, Europeans sent out remote agents, often family relations, to solve these problems. (Neal and Williamson, I, 252–53)

A new kind of shipping business began in the twelfth century, the ***commenda***. Previously a ship captain would use his own money to buy goods and hire a crew. When the goods were sold, the crew would be paid off, the captain would keep the rest of the money, and the process would begin again. Under the *commenda*, a private investor or a group of investors would lend money to a traveling party that was expected to invest in a commercial operation for the duration of a round-trip voyage. The lenders assumed the risks and would get 75 percent of the profits. (Lopez, 76) This led to the establishment of another business by 1318: marine insurance. Insurance rates were 10 to 15 percent of the cargo's value. (Neal and Williamson, I, 253) The port cities of Italy dominated marine insurance.

These contracts made long-distance trade much more efficient and many early ones specified what goods would be sold, to whom, and at what price. By one estimate, the Italian city of Genoa's trade increased fourfold from 1274 to 1293. Families of merchants diversified among a home office, carriers and branches. They pressed for and gained better and more secure roads, bridges, and passes through the Alps Mountains. The growth of trade enabled the Europeans of the Middle Ages to transform farm surpluses into usable money in a way the ancients never had. This is a form of **monetizing national assets**.

There were also improvements in shipping technology. In 1104, Venice opened a central shipyard and systematically improved ship design. The compass and other innovations allowed Venice to undertake two round-trip voyages each year to Alexandria, Egypt, before the weather turned bad. Alexandria was the key trading city for South Asian goods coming up the Red Sea. In 1291, the Genoese drove off a Moroccan fleet blocking the Straits of Gibraltar and ensured a safe sea voyage from Italy to Flanders, the other wealth center. (Maddison 2001, 23, 55)

The Fairs

A key development for land trade was the fair. The Count of Champagne held a famous fair regularly where he set up booths and paid for police and money-changers who would convert different coins to the silver coins of the town of Troyes. This became so widespread that gold and silver to this day are measured in "troy" ounces and pounds. Officials of the fair tried to minimize the need to carry coins by matching the merchants' credits and debits at the end of the fair to see how much could be canceled. This is called **debt clearing**. The remainder would have to be paid in coin, or a bill of exchange brought to the fair, or a new bill would be written that the merchant could bring to the next fair. To speed business up, officials weighed and tested coins, put them into sacks, and sewed them shut. (Kindleberger 1993, 22, 39) Thus, you did not have to count a bunch of coins, just pay in sacks and then a few coins. The Count wanted to attract merchants from distant Italy to his fair so he paid the barons along the route to protect the traveling merchants. What did the Count get out of this? He collected sales taxes that more than paid for the expenses. Every great lord, seeking revenue, tried to set up his own fair. Most of them failed, a few became specialized. Kings and nobles in 1100 had been hostile to merchants, seeing them as spies or parasites. By 1200, rulers greedily encouraged the merchants.

The Growth of the Towns

In the time of Charlemagne, there had been no western European cities with more than ten thousand persons. Four hundred years later, cities and towns were growing rapidly. The Italian cities led the way, but Flanders (part of Belgium today) also grew important by 1000. This area had been famous for its woolen cloth even before the Roman Empire. It had easy access to Scandinavia and up the Rhine River to the German towns. It was making so much woolen cloth that it soon had to import raw wool from England. Before 1300, the direct sea route to Italy was very dangerous, so merchants used the overland route instead. This became much traveled after 1225 when the St. Gotthard Pass across the Alps opened.

Joint-Stock Companies

The harnessing of waterpower in water mills was a crucial part of medieval development. Local nobles controlled and financed some of these. The eleventh century also saw the first primitive joint-stock ventures. A number of partners would buy shares in a project, usually a flour mill, employ laborers to construct the mill, and share in the profits according to the percentage owned. The Société du Bazacle of Toulouse financed the mills of the Garonne River in southwestern France. (Cipolla, 160) The problem was that the partnerships were short-lived and the partners tried to squeeze as much profit out as quickly as possible. The *commenda* was a form of joint-stock agreement but only existed for individual trips and not continuing businesses. West Europeans built dozens of mills in the mid-twelfth century.

Accounting

Arabic numerals (actually originating in South Asia) replaced Roman numerals after the Italian mathematician Leonardo Fibonacci popularized them in 1202. It is far easier to do both simple and complex mathematical operations with Arabic numerals, and Roman numerals have pretty much disappeared except for the Super Bowl. The fourteenth century saw the invention of **double-entry bookkeeping**. An accountant kept credits and debits in separate columns and the profits made or lost from a transaction. Single-entry bookkeeping had only recorded the debts owed and the proprietor would not know until the end of the year whether there was a profit or a loss. Single-entry bookkeeping cost less but did not distinguish between capital and revenue and made the concealment of fraud easy. Accountants had noticed that receipt of cash involved two entries: a discharge in the account of the debtor and a charge in the record of the cashier. This was a rational way of dealing with money and keeping accounts. It was used in Genoa as early as 1340. (Neal and Williamson, I, 280) In the sixteenth century, double-entry bookkeeping spread to the northern areas of Europe, including England. (Cipolla, 163) Early writers on capitalism such as Werner Sombart and Max Weber felt that double-entry bookkeeping was the critical breakthrough for capitalism.

AN IDEOLOGY FOR CAPITALISM

The Usury Problem

By 1250, capitalism was running into the prohibition on usury and the prevailing Christian ethic represented by St. Francis and others who condemned wealth. A crisis of conscience set in among capitalists about loaning money for interest. This threatened economic development. The concept of a prohibition on usury had its source from Luke 6:34-35:

> And if ye lend to them of whom ye hope to receive, what thank have ye? Even sinners lend to sinners, to receive again as much. But love your enemies and do them good, and lend, never despairing; and your reward shall be great.

A usury ban had grown in the Church from 400 to 1050; Charlemagne's law code of 806 forbade it and established punishments. The Church was trying to protect the peasants from greedy landlords who would get them into debt and then take their land. These landlords sometimes charged interest at a weekly rate that would amount to 50 percent a year. The Church's Second Lateran Council of 1139 explicitly called usury a sin. The Fourth Lateran Council of 1215 excepted Jews from obedience to this Christian regulation. The interest rates of Jewish moneylenders could be as high as 33 percent. An unscrupulous Christian offered a loan at 20 percent in 1161. (Lopez and Raymond, 158–59)

A poverty movement grew strong in Western Europe in reaction against the growing wealth and obvious luxury. It emphasized the words of Jesus against the moneychangers in the temple. (Matthew 21:12) Jesus had also said "It is easier for a camel to go through the eye of a needle than for a rich man to enter the kingdom of God." (Mark 10:25) Not all Christians obeyed the usury prohibition. They employed tricks such as having the loan repaid in a different currency, which obscured an interest rate. Some charged late fees with an impossible due date set. (Neal and Williamson, I, 256) Enough Christians did obey the usury prohibition that there was an increasing shortage of credit in mid-thirteenth century Europe. This was the point where Europe could have easily gone down the path of the Islamic world.

Aquinas' Solution

A scholar of the church named **Thomas Aquinas** solved the usury problem in 1268. Aquinas wrote of the difference between usury and investment. The key is the element of risk. In Aquinas' view, it is usury only if you know you are going to get your money back. If you get a peasant in your debt and can take his land, that is usury; if you invest in shipping and commerce, you run the risk of the ship being sunk by a storm or taken by pirates and losing your entire investment. (Braudel, II, 562) In the mid-fourteenth century, the Catholic Church formally modified its prohibition on usury to accept Aquinas' changes.

Aquinas provided an ideological basis for investment and capitalism by making money respectable. After Aquinas, there was a great surge of civic pride. People were proud of their wealth and showed it off by giving lavishly to the church. Many magnificent gothic cathedrals began construction between 1250 and 1350. They remain as monuments to the birth of capitalism. The Cathedral of Chartres was an economic market: food and firewood were sold at the southern door, manufactured goods at the northern door, prospective workers and employers met in the side aisles, wine merchants sold in the coolness of the crypt, and the southern cloister was reserved for (yes) moneychangers.

Aquinas' distinction still guides public perception of wealth. We admire those who have taken risks or at least say they have taken risks—we call them "entrepreneurs" and forgive them even if they break some laws. England legally allowed all forms of charging interest in 1545 but capped the yearly rate at 10 percent. (Kindleberger 1993, 43) American state laws long outlawed "usury" by which they meant the charging of interest above a certain rate. That was seen as unfair profit. In the 1970s, credit card companies moved to states that had no usury laws so they could charge high rates on their cards. Some "paycheck advance" stores charge higher rates than the usurers of medieval Europe! But Aquinas put the first big hole in the barrier of usury that has led to the "anything goes" world of finance today.

THE CALAMITOUS FOURTEENTH CENTURY

The "Little Ice Age" (1250–1850)

After nine thousand years of some of the warmest weather of the last million years, the world began to cool off with disastrous consequences. Fields in the high altitudes were abandoned, glaciers marched down the Alps, arable land in Scandinavia shrank, more icebergs drifted further south in the Atlantic and made navigation difficult. Icebergs cut off Greenland from Europe. Herring disappeared from the Baltic Sea. There was a disastrous flood in low-lying Holland. Farmers could no longer grow grapes in England. There were widespread famines and epidemics from 1313 to 1317. People were more vulnerable to disease. Price inflation started around 1200 as the population grew faster than the supply of goods; prices rose perhaps 0.5% per year on average from 1225 to 1345. (Fischer, 17)

The Supercompanies

At the beginning of the fourteenth century, a number of large businesses appeared, based out of Florence. At that point northern Italy was probably the richest region in the world. Seventy percent of Florentine men were literate. (Neal and

Williamson, I, 269, 291) They grew from merchant bankers who had become wealthy enough with branch offices to manage and finance the woolen textile trade from the beginning where the sheep were sheared for wool to the end where woolen goods were sold. In the 1320s, Florence began to produce more luxury woolens and needed a regular supply of fine English wools. They were not interested in manufacturing; they "put out" manufacturing to the peasants who lived outside the city walls. They negotiated contracts years in advance for discount prices. These companies were organized by partners on a joint-stock basis. One such supercompany, the Peruzzi, had seventeen partners with unlimited liability and 133 employees. The papacy at the time had 250 administrators, most kings had fewer.

The Peruzzi, Bardi, and Frescobaldi companies collapsed between 1343 and 1348. The fourteenth century generally saw economic stagnation. The worsening of the climate increased agricultural failure; many precious metal mines were exhausted or flooded with water because they did not have pumps with adequate power to keep the mines dry. The bankruptcy of states kept banking precarious. Two of the supercompanies collapsed in 1348 when King Edward III of England defaulted on his loans. (Kindleberger 1993, 45) In 1291, the Muslims drove out the last crusaders, hampering Mediterranean trade.

Bubonic/Pneumonic Plague (1347–50)

Changes in temperature affect weather patterns. The Little Ice Age shifted the wind patterns east with Europe getting more wet Atlantic weather, and the hot desert winds from Africa blowing into Central Asia. Sometime after 1300, rodents in the plague-endemic areas of the Gobi desert in Central Asia began to move east, and plague hit the Mongol Empire in the

1320s. The plague moved to China in the 1330s and then slowly moved west along the Silk Road with the Mongols and Italian traders. The main epidemic of 1347–1350 and the subsequent epidemics over the next fifty years killed at least 33 percent of Europe's population. The plague would reappear periodically well into the seventeenth century when the Norwegian (brown) rat replaced the black rat. The fleas that carry the plague like the taste of brown rat less than black rat and are less likely to land on, bite, and infect this rat. The flea that infests the brown rat is less of a plague carrier because it does not care for human blood.

Panic and demoralization swept Europe. Some fanatics said that Jews had poisoned the wells. Despite attempts by the Pope to denounce this lie, there were many anti-Jewish massacres. The plague had long-lasting social effects. It devastated the labor market, and the surviving workers found that their labor was much more valuable. If Europe had been approaching a balance in the 1320s between capital and labor that would discourage further capitalist development, the plague surely upended that. (*Cambridge Economic History*, IV, 68, 85) Labor efficiency was needed more than ever. On the manors, serfs demanded more rights and an end to their labor services and fees. (Neal and Williamson, I, 236–37) When lords in England refused, there was a massive **Peasants' War** (1381). Governments passed laws to cap wages paid to city workers, but this led to riots in the towns. The free market had prevailed. This was a major blow to manorialism, which was already rotten because people no longer needed the lords' protection against invaders.

THE REVIVAL OF BANKING

Even before the disasters of the 1300s, cities developed a public credit market. As early as the 1200s, Venice was taking loans in exchange for paper that effectively yielded 5 percent a year. This was at a time when a private loan would bear 20 percent interest. (Braudel, II, 521) "Venice started a government bond market by demanding compulsory loans on which interest was paid regularly." (Maddison 2001, 52) The Italian city of Florence in the fourteenth century increased its debt level from fifty thousand florins to three million by using overdrafts and credits. For the first time, Europeans saw the possibility of overcoming the limits imposed by precious metal supplies. The kings of Castile issued *juros* in the 1370s. In the early 1530s, Venice sold tax-free bonds on the open market. (Neal and Williamson I, 295–98; Braudel II, 522; Cipolla, 199)

After the fourteenth-century setbacks, the capitalist machinery resumed its expansion in the fifteenth century. After 1460 there was better technology to pump water out of mines. Either horses or more powerful water wheels drove the pumps. This allowed some mines to reopen. The Europeans also rediscovered the ancient smelting process to separate copper from silver ore. By 1450, the per capita GDP in West Europe had exceeded that of China, setting the pattern that has persisted to the present day. By 1321, bankers in Venice had developed **fractional reserve banking**. (Cipolla, 181) This means that the bank only kept a fraction of its deposits on site at any given time. It was highly unlikely that all of a bank's depositors would show up at once demanding all of their money. As long as the bank kept enough to meet reasonable demand, it could lend out the rest at profitable interest. Thus the roles of deposit bankers and merchant bankers began to merge. (Maddison 2001, 42) The problem was that when depositors got nervous, they would all run to the bank and pull out all of their money. A **bank run** thus became the most dreaded event and banks worked hard to quell any panics. Bank runs continued in the United States into the 1930s. The U.S. government as of 2015 guarantees up to $250,000 in deposits so depositors will feel secure and banks can invest most of their reserves without fear of a run.

The Medici

Unlike the supercompanies of a century before, the Medici family of Florence was a major investor in woolen and silk manufacturing. It established a bank in Rome in 1397 and became the major banker to the Papacy. The Medicis also had branches in Genoa, Venice and Milan. **Cosimo De Medici** (1389–1464) built up a network of patronage from favors and dominated Florence after 1433. Cosimo's grandson **Lorenzo the Magnificent** (1449–1492) was a great patron of the arts but not a very good businessman. His finances became increasingly mixed up with those of the city of Florence and the bank failed in 1494. Italy's economic problems grew when the Ottoman Turks destroyed the Byzantine Empire and then shut the Venetians out of Black Sea trade. The Ottomans took Alexandria in 1517 and ended most of that city's trade with Venice. (Maddison 2001, 53)

Jacques Coeur (c.1395-1456)

This leading merchant in Bourges became a supplier to the French government in 1418. When the future king was exiled to Bourges, he became friends with Coeur. In 1427, Coeur became master of the Bourges mint. He traveled to the eastern Mediterranean in the 1430s, made treaties with the Alexandrians, and became the main supplier of spices to southern France. From 1438 until 1451, he was treasurer of France. He became richer than ever by gaining mining rights, revitalizing the mines, and selling ore to other countries. Coeur's riches allowed France to defeat England and end the Hundred Years' War. But then his debtors and enemies brought false charges against him, forced him to flee, and confiscated much of his fortune and business. The king stood aside as the man who won his kingdom died in disgrace.

The Fuggers

Augsburg was a key city on the overland trade route between northern Italy and Flanders. After 1370, Augsburg merchants such as the Fuggers accumulated wealth by buying raw cotton in Venice and Milan and advancing credit to the Swabian weavers to make fustian, a mixture of cotton and linen. Southern German fustian was much cheaper and even penetrated Italy after 1400. Meanwhile the German and Swiss merchants began to replace the Italians as marketers of cotton goods. Augsburg also profited from the mid-fifteenth century revival of mining, and merchants again organized the process but not the manufacturing. In 1487 Duke Sigmund of the Tyrol borrowed from the Fuggers against the collateral of his mining income. This was the start of the Fugger Bank. It reached its height under Jacob Fugger, who died in 1525. The head accountant of the bank went to Italy to learn the double-entry bookkeeping system. (Cipolla, 204) Jacob's nephew Anton steadily mismanaged the business until his death in 1560. The ever-deepening debt of the Habsburg family that dominated the German lands bankrupted the Fuggers.

CONCLUSION

By 1450, western Europe had established the world's first fully-functioning capitalist system. Even as the population regained its earlier level, resources had steadily become more valuable so there was no repeat of the fourteenth century. The Europeans had a well-monetized economy, had built mechanisms for efficient and profitable long-distance trade, and had the model of the joint-stock company. The banking and credit system remained fragile, but bankers took the lessons of the Medicis and the Fuggers to heart. There was an established ideology glorifying profit from risk-taking and the passage of hundreds of years had established the habit of labor efficiency.

TIMELINE

650	Silver coins minted in Frisia and England
800	Ghana grew rich on gold trade
1104	Venice opened central shipyard
1202	Fibonacci popularized Arabic numerals
1250–1450	Kingdom of Mali
1252	Genoa and Florence minted gold coins
1268	Aquinas, *Summa Theologiae*
1280	First eyeglasses
1291	Genoese broke through Strait of Gibraltar
1312–37	Reign of Mansa Musa
1321	Fractional reserve banking in Venice
1343–48	The "Supercompanies" collapsed
1347–50	Black Death appeared in Europe
1381	Peasants' War in England secured rights

1433–64	Cosimo di Medici dominated Florence with his bank
1438–51	Jacques Coeur, treasurer of France
1468–1591	Songhai Empire
1487	Start of Fugger Bank

KEY TERMS

Mali
pawnbrokers
deposit bankers
merchant bankers
Knights Templar
serfs
Commenda
double-entry bookkeeping
Thomas Aquinas
the "Little Ice Age"
Bubonic/Pneumonic Plague
Peasants' War
fractional reserve banking
Medicis
Fuggers

Chapter 5

CAPITALISM IN ACTION

In 1291, the same year that the Muslims drove the last Crusaders from Acre, two brothers from Genoa sailed off into the Atlantic to explore and recreate the legendary voyage around Africa. They were never heard from again. The Europeans had tried to expand beyond their continent twice since the fall of the Western Roman Empire. The Vikings had hopped across the North Atlantic islands all the way to North America, but their distant colonies in Newfoundland and Greenland failed. Their greatest achievement had been the conquest of sparsely-populated Iceland. The Crusades had been a mightier effort, but after two hundred years, the Muslims had thrown them out. As we will see in this chapter, by 1450 the Europeans were successfully expanding down the African coast. By 1500, they had made permanent contact with south Asia and the Americas. What changed fundamentally between 1291 and 1450? The rise of European nationalism is part of the answer: intensified competition drove the nations to outdo the others. R. Bin Wong and J.L. Rosenthal saw this as the critical difference between Europe and China. (Neal and Williamson, I, 154) The larger part is the creation of a capitalist system, outlined in the last chapter. Stronger economic organization made European expansion, exploitation, and settlement possible.

THE MOVE TO THE ATLANTIC

Early Exploration

The last chapter mentioned that Italians began to mint gold coins in 1252 made from African gold. The Europeans knew that gold came from somewhere to the south, but Mansa Musa's spectacular pilgrimage of 1324/25 gave them a new appreciation of African wealth. The king of Mali's caravan included a hundred camels each carrying at least a hundred pounds of gold. That is $208 million at the 2014 valuation of gold! It inspired the king of Portugal, Afonso IV, to establish direct contact with the gold sources of western Africa. There was a further need because Europe was suffering from a shortage of silver starting in the 1340s. In 1346, a Spanish sailor was shipwrecked looking for the sea route to Mali. Portugal had scanty natural resources and a population of one million at most. It begged, borrowed, and stole money to finance these voyages.

As early as the 1290s, Europeans were traveling to the Canary Islands. Wind patterns, reinforced by the Canaries current, made it easy to sail to them, but sailing against the wind and current back to Europe posed a major challenge. Contact was small-scale, and the Canary Islanders (Guanches) often hostile. The Portuguese officially discovered the Canaries in 1341, but the plague delayed their attempts to exploit them. Around the same time, the Azores and Madeiras start appearing on maps, but the Portuguese kept these secret until they officially claimed them in the 1420s and 1430s. These early explorations of the Atlantic and the Moroccan coast yielded no profit. No individual or business could afford such sustained losses. In 1469, the King of Portugal leased some of the possessions and rights to a businessman, who then made a fortune. That was more than 120 years into the process. One can compare this to moon exploration: only the state could afford to finance this.

That began to change in the 1420s. **Prince Henry** (d.1460), son of the Portuguese king, promoted and financed Atlantic exploration in order to trade with the African gold kingdom and fulfill the glorious destiny foretold by his horoscope. (Parry, 35–36) In 1421, Portuguese ships sailed past Cape Chaunar, which lies east of the northern Canaries. They also settled Madeira island, cleared it with fire so they could plant, and released rabbits on the neighboring island of Porto Santo. Finally, they were making some money off of exploration. Portuguese captains were given a lengthy questionnaire on all the new places they reached, so the authorities would know the religion, political system, money system, and culture of each place the next time they sent out a captain. (Landes, 92) The Portuguese launched an attack on the Canaries but were driven off by the Castilians, who had taken the lead in slaughtering the natives. This was a tough fight that would last until 1496 and lead to the extermination of the natives. Formidable Cape Bojador with its shallow water extending out three miles and inviting shipwrecks deterred the Portuguese until 1434 when Gil Eanes got around it. He also brought African slaves to the Portuguese capital of Lisbon, opening a new source of profit. From 1450 to 1500, the Europeans enslaved 150,000 Africans.

South of Cape Bojador, strong winds constantly blow from the northeast. The Portuguese discovered in 1431 that if they sailed north into open water beyond the Canaries to the Azores, they could catch a west wind back to Europe. (Crosby, 113) In 1441, they reached Cape Blanco, then built a fortress on nearby Arguin island where they tried to divert the gold trade from the Sahara. By 1520, the Portuguese on the coast were buying about one-quarter of West Africa's gold production, which amounted to nine hundred pounds. (Klein, 52)

Sometime after 1180, European sailors equipped themselves with the **magnetic compass** from China, which told them direction, and the **astrolabe** from the Arab world, which told them how far north or south they were. With methodical capitalistic research and development, the Portuguese studied Arab vessels on the Indian Ocean and learned of the lateen sail which was small and triangular. They put together the lateen sail with multiple masts and sternpost rudders from the Chinese to make the **caravel** ship. They started with a fifty ton caravel in the 1440s. (That means that the ship could carry fifty tons of cargo). By 1500, the Portuguese were building two hundred ton caravels with a third mast and a combination of triangular and square sails that could move in almost any wind. These heavy ships could carry cannons and were highly maneuverable. They carefully made ever-better maps, sea charts, and logs with descriptions. They kept them very secret. In 1484, King John II convened a meeting of mathematicians to determine the best way of figuring out latitude by observing the sun. (Parry, 94)

A turning point came in 1452, when the first water-driven sugar mill opened on Madeira. Three years later, Madeira exported about seventy tons of sugar. After 1500, it exported about seventeen hundred tons of sugar a year. Portugal brought in hundreds of slaves, mostly from the Canary Islands, to work in the sugar fields. (Crosby, 77–79) Sugar plantations began in the Canary Islands themselves in 1484. (Crosby, 96) By 1490, the price of sugar had fallen by two-thirds. Antwerp in the Netherlands had emerged as a major sugar refining center. The European demand for sugar kept growing and growing, especially as new delights appeared such as coffee, chocolate, and tea that could be used with sugar. The Portuguese crown took up to one-third of the sale proceeds, finally rewarding the money invested by Afonso IV and Prince Henry. (Landes, 70)

In the 1450s, the Portuguese pushed up the Gambia River and found that the Kingdom of Mali had been defeated. They finally reached the "Gold Coast" of Africa (present-day Ghana) and set up a gold-trading post at Elmina in 1482. The Portuguese sold North African cloth and copper. They could not venture into the interior because of disease. In 1483, they reached the mouth of the Congo River. The king of Portugal sent a group of eight into Africa; only one survived. On the coast, the Portuguese set up colonies and sugar plantations worked by slaves. After 1530, they had gained most of the gold they could and slave trading became more lucrative. The Portuguese made a final attempt in 1569 by sending a thousand soldiers up the Zambezi River in East Africa to take the gold fields. The expedition failed, and most of the men died of malaria. (Klein, 52–54) The initial goal of direct trade with the gold kingdoms had failed, but the Portuguese had claimed a greater prize.

On to the Indies

By the late fifteenth century, reaching India had become the main goal of the Portuguese. They wanted to outflank the Muslims who controlled the rich spice trade with southern and southeastern Asia. It had taken the Portuguese over a hundred years to get to the mouth of the Congo River, but only four years later their mastery of the seas had grown so much that they reached the Cape of Good Hope, the southern tip of Africa. The European diet was very bland and relied on bread, gruel, cabbage, turnips, peas, lentils, and onions. Spices could help preserve food or cover the taste if it rotted a little. The main spices (pepper, cinnamon, cloves, ginger, and nutmeg) came through the Middle East to Beirut and Alexandria.

In 1487, the Portuguese captain **Bartholomew Dias** reached the Cape of Good Hope with three ships. His crew's fatigue from this long trip forced him to turn back before he could explore the Indian Ocean. The Portuguese now frantically tried to raise money for the next trip and sent spies to scout trade conditions in India, Persia, and eastern Africa. (Parry, 138–39) In 1498 **Vasco Da Gama** reached India on Portugal's behalf, despite Jakob Fugger's refusal to fund him. Da Gama's large vessels (two specials at two hundred tons, a fifty-ton ship, and a supply ship) and cannon made him master of the Indian Ocean. He landed in Melindi on the East African coast and secured the services of an expert on Indian Ocean currents and winds, who brought him to India in about three weeks. The Indians realized that he was disrupting trade and drove him out. Da Gama limped back with two-thirds of his men dead but did make some money from spices that he stole from another ship. (Landes, 88) The next voyage lasted from 1500 to 1501 under **Pedro Cabral**. He lost seven ships of twelve (including the one commanded by Bartholomew Dias) but came back with seven hundred tons of cinnamon. Antwerp, already a sugar center, became the main distributor of spices. (*Cambridge Economic History*, IV, 164) Da Gama came back to Asia with twenty ships and many troops in 1502. His fleet frightened the Indian cities by flinging shot as far as three hundred yards, and his sailors mutilated people. (Parry, 119–122) He returned to Portugal in 1503 with thirteen ships and spices equal to a year's supply. It made a profit of 3,000 percent. The Portuguese then discovered the law of supply and demand: Da Gama's pepper flooded the market and caused the price to fall 90 percent. At the 1509 **Battle of Diu** off the Indian coast the Portuguese defeated a Muslim fleet. By 1520, all the European ships had bronze or brass cannon that could fire balls up to sixty pounds. In 1510, the Portuguese conquered Goa off the western Indian coast and built a permanent naval base. (Parry, 144) They soon reached the Strait of Malacca near Singapore and made contact with the Spice Islands. They opened trade with Japan in 1542. Starting from humble beginnings and repeatedly without money, the Portuguese had used capitalism to create a lucrative trade route with bases from Japan through China, India, Persia, East Africa, West Africa, and back to Europe.

Spanish Exploration

The Spanish had been watching the Portuguese progress with a jealous eye. They were locked in a ninety-year war with the Canary Islanders and had no knowledge of the currents and winds south of Cape Bojador. Dias' discovery of the passage to India in 1487 became general knowledge, and the Spanish desired to beat the Portuguese to the Spice Islands. In 1492, the Spanish rulers drove the Muslims out of Spain and were ready to finance their own explorations. A Genoese captain named **Christopher Columbus** told them that, based on his calculations of the size of the earth, he could beat the Portuguese to the Spice Islands by sailing due west. Columbus had been rejected by Portugal in 1484. He had stated that Japan was 2,760 miles west of Portugal, but it is actually 10,600 miles. (Parry, 150) The geographers at the court knew the world was much bigger and urged the monarchs to disregard Columbus, but in the end Queen Isabella financed almost 90 percent of his first two voyages. (*Cambridge Economic History*, IV, 227) Columbus believed that he reached the Indies but actually landed in the Carribean. This is why those islands are called the West Indies.

THE PUTTING-OUT SYSTEM

Medieval Guilds

As towns grew in western Europe after 1200, manufacturing had prospered. **Guilds** developed throughout the thirteenth century. Some were guilds of merchants that tried to forbid their workers from organizing. Others were brotherhoods of craftsmen where one would advance from apprentice learning the craft to being a journeyman and finally to master when one completed a "masterpiece." Only the masters had the right to own a workshop in or near his residence. As we have seen, labor became more valuable in the plague-ridden late fourteenth century. Guilds dictated wages, prices, and ensured the quality of the goods. No one could open a workshop in a town without the guild's permission.

At first, the guilds were fairly fluid. As the demand of the towns and cities grew, they welcomed newcomers with skills to open new workshops. Journeymen had a reasonable hope of rising to a mastership. The guilds were strongest in the wealth centers of Italy and the Low Countries and the central and southern Rhineland that connected them. Workers' guilds had their greatest power in metalworking, leatherworking, and butchering either because there was strong demand for the products or the craft required a considerable level of skill.

Merchants and Cottage Industry

The guilds in spinning and weaving had never been very strong because many continued to make their own clothes at home. The cloth merchants' guild kept workers' wages low. When the plague reduced the labor supply, workers rioted in the towns to demand a better deal. The rise in wages in the late fourteenth and fifteenth centuries convinced merchants to seek alternatives. Capitalism again sprang into action finding a way to use the limited labor force more efficiently. Merchants could travel just outside the city walls and find peasants who had long stretches of underemployment outside of the planting and harvest seasons. The end of feudal services had given them more free time. The merchants "put out" manufacturing by supplying peasants with the raw materials and sometimes the necessary tools. Evidence of this can be found as early as twelfth-century Flanders. (Neal and Williamson, I, 243) The putting-out system in textile manufacturing undercut the workers' guilds. In a shrinking market, masters became more selfish and raised the standards again and again so that journeymen who could not inherit a master's position had little hope of moving up. This destroyed the guild system in England; only government intervention kept it alive in France, because the government saw it as a tax source. The merchant now became supreme, replacing the manufacturer.

Country workers struck back in their own ways against low pay. They demanded higher wages and more leisure. They would take multiple contracts and then sell their product at a higher price to another merchant. Their quality was often low. The father of a family might take the pay, spend it on alcohol for a week, recover, then spend three days and nights driving his wife and children to get the next job done. Peasants cheated by adding cheap filling material. There were no large factories built at this time because that would involve a larger overhead cost (the land and building) than any potential savings from concentrating labor. Only in the heat-using industries such as glassmaking, iron, fulling, and brewing were savings by concentration sufficient. Only on the European continent did some heavily-subsidized merchants build "manufactories."

Most guilds collapsed except in places where cities were very strong and controlled by the elites. Cities in early modern Europe had unemployment rates of at least 20 percent. In hard economic times, one-third of the workforce could be jobless. Many died in poverty. Migration from the countryside slowed down because of the uncertainty of making a living. The cities that prospered tended to be government capitals such as London, Paris, Berlin, and Vienna.

A First Industrial Revolution?

The wave of modern wars that had opened with France's invasion of Italy in 1494 led to great demand in the areas of mining, armaments, and ship building. This led historian John Nef to proclaim that a first industrial revolution had occurred in England between 1540 and 1640, especially in metal manufacturing after the arrival of the blast furnace. The putting-out system accelerated around 1600 and changed Lancashire, the precise area transformed two hundred years later by another revolution in textiles. Massive water wheels supplied mechanical power, and woodcutters cleared entire forests to provide heat. Paper mills and sugar mills were entirely new industries growing from the printing press and the import of sugar. The output of coal increased eightfold and required more powerful pumps driven by horse and water wheels. Nef estimated that by 1640, Britain was producing three to four times the amount of coal as continental Europe.

Nef provided a vigorous picture of capitalism in action in England of 1600, but even he conceded that there was a falling off after 1640. Coal could provide heat in a number of industries, but not yet the critical manufacturing of iron, for reasons that will be explained. The rising price of timber and charcoal choked off iron growth. As an energy contributor, coal was barely perceptible on the global scale before 1800. In Britain, it started from a very low level. The Industrial Revolution, as we shall see, not only involved a basic shift to fossil fuels but to a wide variety of labor-intensifying machines as well as the steam engine.

Industrious Revolution?

This term was coined by the Japanese scholar Akira Hayami when he examined Japanese economic development before its industrial revolution. He found that even before industrialization, Japan's productivity grew primarily because its people were working more hours. Jan de Vries suggested that something similar occurred in Europe in the seventeenth and eighteenth centuries. He saw this not as exploitation but rather that Europeans wanted more money to buy goods, especially the luxury goods that became more widespread after trade expanded with Asia. Some connected it with the Protestant Reformation's elimination of many religious holidays and an alleged Protestant emphasis on hard work.

Finding the truth is difficult. Angus Maddison estimates that per capita real GDP growth from 1500 to 1820 averaged 0.1% per year in East Europe, which would match the 270 good years of the ancient world. But it was 50 percent higher in West Europe, and total growth over the 320 years was 59 percent. (Maddison 2001, 264–65) Great Britain and the Netherlands, both Protestant-led countries, grew the fastest. But strongly

Protestant Norway, Denmark, and Sweden grew no faster than Catholic Austria or France. There was no difference in the economic performance of Catholic from Protestant cantons in Switzerland. Furthermore, wealth in the Netherlands fell by about 14 percent in the eighteenth century. Gregory Clark and Ysbrand van der Werf have studied working hours in several English sectors and deny there was a big increase in working hours. French and English records of the middle ages suggest that people worked between 150 to 170 days a year, but before 1789, the French government still guaranteed fifty-two Sundays, ninety rest days, and thirty-eight holidays. This leaves 185 days for work, not a substantial increase. Nor is it likely that the hours worked per day increased in this time since artificial light was not widespread. Protestant countries show no evidence of working more hours than Catholic nations.

From this, it would seem that for Europe, the big increase in working hours came with the Industrial Revolution, not before it.

THE MOVE TO THE PACIFIC

In 1513, the Portuguese reached Quanzhou, but the Chinese resisted opening trade to them. It was not until after 1549, when China banned Japanese trade, that the Portuguese seized the opportunity to manage Chinese trade. From 1519 to 1522, Ferdinand Magellan and his crew had circled the world, proving how big it was and aiding geographers. The key to opening the Pacific came in 1564–65 when the navigator-turned-monk Andres de Urdaneta used the westerlies to go from Mexico to the Philippines, then used the summer monsoon to go north, catch the Japan current to the wind zone across the ocean to California, then went back down the North American coast to Mexico. The trip from Manila to Acapulco took between eight and ten weeks. (*Cambridge Economic History*, IV, 209) Ships brought Chinese silk across the Pacific in exchange for Peruvian silver.

CONCLUSION

The Portuguese and Spanish in the fifteenth century created the model for the Atlantic economy that would last for more than three hundred years. It was based on sugar cane. Not only was the European population growing, but the desire by each individual for sugar grew. As sugar production became more widespread and efficient, the price fell so people could consume more sugar without paying more. The sugar was grown on plantations, and African slaves provided the labor. From its cradle in Madeira, the system would spread like a disease and take over the islands of the Caribbean Sea and the Brazilian coast. It would change the lives of tens of millions of people.

The Portuguese had also created a long-distance sea trade to Asia. This does not mean that they controlled or ran the Asian trade. They did not even destroy the old overland route along the Silk Road where the Italian merchants continued to make profit. The trade in the Indian Ocean went about in the sixteenth century almost as it had in the fifteenth. The European role became a little more prominent in the China seas trade as the Chinese/Korean/Japanese dynamic shifted several times. At the same time, commercial textile manufacturing was being given to underemployed peasants. They were happy to get supplemental wages, the consumers were happy to get cheaper clothing, and the merchants were happy to pad their profits. The ruined city workshops and their employees were soon forgotten. Capitalism had arrived on the world stage.

TIMELINE

1324/25	Mansa Musa's pilgrimage to Mecca
1420s	Sugar planted on Madeira island
1434	Portuguese rounded Cape Bojador
1483	Portuguese reached mouth of Congo River
1484	Sugar plantations on the Canary Islands
1487	Bartholomew Dias rounded Cape of Good Hope
1492	Columbus reached America
1498	Vasco da Gama reached India
1509	Battle of Diu
1513	Portuguese reached Quanzhou
1519–22	Magellan and crew sailed around the world
1542	Portuguese opened trade with Japan
1564/5	Northern Pacific route discovered

KEY TERMS

caravel
Vasco da Gama
Battle of Diu
Christopher Columbus

Chapter 6

NATIONAL ECONOMIC PLANNING AND FINANCE

The rise of capitalism and the creation of a global trade network revolutionized trade and money. From the mid-fifteenth century, European population, money supply, and prices began to increase to unprecedented levels. This shocked and transformed European society. Nationalism and capitalism led to attempts to plan and guide a national economy. War and inflation led governments to borrow more money than ever before. Gradually, they created a system of structured debt and earned the confidence of creditors.

THE MONEY REVOLUTION

Population, Productivity, and Prices

From the fall of the Roman Empire into the Late Middle Ages, prices were stable over the long term. There might be successive years of famine that drove food prices higher, but then the prices would fall because people died and the production recovered. Even the disruption of the bubonic plague and the rise in wages did not create a permanent new level of higher prices.

In the late 1400s, prices began to rise and did not fall. The rise in prices was not matched by increased wages so that living standard of the wage-earning workforce (which had risen in the previous hundred years) began to fall back. A new phenomenon had appeared in Europe: **price inflation**. What causes inflation? We know it has something to do with the money supply. In the sixteenth century, money supply in Europe was simple: coins and metals used in trade. Most economics textbooks will pair money supply with "velocity" (that is the speed of transactions that circulate money) because history shows that inflation does not always march in lockstep with money supply. But velocity is really a fiction that is not measured independently, just used to explain the variance between money supply and inflation. It seems clear that there are other independent factors affecting prices. One is population. Even human beings without a penny to their names can increase demand because of their ability to beg, borrow, or steal. The law of supply and demand operates here: prices rise with greater demand or lower supply, they fall with lower demand and higher supply. The growth of European population in the high middle ages had caused modest price inflation. Prices fell when the Portuguese brought pepper from Asia. Productivity also affects prices. The more efficiently something is produced and transported, even if wages rise, the more the price will tend to fall. Productivity rises can powerfully balance increases in money supply and population and even cause **deflation**, which is when most prices and costs are falling.

The population of Europe west of the Oder River and the bend of the Danube River had fallen from about fifty-eight million in 1350 to about thirty-eight million in 1400, a little over one-third. By 1500, it was about fifty-three million, and had reached about sixty million by 1550. A population that had seemed to exceed the carrying capacity of the land and to approach the value of all capital after 1300 did not fall into crisis after 1550. What had changed in 250 years? The total capital had become more valuable with various resources and the Europeans had an accelerating ability to claim more resources. This growing population put pressure on the forests and food supply and certain manufactured goods. In England, wages kept pace with manufactured goods but fell far behind the prices of grain, livestock, and wood. (Fischer, 74) It may also be that the growth in farm productivity fell a bit after the great medieval gains of the three-field system and better use of animals. Productivity grew in the Po River valley of northern Italy as the old manors broke into smaller farms intensively farmed by the large population. But in the rest of Europe, production seemed to grow only because more land and labor were added (extensive production). Farmers again plowed poor soils that had rested since the bubonic plague. Spain failed to maintain the elaborate irrigation system of the south built by the Muslims and its land was farmed very inefficiently or left for sheep to graze. (Cameron, 110)

The period from 1450 and 1550 saw a modest increase in the money supply. The Portuguese gained a small amount of gold from West Africa. More significant was the use of mercury to extract silver from ore. A major jump in the money supply began in 1512 with the discovery of the Joachimsthaler silver mine in Bohemia. So much silver would come from this source that it gave its name "thaler" (which is German for "valley") to the silver coins of this area. This is the origin of the word dollar.

The Taking of Mexico and Peru

When Columbus landed in the Americas, there were two powerful empires. The Aztec empire, centered in the valley of Mexico, was the latest in a series of empires whose economy rested on growing corn. In the Andes mountains of Peru, the Incan empire had grown rich growing potatoes, another crop as yet unknown in Europe. **Hernando Cortes** with six hundred soldiers made contact with the Aztecs in Mexico and their enemies. Aided by the Aztecs' foes and measles which ravaged the Indians, Cortes took over the area in 1521. From 1531 to 1539 **Francisco Pizarro** with 175 troops overthrew the Incan empire in Peru having been attracted by reports of a civil war in the empire. Pizarro then fought other Spanish leaders until his death in 1541. (Parry, 166–73)

Silver and Slavery

In a short period of time, the Spanish had organized Peru and Mexico into viceroyalties and set up operations. Measles and smallpox had killed the natives off at an astonishing rate, doing much more harm than the Spanish weapons. The Spanish grabbed those that remained and forced them to work in the gold and silver mines. Most of the Spanish who came to America at this time were men and minor nobles, and many of them took Indian women for wives. The Church had followed the *conquistadors* and determined that the Indians should not be exploited. They set up missions and employed Indians to keep them out of the mining companies' hands. Laws of 1542 forbade the use of Indians as chattel slaves. (Neal and Williamson, I, 412) The companies, especially in Portuguese Brazil, turned to a new source of labor: slaves from Africa. At first slaving raids in Africa had been run-and-grab affairs, but as the Africans learned to avoid the Portuguese ships, the slavers used new tactics. The Portuguese and Spanish made contact with powerful tribes that were willing to sell prisoners of war from other tribes into slavery. In this way, they gained access to the interior of western Africa that they never could have gained by themselves. In 1570, the Portuguese planted sugar in Brazil, drawing that area into the ever-growing sugar empire. By 1585, Brazil had about fourteen thousand African slaves. (*Cambridge Economic History* IV, 314) Over the next eighty years, Brazil was the biggest supplier of cane sugar to Europe. (*Cambridge Economic History* IV, 202)

The Flow of Silver

Vast amounts of gold and silver came from the mines. In 1545, the Peruvian mine of **Potosi** opened. The Americas prospered with universities established in Lima and Mexico City in the 1550s. The Spanish government took 20 percent of the metal as tax. The Spanish mined thirty-five million pounds of silver ($6.9 billion worth in 2015 value) and 407,000 pounds of gold ($5.9 billion). Portugal and Spain, and the Dutch ports through which the silver flowed, became the center of the world. The French and English did not participate much in this exploration. They were occupied with domestic problems and content to raid the treasure ships. Spanish king **Philip II** (1556–1598) instituted convoys in 1564 to protect the ships from pirates. In the 1570s, the value of imported American treasure tripled. (Fischer, 82) In 1580, Spain inherited the Portuguese possessions and fleet as well, boosting its commercial power. The realm was incredibly diverse. In good conditions, from Lisbon or Seville, one could travel to Madrid in four days. It took ten days to reach Brussels, the center of Spanish power in the Netherlands, and two weeks to Milan, their center in northern Italy. Rome was four weeks away. America was six weeks by ship, and Manila in the Pacific Philippines would take four to six months.

Some tried to avoid Spanish taxation by taking the Peruvian silver overland and then down the Plata River. Argentina gets its name of "land of silver" not from any silver mines but because that was the export point of silver for smugglers. (Braudel II, 161) In 1580, Buenos Aires was founded at the mouth of the Plata. This in turn opened the rich plain of Argentina to farm settlement.

The Price Revolution

After 1470, prices rose noticeably in northern Italy and southern Germany. This trend spread to France and England in the 1480s and later to other places. (Fischer, 70) Inflation rose about 1 percent a year. That does not sound like very much but with compounding from 1500 to 1650, prices increased about 300 percent.

As silver poured into Europe via Spain, prices rose. Much of the inflation, as noted above, is not attributable to money growth but rather to population growth and the demand for goods, especially food and fuel. Prices rose most steeply before 1565, but bullion imports peaked between 1580 and 1620, and one-third of all the precious metal mined in the Americas ended up in East Asia. (Braudel II, 198) The velocity of money grew with the final end of the usury prohibition in Christendom. In 1541, Spanish king Charles V legalized loans at interest and capped the rate at 12 percent. (*Cambridge Economic History* V, 300) The Protestant reformer John Calvin announced the end of the usury ban around 1545 and the Catholic Council of Trent accepted Aquinas' definition officially in 1563, which meant its end in Catholic Europe.

Most economics textbooks will tell you that unexpected inflation is bad for people on fixed income and creditors, but good for debtors and those who make profit. Why? If you borrow $100 at no interest and there is 7 percent a year price inflation over ten years, the $100 is only worth $50, so effectively you never had to pay back half the loan. A person on fixed income who is receiving $10,000 a year will only be getting half of that after ten years in real terms. Small wonder that Social Security pensions have a cost of living adjustment every year, and politicians dare not eliminate this.

Social Developments in Western and Eastern Europe

The Price Revolution shook up society. In the towns, it combined with the putting-out system to make for more distinct classes. Merchants benefited because they could raise their retail prices and increase profits. Journeymen could not demand higher pay because their work was being outsourced beyond city walls. When they tried to form secret brotherhoods, the governments suspected them of subversion and suppressed them.

The inflation hurt those landlords who rented land to a family for eternity at a fixed rent. This meant a **crisis of the nobility**; it could no longer keep the old political and economic power it had held in medieval Europe. As long as the family had the lease, the landlords made steadily less rent in real terms. Many of them, even nobles, sold their land and ceased to be lords of the manor. Many spent their lives serving the king in the army, the government, or as a diplomat. Other nobles tried to rebel against their king or force rent hikes on the peasants. This always ended badly. Some nobles tried to make up for their diminished rents by taking loans and defaulted.

This led to a new merchant nobility of landowners who bought land or gained it in foreclosure. Many tenants had lost their leases over the years, and some had deliberately destroyed them in the violence of the fourteenth century when they were pushing for lower rents. In Western Europe, landlords responded with new, reasonable contracts, but in Eastern Europe, they worked with the kings to force the peasants into serfdom. Powerful German, Polish, Hungarian, and Russian nobles emerged, their wealth based on vastly increased days of free labor by the serfs. (Braudel II, 267)

Impact on Government Borrowing

Governments were both borrowers and on fixed income. Their taxes were stable, but they owed money. The money for wars had drained them. Taxes fell heavily on the poorest; the church owned a large amount of tax-free land while nobles often paid little or nothing in taxes. Governments used different methods to close the budget gap: they borrowed from merchant bankers; devalued coins by reducing their gold and silver content; sold government offices; and sold charters to towns for cash. This was the era of the Protestant Reformation: if a prince or king turned Protestant, he would usually seize the land of the church. In France, debt became a permanent feature under King Francis I. (Cameron, 150) He began in 1522 by borrowing 200,000 *livres* at 12½ percent interest. He borrowed heavily to pay for wars on the credit markets of Antwerp and Lyon, sold crown lands, raised taxes, and sold almost meaningless judicial and administrative offices. Nevertheless, the French crown ran out of money in the mid-1570s and had a partial default on its debts in the 1590s. By 1642, the French debt was at 600 million *livres* with interest payments on the debt taking up more than half of the state's revenue. Even the Pope had to borrow at 10 percent interest. (Cipolla 38–39, 48) In England and Holland, the central government quarreled with the elected representative bodies over levying taxes. A civil war in England ended with the king getting his head cut off. In the Netherlands, religious conflict and a backlash against Philip II's control led to a revolt and independence for the northern part in 1609. This part would be known as the United Provinces or just plain Netherlands distinct from the Spanish Netherlands (present-day Belgium).

THE SPANISH ECONOMY

One might think that controlling the mines of Mexico and Peru would lead Spain to permanent prosperity, but it did not happen. An abundance of natural resources, especially one natural resource, is sometimes a curse rather than a blessing. In our time, countries as different as Britain and Indonesia have wasted the money from temporary oil riches and wound up worse off than ever. The revenue from metal taxes made up 20 to 25 percent of Spain's total revenues. As early as 1544, Spain was already pledging two-thirds of this revenue to pay the debt. Interest rates were very high. *Juros* that were backed by promised tax revenue yielded 7 percent a year interest while the unsecured *ascientos* were traded at 14 to 20 percent interest a year. The Spanish debt rose from three million ducats in 1504 to eighty million by 1598. In 1557, Phillip converted the debt of Spain to 5 percent bonds. (*Cambridge Economic History*, V, 370–71) His creditors condemned this as a bankruptcy. Phillip made additional financial overhauls in 1575 and 1596. After Phillip II, Spain had bankruptcies in 1607, 1627, 1647, 1653, and 1680. (Cameron, 135) It wasted most of this money on religious wars. In the 1590s, Phillip had to levy a new excise tax. The burden on the average Castilian taxpayer rose 430 percent. Because Phillip was leading religious wars, the church in Spain turned over half of its revenues by 1574.

Spanish Demographics

The Spanish population rose rapidly in the sixteenth century. Population rose especially in the cities. Seville tripled its population from 34,000 to 95,000 from 1534 to 1561 and had 150,000 residents by 1640. This put pressure on land use and grain supplies. Spain had to become a net importer of grain, especially from Sicily, which Turkish pirates regularly threatened. Before 1560, Castilian prices had doubled. From 1516 to 1556, the wheat price in Andalusia rose 109%, olive oil 197%, and wine 655%. Farm production grew, but only because more land was brought under cultivation, not because productivity increased. The towns prospered, but their trade was in foreign-made goods financed by foreigners. Castilian textiles flourished for a time, but then became too expensive due to low productivity and low quality. Spanish merchants never formed a class. Many put their profits into land and retired.

The Decline of Spain

Inequality and religious discrimination were decisive in bringing down the Spanish economy. In 1492, Ferdinand and Isabella forced between 120,000 and 150,000 Jews out. (Cameron, 139) In 1502, they forced the Muslims to convert or leave. This intolerance spread to Portugal, where riots killed two thousand Jewish converts to Christianity in 1506. (Landes, 133) Eventually, Spain would not even tolerate Muslims who had converted to Christianity. Agriculture, especially in the dry southern part of Spain, depended on an intricate system of irrigation that the Muslims had established. The ouster of non-Christians and large absentee estates led to this system breaking down. By 1500, the crown, the church and 2 to 3 percent of the population owned 97 percent of the farmland. This got worse in the sixteenth century. Phillip II sold much of the crown's land and was allowed by the Pope to sell large amounts of Church land to fight the religious wars. Most of the people doing the actual labor had no incentive to improve the land or use more efficient processes. As the price of wheat and bread rose, the Spanish crown capped the price in 1539. (Cameron, 135) Many farms were abandoned and more land was given over to sheepraising that tore up the land. Spanish wool was sent to Flanders and Italy rather than to domestic manufacturing. (*Cambridge Economic History* IV, 160) The productivity of Spanish agriculture was probably the lowest in Western Europe. The agricultural base had collapsed, and the king had trouble paying his bills.

The End of the Inflation

The Price Revolution slowed and ended in the early 1600s as the factors that drove it subsided. The rapid population growth stopped, and in some areas the population fell. There was massive famine from poor weather in the 1590s, and disease killed many more. The Thirty Years' War devastated the German lands from 1618 to 1648 and killed at least one-quarter of the people. This was the last of the religious wars and set back German economic development for 150 years. After 1620, the pace of silver mining slowed even as repeated defaults by many governments had destroyed much of the credit supply and made other lenders hesitant. David Hackett Fischer calls the period of price stability from 1660 to 1730, "the equilibrium of the Enlightenment."

MERCANTILISM

The Rise of the Netherlands

In the late Middle Ages, the Netherlands (or "Low Countries" including today's kingdoms of the Netherlands and Belgium) were already wealthy from trade and manufacture. Flanders centered on Bruges and Antwerp had been particularly prosperous. Around 1500, they began to shift their approach to farming because their density of population was much higher than most other areas. They focused on growing cash crops and increased their farmland by about 33 percent using windmills to pump out seawater from an enclosed area. (DeVries and van der Woude, 31) Farmers raised high-value livestock, especially dairy animals that would produce milk, butter, and cheese. The Netherlands became a major cheese producer even as it imported perhaps one-quarter of its grain needs. (Cameron, 113, 154) It pulled massive amounts of grain from the Polish plains as the shipping trade of the port of Danzig grew tenfold from 1490 to 1550. Dutch fleets brought fish from the western Atlantic and meat came from the Danish lowlands. (*Cambridge Economic History*, IV, 77–78) The Dutch also began experimenting with new crop rotations and farming techniques.

During the religious wars, Belgium had the misfortune to be recaptured by Spain. This meant that Flanders, a leading economic area for centuries, was chained to the dead weight of Spain. It drove out Jews, former Jews, and Protestants. The violence of the war drove out others. The wars damaged Antwerp, then the Dutch blockaded it. (*Cambridge Economic History*, IV, 169) About 10 percent of the south's people moved to the north, 150,000 in all. (Maddison 2001, 79) The northern area of Holland, centered around Amsterdam and Rotterdam, promoted religious freedom and took in talented people of all religious faiths. It only had a million people, fewer than England or France, but it would build a remarkable economic record. (Landes, 137)

The foundation of Dutch success rested upon the profit from shipping and banking. Shipping capacity grew from sixty thousand metric tons in 1470 to 232,000 tons in 1570 and then 568,000 tons in 1670. Huge six hundred ton ships plied the Asian routes. They also developed a new type of ship that could transport bulky, low-value goods such as grain and timber from the Baltic efficiently and profitably. (Cameron 188; Cipolla, 258) The number of Baltic ships going though the Danish Sound quadrupled in the sixteenth century. (*Cambridge Economic History*, IV, 170) The Dutch controlled most northern Atlantic shipping in the seventeenth century. The Dutch retaliated after the Spanish closed their ports in 1585. (Landes, 140) By 1625, the Dutch had taken control of the spice trade. (*Cambridge Economic History*, IV, 189) They forced the Portuguese out of the Spice Islands, took Sri Lanka, and in 1606 found a faster route to those islands by going below 40° S of latitude, where they found the west winds of the "roaring forties." (Cameron, 122) They could take these speedy winds almost to the western coast of Australia, then turn north. This route also had the advantage of avoiding the monsoon winds that shut down trade for half the year. (*Cambridge Economic History*, IV, 195) From 1639 until 1853, the Dutch were the only westerners allowed to trade with Japan. The Dutch conducted more Asian trade than the Portuguese ever had. Trade activity diminished in the Arabian Sea as the Dutch pulled trade south to the East African/Indian/Indonesian axis. The Dutch were able to gain a monopoly over spices by 1700 when they took military control of the Indonesian islands by 1700. They established a center at Batavia (present-day Jakarta) that controlled the Sunda Strait. (Parry, 200, 250–51)

The First Modern Economy?

Jan de Vries and Ad van der Woude have written that the Dutch in the seventeenth century had reached a new height of economic development and that they deserve the honor of having the world's first modern economy. (693–94) Some of the reasons are rather circular: it is modern because it has been continuously modern. Well, so have most of the other European countries. The state's support of property rights is an issue we discussed in the first chapter. It was also not notably ahead of some other western European nations in providing "reasonably free and pervasive markets in commodities, land, capital, and labor." The Netherlands was notably ahead and "modern" in its high level of farm productivity. This allowed more people to do something other than farm and also led to a much larger proportion of the Dutch population living in cities. By the late eighteenth century, perhaps 60 percent of the population of Holland and 50 percent of the district of Utrecht lived in cities. (59) Literacy was particularly high. Even in a rural province, 75 percent of the farmers could sign their own names. (*Cambridge Economic History*, V, 102) I should note that the trend stalled in the nineteenth century suggesting a flaw in the "continuously modern" narrative.

De Vries and van der Woude also note that the ratio of capital to labor and energy to worker was the highest in the world in the seventeenth and eighteenth centuries. After 1600, the Dutch had more money in circulation per person than anyone else. (De Vries and van der Woude, 89) A large number worked full-time or part-time at wage labor. (Neal and Williamson, I, 323–24) From their unpromising swampy land, the Dutch had built a highly productive area, had given value to their resources, and (perhaps most significantly) made the move toward fossil fuels. The Dutch burned tremendous amounts of **peat** for energy. Peat is compressed plant matter that given a few million years of heat and pressure, would turn into coal. Certainly on a per person basis the increase in energy produced exceeded the English coal burning in the sixteenth and early seventeenth centuries. Peat took the place of wood and charcoal from wood as energy sources. Manufacturers used the heat to make bricks, glass, and beer. (Cipolla, 256) Wood is a limited resource that is quickly exhausted and slowly renewed. Fossil fuels at first seemed limitless and allowed a massive application of energy that in turn raised productivity and wealth. Aside from peat, the Dutch also built many powerful windmills that could generate twenty or thirty horsepower. (Cipolla, 144) Wind-powered saws and cranes accelerated the building of Dutch ships. (*Cambridge Economic History*, V, 531) Canals were easy to build and provided cheaper transportation than roads. The Netherlands was also the first modern economy because it had a long-term rate of growth in per capita GDP. From 1400 to 1700, Dutch growth averaged 0.5% per year, faster than ancient Roman economic growth. From 1600 to the 1820s, the Dutch were the richest Europeans. (Maddison, 2001, 75, 90)

Describing Mercantilism

This was an early attempt at national economic planning practiced by England, France, and Spain among others. The Netherlands, as a much smaller country with much smaller overseas colonies than others, tended to promote free trade and open relations. The practice built on the sixteenth-century idea of **bullionism**: governments should hoard gold and silver by running trade surpluses. (Cameron, 133) Since measuring economic activity was very difficult, governments had trouble judging effects of their policies. Since at least the 1300s,

European countries had banned the export of certain valuable items such as grain, cattle, and iron. (Braudel, II, 544)

Rondo Cameron was correct when he warned historians not to think of mercantilism as a master economic plan. It was a series of policies loosely related to promote bullionism. Governments would foster or subsidize industries they deemed important, impose high tariffs, rigidly regulate prices and qualities of manufactured goods, sponsor royal monopolies, and encourage colonial expansion as a way of getting more raw materials without having to import them from another country and to create a market for manufactured goods. The mercantilists hated guilds because they hindered a national policy to promote special interests. In England the guilds were destroyed, in France they were kept alive by the state as a way to get more taxes. States condemned begging, which had become noticeable in the large cities. England introduced the first workhouses for debtors. France created a silk spinning and weaving industry. England passed **Navigation Acts** in 1651 and 1660 stating that goods had to be carried in English ships if traveling between England and its colonies. "English" meant that the owner, master, and three-fourths of the crew had to be of that nationality. (Cameron, 130–31, 159) Manufactured goods from foreign countries had to stop in Britain before they went to the colonies. Raw materials from their colonies had to stop in Britain first. This ensured that English ships carried Baltic lumber and grain. (Hugill, 58) England abolished local tariffs, but it took longer elsewhere.

The (English) East India Company made huge profits bringing in cotton goods (calicoes) from India. The Company was bringing in sixty times as much Indian cloth in the 1680s as it had in 1620. (Landes, 154) Around 1650, Indian textiles became the leading European import from Asia. (Broadberry and O'Rourke, I, 106) For the mercantilists, this was a nightmare. The English **Calico Act** (1701) prohibited the import of printed cloth from India. This was still not very effective, so a Second Calico Act of 1725 forbade the display or consumption of Indian printed cotton goods. (Cameron, 159) The English also banned American-made hats in 1733. (*Cambridge Economic History*, IV, 269) France imposed tariffs on foreign goods in edicts of 1664 and 1667 and banned calicoes in 1686. (Braudel, II, 544; Maddison 2001, 85) France in 1717 ordered that anyone caught selling Indian cottons in France would be sent to the rowing galleys in slavery. (Braudel, II, 180) Angry Parisian merchants wanted more radical measures: reward people to attack and strip women in the street of their Indian clothes or perhaps dress all the prostitutes in Indian cotton so it would become unfashionable. (Braudel, II, 178) Spain did not want Chinese silk taking over the American market, so in 1604 it banned the shipment of Chinese cloth to Peru, and then in 1636 it banned trade between Peru and Mexico. The Spanish American ports could only trade with Cadiz and Seville. (Braudel, II, 152) In 1701, a grandson of French king Louis XIV became king of Spain and brought in French-style mercantilism. Spain banned Asian textiles, ordered the army to buy Spanish-made goods, and set up factories to make luxury goods. (*Cambridge Economic History*, V, 482)

Mercantilism and the policy of running trade surpluses also encouraged European countries to gain colonies. Even if they did not provide the precious metals of gold and silver, colonies could provide sugar and other raw materials. The Europeans could also force the colonies to buy only goods made in the home country and could even forbid the manufacturing of certain items in the colonies. The colonists would have to pay for the value added by manufacturing and thus wealth would be transferred to Europe. This caused economic disruption in areas such as North America that were money poor and also caused resentment among colonial businessmen. It would be a cause of revolutions throughout the Americas in the late eighteenth and early nineteenth centuries that threw out the British, Spanish, and Portuguese. For example, smugglers of cheap Dutch tea played a role in the "Boston Tea Party" right before the American Revolution.

The desire for colonies and the belief that the Europeans could economically exploit them led to colonial wars. England seized New Amsterdam from the Dutch in 1664 and renamed it New York. Colonial wars combined with the European wars of the French king Louis XIV (personal rule 1661–1715).

Immortal Corporation

The Dutch traders had first come to Asia working with the Portuguese when they were all possessed by Phillip II. The Dutch learned the secrets of winds, currents, and maps. During the religious wars, Phillip had foolishly used the Portuguese pepper fleet as part of his naval battles with other European powers. When the English sank most of those ships in 1588, the Dutch saw an opening. They broke the Spanish/Portuguese monopoly in Asia. Merchants required investment and the goodwill of the central government. The Dutch granted special charters which gave them exclusive rights over a specific area, such as the **Dutch East India Company,** which was founded in 1602, but reformed as immortal as of 1612. Previously, all companies had been partnerships. Under the charters, when one of the partners died or left, the corporation had to be dissolved and reformed. Now, when a shareholder died, his shares would be sold or reassigned. Instead of pulling their investment out, the owners were only allowed to sell the shares to another investor. (*Cambridge Economic History*, IV, 257)

Soon, the buying and selling of shares in the Company became a brisk business of its own. On average from 1602 to 1795, the Company paid dividends of 18 percent a year, an amazing figure then or now though most of it was concentrated in the 1602 to 1650 period. (De Vries and van der Woude, 462) The Dutch East India Company would not break up; this fostered an interest in long-term development and future profits, rather than quick riches. The Company and associated shipping and military occupations brought even more people into the salaried labor force and the money economy. (Neal and Williamson, I, 326–27)

Immortal turned out to be a misleading term. Companies, like people, seem doomed to go through a cycle of birth, growth, maturity, aging, senility, and death. The Dutch East India Company became obsessed with its dividend payments at the cost of paying its employees properly. Asian politics turned against the Dutch, as the Chinese drove them out of Taiwan, the Japanese sharply restricted trade, and government changes forced them out of parts of Persia and India. Company debt tripled from 1670 to 1690. (De Vries and van der Woude, 434–35, 449) Many captains and sailors, out of sight of Amsterdam, opened their own side businesses and devoted their energies to those instead of the Company. Trade volume grew in the China Seas and the Indian Ocean with Dutch traders a part of it but not running it and taking most of the profit. Corruption became rampant. The accounting system cannot be deciphered today and likely was not understood then. (Landes, 145–48) The Dutch phase of the American Revolution in the 1780s ruined the Company. In 1795, the Dutch government took the Company over. Immortality turned out to mean 193 years, but it was the thought that counted.

NATIONAL BANKS AND FINANCE

Public Banks

Medieval banking had been in private hands and often clashed with the greed of kings, nobles, and other political leaders. The Medicis had mixed public and private functions to the business' ruin. The northern Italian cities of Genoa (in 1407) and Venice (in 1587) took the lead in establishing government-run banks that would work closely with the city mints that melted down "bad" coins that had been damaged or deliberately mutilated and reminted them. The government would deposit its tax revenue and then draw upon those funds as needed. These banks were run under strict rules. They were not supposed to engage in fractional reserve banking because the city, as the main customer, might need all of its money at once. The banks did solicit private deposits and likely broke the rules so they could lend at interest and make profit.

In 1609, the Dutch government signed an agreement with a group of Dutch banks to establish the Wisselbank, which is better known as the **Bank of Amsterdam**. (Kindleberger 1993, 48) This built on the Italian model, but the Bank made profits from other activities. It served as a supreme moneychanger as Dutch traders were bringing back hundreds of different coins from around Europe and Asia. Each exchange brought profit from commission. The Bank also minted gold coins and profited from that. The city of Amsterdam ordered that all large bills held by merchants had to be exchanged for Bank money. It plowed these profits into investments and gained further commissions by advising the rich where to put their money. The Bank often made loans to the state of Holland, even beyond the volume of its assets. (*Cambridge Economic*

History, V, 337, 340) This was illegal but gave the Dutch state the ability to hire soldiers and ships and keep its independence from France. As with the Dutch East India Company, the Bank ran into insolvency in the 1780s when it made large loans to the government during the American Revolution. (Kindleberger 1993, 50)

Why did the Dutch not Industrialize?

The Dutch were in the leading position of wealth, but did not take the next step and industrialize the country. Instead, economic growth slowed by 1680, and there was a long stagnation through the eighteenth century. The most serious problem was that the Dutch Republic was very small. (*Cambridge Economic History*, V, 25–27) It was richer than France, but France undoubtedly had a bigger GDP. In 1672, Louis XIV invaded the Netherlands. His army was four times larger than that of the Dutch and within two months had captured Utrecht and was threatening Amsterdam. The Dutch in desperation broke the dikes and flooded most of the country forcing Louis to pull out his army. Naval and colonial wars against England also wore down the Dutch. An estimate of the time stated that Dutch per capita taxes were twice as high as those in Britain and France. (40) After 1713, the Netherlands was no longer a political power but it remained a major economic power and lived off the capital accumulations of the previous two hundred years. It was a major lender to both Britain and France.

The Dutch had many of the same ingredients that will explain why England was the first to industrialize. The canals lowered their transport costs (though not quite as much as England's). They had a solid credit system, and their farm productivity reduced prices and encouraged a domestic market. However, there were two fatal flaws. First, their small size made it impossible to have a large enough domestic market to create economies of scale and tariffs meant they would not be able to export large volumes of materials. The Dutch in promoting cash crops had to import much of their food, which blunted the price advantage. Second, the Dutch lacked coal and iron. Peat does not have the energy density of coal, and the Dutch were already importing coal from England in their golden age. There were no large forests to exploit for energy. The Dutch did not industrialize first, nor were they second or third. The country in fact lagged far behind many nations. Indeed the Dutch never had a labor force where there were more people in industry than in farming or services. Around 1900, it went straight from a farming plurality to a service plurality.

NATIONAL FINANCE

Establishment of the Bank of England (1694)

As the Dutch colonies were taken and the French pressed the Dutch fiercely, the colonial wars became global conflicts between Britain and France. They grew ever more expensive. France had three times the land and four times the people of England. In 1688 English debt was £664,000. Then came another war with France fought in Europe, America, and on the high seas. Within six years, the debt had almost doubled. The government borrowed £1.2 million from a group of rich men to pay back existing debt and provide for new spending. The lenders gained the right to run the new Bank of England and would also get back an 8 percent return on their loan. The Bank of England held government accounts, issued banknotes, and granted secured loans drawing on negotiated securities. Taking this path instead of defaulting or unilaterally rescheduling the loans assured creditors and provided England with new sources of credit. It gave England tremendous fiscal backing that France did not have and compensated for the French advantage in land and people.

At the same time it borrowed money, England established a new land tax that effectively doubled British tax income. The average Englishman paid twice as much as the average Frenchman. About 9 percent of the British GDP was collected in taxes, which was an astonishing figure for the time. Around the world, the only other place that may have collected so much was Japan. The land tax was collected by local assessors and collectors who sent the money to the country receiver and on to the Exchequer in London. It provided about two-thirds of all tax revenues in 1697 and was highly symbolic because the landowners of England had claimed a major stake in government after 1688. It was important for the English people to see that the men who were running the government were prepared to pay for it.

This happy state of affairs did not last. The rich landowners who ran the Parliament never reset the property values, so gradually less tax was collected on land. After 1714, taxes on goods and consumption such as alcoholic beverages, salt, leather and candles, which fell more on the poor, accounted for more tax revenue than the land tax. (Brewer, 89–101) The refusal to pay their fair share of land tax led to the decision to tax the American colonies to pay off the war debt after 1763. This in turn led to the American Revolution.

The Sinking Fund

The English wars against Louis XIV and France ended in 1713 with both sides exhausted and deeply in debt. The English had a total debt of £36 million with £9 million of floating debt. Many loans had been taken at 6 to 8 percent a year interest. The biggest creditors included the Bank of England, the British East India Company, and the **South Sea Company**. This last company was founded in 1711 and ran the slave trade to Spanish American colonies and other privileges that Spain had surrendered in the peace treaty. The government borrowed the £9 million from the South Sea Company to pay off the floating debt and would pay shareholders £576,000 per year, a 6.4% loan.

In 1717, Britain announced the establishment of a **Sinking Fund**. This was a plan to retire part of the debt each year until there was nothing left. The government would also issue new bonds at lower interest rates to replace the wartime bonds. About £6 million of debt was actually retired in the 1720s and 1730s. The interest rate was cut to 5 percent, and the interest on the debt that had to be paid each year was reduced substantially. England would have very deep pockets to draw on in times of war. Low risk meant a steady fall in interest rates which encouraged business expansion. (Brewer, 123–24)

The South Sea Bubble (1720)

In 1720, the British Parliament passed a law allowing creditors holding another £4.6 million of debt to exchange their bonds for an equal value of stock in the South Sea Company. The Company had been profitable and its share price had risen from £68 at its founding in 1711 to £128 in January 1720. The stock boomed as shares reached a value of £210 in late

March and then peaked on June 24 at £1,050. When profits were not up to expectations, the price collapsed. However, the British government took strong actions to reassure the markets by convicting crooked politicians and insider traders. It confiscated the estates of the Company directors and used the money to compensate the former bondholders. No reward was given to speculators, many of whom were ruined because they had borrowed money **on margin** to buy Company stock and could not repay the loan when the stock price collapsed. The South Sea Bubble ended up boosting investor confidence because the government had made good on the debt even when not legally obliged to. The government also stepped in to regulate stock issues, which slowed down the development of the modern corporation. Companies remained partnerships raising money mostly from profits. There was not yet mass ownership of companies.

France and the Mississippi Bubble

France tried to follow the English in modern finance. It had come out of the war in even worse fiscal shape than Britain: it had a debt of 2 billion *livres*, annual income of 145 million, annual expenses of 142 million plus 80 million each year as interest on the debt. For the last few years of the war, it had resorted to printing paper money. (Braudel, II, 396) Louis XIV had outlived his son and grandson. When he died, his four-year-old great-grandson became king with the Duke of Orléans as regent. To fix the budget, Orléans debased the currency by 20 percent and fined the tax farmers, who also held much of the French debt, 80 million *livres*. The Regent met a Scot named **John Law** while playing cards and came to rely on him as chief financial adviser. Law tried to imitate Britain's successful structure. He set up the Banque Royale in imitation of the Bank of England. The Banque assumed a small part of the debt and issued privileged banknotes that could be redeemed for gold and silver. This was a form of paper money, and Law issued it with the explicit purpose of stimulating the French economy. (Kindleberger 1993, 98–99; *Cambridge Economic History*, V, 298) Law worked to overhaul the financial system and fired the corrupt and the incompetent, regardless of their social and political connections. This created a lot of powerful enemies.

In August 1717, Law oversaw the formation of the **Mississippi Company**. This held a monopoly over the lands of the Mississippi Valley (called "Louisiana" in honor of King Louis). In 1718, the Company founded a city at the mouth of the Mississippi and named it New Orleans in honor of the Regent. Law grew bolder in 1719. He proposed getting rid of the entire national debt by swapping it for 300,000 shares of the Company valued at 5,000 *livres* apiece. Like the South Sea bubble occurring at the same time, share prices boomed from 500 *livres* to 15,000. A new word, "millionaire," was coined to describe those whose worth had suddenly risen above a million *livres*. Law was the toast of Paris, and the Regent named him Duke of Arkansas. But in 1720, it became clear that the promised gold and silver in Louisiana did not exist. The share price collapsed from 10,000 *livres* to 200 *livres* as people rushed to sell. (*Cambridge Economic History*, V, 379–80) Then his enemies turned on the Banque Royale, which held a reserve equal only to one-fifth the value of the banknotes it had issued. The nobles, dismissed officials, and rival financiers staged a bank run and forced the Banque Royale to close. By the end of 1720, Law had lost all of his positions, and the Regent was discredited.

Many of Law's ideas were sound and his attempt to use monetary policy to stimulate the economy ahead of its time.

But this skilled gambler (he is said to have invented the card game of poker) went too far. France had gotten rid of much of its debt by cheating 95 percent of the investors with shares that turned out to be worthless and then by lowering the interest rates on bonds to 4 percent. (Kindleberger 1993, 99) Unlike Britain, credit was extremely limited and interest rates were high. French investors tended to put their money into land instead of paper securities. France would not try again for some kind of central bank until 1776 and did not have a stable central bank until 1800. This put it at a severe disadvantage compared to England. The inability to create a debt structure would lead in 1792 to the overthrow and execution of the French king Louis XVI.

CONCLUSION

From the fifteenth to the seventeenth centuries, capitalism transformed society around the world. Population growth, a productivity slowdown, and large flows of treasure from America caused price inflation and undermined the stability of money in Europe. These changes ruined many journeymen workers in the cities and noble landowners in the countryside. Governments needed more tax revenue from their people and the resulting tension cost one king his head. Spain, the biggest beneficiary of American gold and silver, did not prosper thanks to bigotry and religious fanaticism. As world trade grew, European nations attempted early forms of national economic planning and concentrated on increasing their hoards of precious metal. The most prosperous European nation, the Netherlands, refused to implement mercantilism and prospered in the seventeenth century. The Dutch East India Company was a new kind of company, one that was designed to live forever and focus on long-term profit. The

Dutch also pioneered a new kind of bank with the Bank of Amsterdam that was a mutually beneficial public/private partnership. The small size of the Netherlands prevented it from taking the next step to industrialization and soon its larger rivals, England and France, tried to imitate its success.

TIMELINE

1492	Spain expelled the Jews
1502	Spain expelled the Muslims
1512	Joachimsthaler silver mine discovered
1521	Cortes and Spanish overthrew Aztec empire
1539	Pizarro overthrew Incan empire
1545	Potosi mine opened
1556–98	Philip II king of Spain
1570	Portuguese planted sugar in Brazil
1602	Dutch East India Company founded
1609	Dutch Republic gained independence
	Bank of Amsterdam founded
1618–48	Thirty Years' War in Central Europe
1639	Japan restricted European trade to the Dutch
1650	Dutch brought Brazilian sugar cane to British and French West Indies
1651–60	English Navigation Acts
1661–1715	Personal rule of Louis XIV in France
1664	English captured New Amsterdam from Dutch and renamed it New York
1694	Bank of England founded

1700	Dutch gained control of Indonesian islands
1701–25	English Calico Acts
1720	South Sea and Mississippi "Bubbles"
1795	Government took control of Dutch East India Company

KEY TERMS

Hernando Cortes
Potosi
Mercantilism
Navigation Acts
Calico Acts
Dutch East India Company
Bank of Amsterdam
Bank of England
South Sea Bubble
John Law

Chapter 7

THE GLOBAL ECONOMY OF THE EIGHTEENTH CENTURY

People, money, and goods traveled around the world. The Europeans brought wheat and a variety of fruits to the Americas. The "greater yam" was brought from India to West Africa, where it largely replaced the Guinea yams, and then to the Americas. (Parry, 284) Domesticated cattle, sheep, pigs, and horses were brought to the Americas, which had so few large domesticates. Wild horses transformed the plains of North America before the Europeans ever arrived. Indians who learned horse riding became masters of war and the hunt. In the eighteenth century, the Sioux groups combined horses and European guns to dominate the North American plains. Cotton, which has plants in both the Old and New Worlds, benefited from having the best aspects cross-bred to produce a fiber that would conquer the textile world. In 1700, the Asian countries still dwarfed Europe in terms of overall population and size of the economy. The Indian subcontinent had 165 million persons, China had

138 million, Japan had twenty-eight million, the Ottoman Empire that stretched from southeast Europe to North Africa and the Middle East had twenty-four million. (Maddison 2001, 40, 112) Meanwhile, France had twenty-two million persons, Russia fourteen million, Italy thirteen million, Austria eleven million, the British Isles nine million, Spain eight million, and the Netherlands two million. The Americas had only thirteen million persons total. But most of the European nations had much higher productivity and wealth. By Angus Maddison's estimates, China's per capita GDP in 1990 dollars was $600, while the Netherlands was $2,110, Britain's was $1,250, and France's was $986. (Maddison 2001, 264) In the seventeenth century, Western Europe as a whole had passed China in economic size.

COMMERCE AND INDUSTRY

Industry

In Europe, most people still lived in the country. Its largest cities London and Paris had about 600,000 to 700,000 people and by 1789, no more than fifty European cities had over fifty thousand people. Urbanization at that point had little to do with economic advancement. The Mediterranean area still had more large cities than England or France. The cities that grew rapidly in the seventeenth and eighteenth centuries tended to be national capitals such as Berlin, Vienna, and St. Petersburg. In 1739, 50 percent of the British Isles' population engaged in some sort of manufacturing. Not only were most peasants doing part-time work in textiles in the putting-out system, but some were engaged in small-scale metal and leather manufacturing.

Growth of Money

European capitalistic measures spread in size and scope: there were more bills of exchange and credit notes. After a long stretch of peace, England and France engaged in a colonial war from 1740 to 1763 that ranged around the world from Europe to North America to India and the seas in between. The British debt tripled and was larger than the annual British GDP. Because the British debt was well structured and there was strong investor confidence, the interest rate (which is the cost of money) only rose from 2¾% to 4% and some of that was offset by modest price inflation. The expense of wars grew. Raising and spending vast sums of money stimulated the economy. In the last years of the war, British taxes covered less than half of the annual expenses. In the 1760s, the British Parliament steadily raised taxes to pay for the war and then the debt from the war. These were almost entirely excise taxes that fell on the poor while the land tax actually seems to have declined. (Brewer, 97) This caused considerable political unrest in Britain, and when the Parliament tried to impose a small amount of tax on Britain's American colonies, it sparked a revolution. The British debt again nearly doubled, and the war against the Americans essentially ended when the Dutch investors refused to buy any more loans. (Brewer, 30) The British debt was likely twice the size of annual GDP, and the interest rate briefly jumped to 5¼%. Interest on the debt climbed past 60 percent of the income from taxes or about 40 percent of the annual budget. (Brewer, 117)

This in and of itself was not fatal. The Dutch at the time were spending about 70 percent of the annual tax revenue servicing the debt and their interest rates were even lower than those of the British. France by 1789 was paying about 50 percent of its annual budget to pay interest on the debt.

This may sound about the same as the British situation, but France's condition was much worse because the debt was not structured and investors lacked confidence. Different regions paid different tax rates. French nobles paid less in taxes. The church held a large amount of land and was exempt from taxes but paid a "gift" to the Crown that was negotiated and not predictable. Though the tax burden was lighter in France than in England, it was resented as unfair. (Brewer, 130–131) While the Dutch avoided telling the truth about their debt, the French struggles to raise money were very public.

Commerce

During the seventeenth century, the Dutch, British, and French seized control of the main merchant routes to Europe. In the eighteenth century, many other nations tried to found companies to compete but lacked capital or strong diplomatic, military, and naval support. The three big commercial countries stayed on top by hook or by crook. France and Britain continued to use mercantilist principles with high levels of domestic production. By the 1780s, French and British led foreign trade volume and slowly squeezed out the Dutch just as they had reduced the Dutch colonies. British traded more with the Americas and Asia, while the French concentrated on trade with Europe and the Middle East.

British trade with Russia greatly increased in the eighteenth century. British imports rose fifteenfold as they bought timber, grain, and naval stores from the Russians. British exports rose sixfold by selling manufactured goods, tea, sugar, and tobacco to the Russian landlords who had disposable income. The growth of trade encouraged the landlords to make their estates bigger and more efficient, and the Russian peasants became virtual slaves who could be bought, sold, or rented out. As serfs began to make payments to the lords in cash, Russia became a money economy and was drawn into the capitalist world. (Braudel, III, 448)

THE ISLAMIC WORLD

European trade with the Middle East also grew in the eighteenth and nineteenth centuries. The Islamic legal system and inheritance system caused Muslim firms to fall behind not only European firms but also Christian and Jewish merchants in the Ottoman Empire who had previously used Islamic contracts, courts, and inheritance. (Neal and Williamson, I, 218) There was no concept of a corporate entity in Islamic law and partnerships remained small. Most partnerships were two men, and the largest did not exceed twenty. The usury prohibition continued to restrict investments. With the dominance of the Ottoman Turks and Turkic Mughals in South Asia, the social standing of merchants declined from early Islamic days. The Koran allows for no more than one-third of an estate to go to one heir. The rest is split among children, cousins, and other relatives according to a formula. This might have been fair but it prevented the formation of giant fortunes that might have invested in large-scale projects. Muslim governments intervened in land inheritance to prevent the formation of **microplots** (lands too small or too poor to support a family). This no doubt helped many families but also removed any incentive to improve the lands or adopt the more productive methods pioneered by the Netherlands in the seventeenth century. Islamic agriculture became ever less productive than European agriculture, the sure hallmark of a noncapitalist economy. In the nineteenth century, Egypt and Turkey "westernized" their legal systems and added joint-stock companies and limited-liability corporations to existing organizational forms. Not until the early twentieth century did large Muslim-owned commercial banks emerge.

When Vasco da Gama arrived in India, the Muslim princes who ruled the cities of the north had been able to shut him out. The powerful Hindu state of Vijayanagar in the south had been more welcoming in part because there were significant numbers of Christians there. Muslim princes overwhelmed this state in 1565, but by that time the Portuguese had taken advantage of war in the north to capture bases at Diu and Bombay (present-day Mumbai). The Dutch largely avoided India. The British who arrived after 1600 had a hard time maintaining relations with Muslim princes. In 1661, the King of England married a Portuguese princess and received Bombay. In 1686, the British established an eastern base, Calcutta, in the defensible swamps of the Ganges delta. (Parry, 247, 257) They would form a mutually profitable partnership with the Indian merchants of the Bengal. (Neal and Williamson, I, 167)

Muslims had long justified slavery by stating that prisoners of war could be sold into slavery. During the early Middle Ages, many eastern Europeans had been sold to the Muslim world. From 650 to 1600, the Muslims sold almost five million Africans across the Sahara into slavery. In the seventeenth century, the sultan of Oman had ousted the Portuguese from many of their trading posts and fortresses along the Arabian and east African coasts, including Muscat in 1648 and Mombasa in 1698. (Klein, 68) In the middle of the eighteenth century, the French decided to develop their islands in the Indian Ocean and imported slaves from East Africa, an area that had not been part of the Atlantic slave trade. Pierre Poivre planted spices on Mauritius in 1747. Coffee grew as a cash crop on Reunion and the Dutch colony of Java. Slaves also flowed throughout the Muslim world. Zanzibar, under Oman's control, became the major slave trading center. The French were buying about fifty-five hundred slaves a year, but even more were going to Muscat and India.

The Muscat prince **Sayyid Said** (ruled 1806–1856) had projected Arab power in the Indian Ocean as the British and French dueled for power. When the British defeated Napoleon, they asserted their power along the Indian and Arabian coasts and forced Said to focus on East Africa. In the 1830s, he conquered Mombasa and moved his center to Zanzibar. He encouraged Indian bankers to immigrate, practice their religion freely, and run finance and trade in the capital. He also promoted the growing of cloves as a cash crop. Swahili and Arab traders moved into the interior from the trading cities in order to revive the slave trade. Said developed Arab trading centers along Lake Tanganyika and elsewhere. They traded guns for ivory and slaves. After the 1850s, traders turned tribes against each other as they introduced guns in large numbers, and major slave trading began. Strong tribes in the area of modern Kenya, Rwanda, and Uganda kept the Arab traders out. To the south in the lake region and Congo River watershed, Swahili, Arab, and African adventurers formed their own armies and looted and enslaved freely. In 1860, one hundred thousand slaves lived on Zanzibar with four thousand owned by the sultan himself.

TEMPERATE AMERICA

North American Indians practiced extensive agriculture after corn arrived from Mexico, but they may not have established cities despite a major trade in copper in the Great Lakes region. They never got beyond copper in industrial metals. Cahokia near St. Louis may have been a city around 1150, but the Indians abandoned the great mounds of the Mississippi by 1600. We have no historical records, but one hypothesis is that the mound-builders were wiped out by European diseases long before any actual Europeans appeared. (Crosby, 210–13) There were ten different cultural groups comprising dozens of tribes with very different traditions. European exploration was slow because there was no obvious wealth as there had been in Mexico and Peru. In the sixteenth century, the Spanish explored the American southwest, while the French and British mapped the Atlantic coast and rivers. The Spanish attempts to colonize Florida and the southeast failed several times due to disease and the hostility of natives. In 1565, they founded St. Augustine, Florida. It took a long time to secure Florida and they did not expand northwards. They did not occupy Texas until 1720.

In the seventeenth century, Europeans established settlements along the Atlantic coast, starting with Newfoundland in 1583 as the first British area, followed by Virginia in 1584. The private London Company founded **Jamestown colony**, Virginia, in 1607, but the government revoked its charter in 1624 because the colony never paid a dividend, and Virginia became a Crown colony. (Parry, 217) **Plymouth colony** in Massachusetts Bay began in 1620 followed by Connecticut, Rhode Island, and Maryland. North America produced a number of cash crops, starting with tobacco. Slaves first came to Virginia in 1619 to work on the large tobacco plantations. At the same time, the French built trading centers further north in the St. Lawrence River area of Canada. The fur trade spurred the exploration of the interior. The Indians had previously regarded the beaver as a useless animal, but now beaver pelts to make felt hats fetched enormous wealth. (Neal and Williamson, I, 472) In 1770 much of North America west of the Missouri River was still unknown to the Europeans.

British/Spanish Colonial Differences

The British colonies, from very modest beginnings, would grow into the United States, for a time the biggest and most wealthy economy in the world. Mexico, which had started so spectacularly, has never risen to that level. The population of British North America rose 900 percent from 1700 to 1820, but only 50 percent in Mexico. Why? The first reason is that Spain imposed a much bigger drain of resources on Mexico. Angus Maddison estimated that there was an official tribute amounting to almost 3 percent of Mexican GDP. Another drain came from Spaniards returning to Europe after making their fortune in America. Like Spain itself, there was great inequality, and the richest were constantly draining wealth out of Mexico. Thirdly, Spanish mercantilism was more onerous than British mercantilism. Fourthly, The British colonies had a more educated population. Finally, British Americans had the opportunity to choose among a variety of different colonies (the thirteen that would rebel, the Canadas, and the Floridas) while Spanish Mexico was very centralized. (Maddison 2001, 107–8)

THE "TRIANGLE TRADE"

The majority of foreign European trade related to the Americas and Africa. The key was sugar, grown in the Madeira and Canary islands early on, then planted abundantly in the West Indies. By 1580, the Portuguese had transplanted the Madeira sugar/slave plantation to the Brazilian coast. At first, the Portuguese attacked and grabbed slaves, but by 1445, they were trading for slaves from the Berbers south of Cape Bojador. (Klein, 51) They easily fit into the Muslim-organized slave trade of West Africa that had existed for hundreds of years.

(Parry, 259) Then after 1512, they opened a new slave trade at the mouth of the Congo River. In 1576, they shifted their center of operations south to the port of Luanda. Favorable winds could bring a slave ship quickly across the south Atlantic from Luanda to Brazil. Between 1580 and 1630, the Portuguese brought about 170,000 Africans to Brazil. Another 300,000 were enslaved and brought to Brazil between 1630 and 1700. (Klein, 11, 28, 31) Brazil traded iron, wine, tobacco, brandies, textiles, guns, and beads for Angolan slaves. The slave trade was accelerating.

The British began to grow sugar on Barbados in 1640 and brought in six thousand African slaves, and the French planted sugar on Guadaloupe and Martinique. By 1700, there were fifty thousand slaves in Barbados. In the 1730s, Jamaica became the British sugar center with over one hundred thousand Africans arriving since the British takeover in 1655. (Klein, 30–32) Crushing, boiling and refining sugar was hot and dangerous work. It was very easy to lose a finger in the cane crusher. Boiling sugar often caused serious burns. By definition, the work on this tropical plant had to be done under a broiling sun with high humidity on lands filled with poisonous animals and insects and tropical diseases. This work was sometimes done in twenty-hour shifts, increasing the risk. (Landes, 117, 123) Speed was important because cane must be brought to the sugar mill within hours of harvest. (*Cambridge Economic History*, IV, 290) Producing sugar was not for the family farmer because it needed massive investment to build the boilers, the tanks, and the crushing mills. (Landes, 115) Sugar would be manufactured into rum and other spirits. These were traded in Africa along with gunpowder, flints, and textiles for slaves, thus the name "Triangle Trade." Textiles made in Europe and southern Asia were by far the largest item traded for slaves. This was done on different ships made for the specific purposes, not one ship doing all parts of the trade. (Klein, 87)

From 1662 to 1850, some 9.5 million slaves were brought from Africa to the Americas; it is estimated that an additional one or two million died during the brutal passage across the Atlantic where slaves were chained together and cramped. There were also significant numbers of deaths from those in pens waiting to be put on the ship. (Klein, 91) It usually took about six months to gather a slave cargo and then another two months to sail across the Atlantic (one month from Luanda to Brazil). (122) In the seventeenth century, up to 20 percent of the slaves died, but after 1700 captains worked harder to speed their cargoes alive across the ocean and the death rate fell to about 12 percent. About once a year, a ship would have more than half its slaves die on the passage. (138–39) Records were not carefully kept and some estimates range to 13 million captured or killed. Some slave areas grew up as the result of wars, such as Ashanti wars of expansion after the 1680s or the Senegambian religious wars of the 1720s and 1730s. Others developed new slave trades such as the Kingdoms of Dahomey and Oyo on the west African coast and the Kingdom of Kongo on the mouth of the Congo River. (57–63) Europeans would either establish factory-forts or invite African dealers out to ships. Slavery spread in African societies as rulers were eager to make money from a sales tax of about 10 percent. (104) New foods (cassava, greater yam, sweet potato, corn, pineapple) spurred population growth. (*Cambridge Economic History*, IV, 285) The African population actually grew between 1500 and 1820 from forty-six million to seventy-four million though regions of West Africa must have suffered some decline from slavery. (Maddison 2001, 241) Commercial crops such as tobacco, cocoa, and peanuts would come to Africa later. (Klein, 62)

Slaves went to the sugar islands of the West Indies, where death rates were very high, or to the tobacco plantations of Virginia and Maryland. The northern American colonies were not opposed to slavery on principle, but their soil was too thin and farms too small and inefficient for profitable slavery. Slaves in the Americas resisted in a number of ways including killing their children to deprive masters of additional slaves, and suicide. There were rugged mountains and forests in islands such as Jamaica and Hispaniola that could hide runaways. (Parry, 278) By the 1780s, seventy-five thousand Africans a year were arriving as slaves. The high death rate on the plantations, the increasing amount of land being planted, and only one-third of the slaves transported being female created an endless appetite for more slaves. This caused the price of slaves to skyrocket. (Klein, 45, 110, 166)

By 1700, the West Indies accounted for 7 percent of total English trade. (Parry, 265) From 1713 to 1792, Britain imported £162 million, mostly sugar, from the Americas while importing £104 million worth of goods from India and China. In 1710, Britain sent 88 percent of its exports to Europe and 10 percent to North America, the Caribbean, and Africa. By 1774, the balance had shifted to 58.5% versus 37.5%. The British import balance also shifted. In 1710 it imported 64 percent of its overall goods from Europe, 29 percent from North America, Africa, and the Caribbean; by 1774, it was 46 percent versus 42 percent, with the rest from Asia. Slave-produced goods (tobacco, cotton, sugar) accounted for one-fourth of British imports. The sugar economy was based on plantations with absentee British or French owners, managed indirectly, and worked by slaves. While the sixteenth-century monopoly companies built many of the forts and got the trade started, by the eighteenth century, slaving was run by a large number of owners and captains who could become rich from a few successful trips. 49 percent of eighteenth-century Dutch captains made only one slave voyage, 7 percent died on a slave voyage. (Klein, 83) They tended to cluster in a few ports. The English city of Liverpool and the French city of Nantes became rich on the slave trade and slave-produced wares. After 1650, the slave trade to the Americas was very substantial: 610,000 came to Jamaica between 1700 and 1786. Some slaves lived in Europe. By 1630, there were about fifteen thousand African slaves living in the Portuguese capital of Lisbon.

The last area in the Caribbean devoted to sugar production was Saint Domingue (Haiti), the western part of the island of Hispaniola, starting in the 1660s. (Klein, 31) After 1750, Saint Domingue grew explosively exporting sugar and coffee. In the 1763 peace treaty with Britain, France gladly gave up Canada and Louisiana to get back Saint Domingue, Martinique, and Guadaloupe. By 1789, Saint Domingue exported more sugar than all the British colonies combined. (*Cambridge Economic History*, IV, 291) The French West Indies in 1770 had 379,000 slaves in a population of 430,000 (88 percent). (Langley, 97) This increased after 1770 with thirty thousand new slaves arriving each year from 1785 to 1790; even if half died, this still meant seventy-five thousand young slaves. Africans in their twenties comprised the largest group in Saint Domingue.

This racial mix ensured that the American Revolution did not spread to the British West Indies. The planters would have had to arm their slaves if they were to fight the British crown. The goal of successful planters was to return to Europe and enjoy life there. The French armed people of color and even a few Africans in some attacks on the British. The French governors of Saint Domingue sent about five hundred people of color and Africans to fight in the American Revolution. They returned with the idealism of those battles. When Saint Domingue's slave population rebelled and opened a bloody war, Cuba and Jamaica stepped in to increase their sugar and coffee production. (Klein, 39)

But the Atlantic slave trade ended in the nineteenth century. It is a casebook example that economics and profit do not determine all. (Klein, 13) There was a religious revival in late eighteenth-century Britain and one of its cornerstones was the belief that slavery was an offense against God. One of the first blows against slavery came in 1771 when the British chief justice ruled that there could be no slaves in Britain. More doubt was cast on slavery when the slave revolt in Saint Domingue won freedom for its people. The belief grew that free labor was more productive than slave labor and that abolition would increase profits. In 1787, Britain paid a ship to take freed slaves to Sierra Leone in western Africa. Half of these settlers died in the first year, and some became slave dealers. In 1788, Parliament placed the first limits on the manner of carrying slaves. New Jersey, Pennsylvania, Connecticut, Rhode Island, and Massachusetts abolished the slave trade shortly after U.S. independence. In 1792 Denmark said it would abolish the import of slaves as of 1803. In 1799, the British Parliament increased the space requirements for slaves on the ships. Urged by President Thomas Jefferson (himself a slaveowner), the U.S. abolished the import of slaves in 1807. In Britain abolitionists in the House of Commons pressed step by step until the trade was outlawed starting January 1, 1808. Britain would abolish slavery in its colonies in 1834; the French would follow in 1848. The North's victory in the Civil War ended slavery in the United States in 1865. Brazil was one of the last when it ended slavery in 1888.

THE EUROPEAN-ASIAN TRADE IMBALANCE

Since ancient times, a severe trade imbalance had existed between Europe and Asia. The Europeans had little that interested Asians with money, and the masses had no disposable income.

The result was that Europe would trade gold and silver for Asian-manufactured goods such as rugs, chinaware, and cotton cloth. After 1700, Europeans began to find ways to imitate Asian goods. The German city of Meissen cracked the secret of Chinese porcelain manufacture in 1709. European cotton goods came in with the Industrial Revolution after 1780. With the growth of European manufacturing and tariff protection, the trade deficit declined. After 1770, Europe's main import from China was tea. British tea imports over the previous hundred years had grown almost 300 times. The British paid for the tea at Guangzhou after 1720 with raw cotton and opium from Bengal. (Maddison 2001, 86; *Cambridge Economic History* V, 211) This would open a tragic chapter in Chinese history.

China Stagnates

Confucian teachings considered trade and industry morally questionable so an edict of 1433 banned all large ships. Another decree banned maritime trade by Chinese subjects. The bureaucracy grew excessive, and harem and eunuch intrigues consumed political life. One had to pass an examination to enter the civil service, which encouraged conformity and a precise knowledge of classics. One took other exams in order to move up. Passing exams not only required knowledge but the money to pay for a tutor and considerable bribery. The Mongols had tried to put in changes, which gave change a bad reputation in Chinese eyes.

The Ming dynasty took giant steps to feed its people, especially in southern China, which was dependent on rice. It introduced Champa rice from Cambodia, which grows faster (up to two harvests a year) but has somewhat less nutrition. Farmers used fish in the rice fields to fertilize the soil and eat the mosquitoes that carried disease. The population grew from seventy million to 130 million.

The Ming rulers faced a grave threat from the Tungusic **Manchus** after 1600. China expanded its army and raised taxes. This provoked riots in the commercial centers of Suzhou, Beijing, and Hangzhou. Neglect had caused Hangzhou's harbor in the lower Yangzi delta to silt up. Factions tore apart the bureaucracy. Emperor Wanli (ruled 1573–1619) became increasingly frustrated by the bureaucracy's opposition. Finally, he gave up and refused to make decisions and devoted himself to hobbies. He lavished money on his elaborate tomb instead of paying the soldiers, who turned outlaw and often joined the Manchus. Entire provinces revolted.

Chinese bandits and rebels captured Beijing in 1644. The main Ming general preferred to surrender to the Manchus. This event marked the beginning of the Manchu (or **Qing**) Dynasty. The new dynasty reinvigorated China and borrowed from Manchu, Chinese, and Western traditions, although it was not strongly innovative. The Manchus stayed aloof, did not marry Chinese, and stayed out of trade and commerce. China remained caught in the Malthusian trap. Its population grew strongly after 1680 as ground nuts, sweet potato, and corn arrived, but its labor productivity and wealth remained unchanged. (Braudel, I, 46)

The emigre Chinese community grew steadily. Chinese worked as miners in Malaya and laborers in the Philippines. Despite anti-Chinese riots, neighborhoods in Manila and Batavia were repopulated. Some niche trades, such as Batavia to southeast Asia, fell under Chinese control.

The fall of the Ming opened opportunity to other peoples. Korean merchants and craftsmen built up profits. In the 1700s, coinage became more common and credit developed in the main city of Seoul, where about 200,000 of the seven million Koreans lived. Practical power in Vietnam was divided between princes of the **Trinh** family ruling from Hanoi and the **Nguyen** family ruling from Hué. The Nguyens built two massive walls to keep out the northerners. By 1700, the Nguyens had conquered the Saigon area in the south and in 1757 they took the Mekong delta. The Nguyens were more welcoming to the Europeans because they wanted trade and weapons.

Social Consequences of the Global Economy

A new merchant class grew up along the African coast where the Europeans had opened trade. Many of these merchants were Afro-Portuguese, Afro-English, and Afro-French and used their wealth to secure power, land, and build slave armies. They had European weapons and used European military tactics, so even if the Europeans could have found a way around the disease barrier, they would face large and formidable African armies. Chinese and Indian merchants also made profits. The Europeans supplied capital and technical and organizing abilities. Profits of about 10 percent piled up in Britain, France, and Holland. (Klein 54–55, 98) These governments became dependent on the taxes and loans which came largely from the commercial classes. The wealthiest did quite well, the middle class became more comfortable, larger, and more literate. The wealth of the lower classes seems to have declined in eighteenth-century Europe. Commercial families married into the old nobility, so the classes slowly merged. Some wealthy acquired noble titles. Others in the growing middle class grew angry at old nobles who looked down on people rich enough to buy them.

CONCLUSION

The word "globalization" gets thrown around a lot and sometimes people act as if that started in the 1990s. This chapter has shown that many parts of the world were connected in the 1700s. Economists have shown that by the 1820s, the world was decisively globalized, that is, that economic events in one part of the world had a huge impact thousands of miles away. The western world moved decisively ahead of the Islamic and Chinese economic areas in this century. Sugar anchored the "triangle trade" that linked West Africa, West Europe, and the Americas in a profitable and destructive relationship. The profits piled up mostly in western Europe, the Africans mainly felt the destructive effects. The Industrial Revolution would start in Britain and would transform an already developed global economy.

TIMELINE

1607	Jamestown founded in Virginia
1640	British planted sugar in Carribean
1644	Manchus captured Beijing
1686	British established Calcutta on Ganges delta
1740–63	Britain and France fought war around the world
1775–83	War of American Independence
1808	British abolished slave trade
1834	British abolished slavery in colonies
1848	French abolished slavery in colonies
1865	United States abolished slavery

KEY TERMS

Jamestown colony
"Triangle Trade"

Chapter 8

BREAKTHROUGH TO RAPID GROWTH

Up until 1800, the economic history of the world had consisted of good times where the sustained growth over a long period of time amounted to about half-a-percentage point rise in real per capita GDP each year. Bad times saw shrinkage: death and hunger and disease accompanied these years. For most of the world over long stretches there was just stagnation: the population would grow but constantly run up against the Malthusian limit. Any gain in productivity was immediately matched by increased population so the productivity gain would be lost. The per capita GDP and per capita income stayed about the same for centuries.

That was four thousand years of human history. But around the year 1800 came abrupt and shocking changes. More and more areas rose to new levels of prosperity at the same time that the population was growing faster than ever. Two thousand years ago, the world's population was 231 million by one estimate. One thousand years ago, it was 268 million, hardly changed. By 1600, the population had doubled to about 556 million and the world was wealthier. This was especially true in western and central Europe where wealth had doubled with the rise of capitalism. But the wealth of the rest of the world had increased by about 25 percent, not only from contact with the capitalists, but also from major farm improvements in Asia. (Maddison 2001, 28, 46) The next two hundred years, from 1600 to 1800, saw another doubling of world population, to over a billion, but the world's wealth hardly grew, only about 13 percent. In the last two hundred years, world population has increased sevenfold. But even more astonishing at the same time, real per capita GDP has increased eightfold! Put another way, the world's GDP has increased by fifty times in the last two hundred years. By a very rough estimate it took the world forty-three hundred years before 1800 to increase its GDP by fiftyfold. How did this happen? What changed? That is the topic of this chapter.

There are a number of answers, but the main change is in energy consumption. For thousands of years, the amount of energy consumed had grown very slowly. Energy production consisted mainly of burning wood or other plant matter. Animals, including humans, supplied a small amount of energy, although they, too, ran on plant matter. Economic growth was limited in part by the rate at which wood grew or the ability to cut new forests effectively. John Perlin has suggested that the economic histories of Greece and India have been governed by three deforestations and collapses. We have seen how the Dutch got around this by using peat, which is a coal precursor. (Hall and Klitgaard, 51, 62)

In medieval Eurasia, the watermill and windmill harnessed those forces. After 1800, the world turned, at an accelerating rate, to **fossil fuels**. Plant matter and solar energy had been laid down and concentrated over millions of years.

Coal, oil, and natural gas had much higher energy densities than previous sources and provided much more energy than was needed to recover them. **Energy Returned over Energy Invested** (ERoEI) is the critical equation needed along with profitability, of course. The transformation began with coal, and the shift from wood burning to coal was a basic shift of the Industrial Revolution. But oil was almost as transformative. **By the twentieth century, energy became its own independent variable, matching labor and nonenergy capital in shaping economies**. Physicist Reiner Kummel found that energy in fact is a stronger correlate to economic growth than land or capital. (Hall and Klitgaard, 7) What happens when energy growth slows down? We will consider that in the final chapter.

Science and Capitalism

The seventeenth century witnessed what has been billed a "scientific revolution" in Europe. There was rapid scientific advance, especially in physics and astronomy. The most important advance was the development of a scientific method that allowed people to approach many problems in a scientific manner. At the same time, science and technology, which had been largely separate endeavors, were united. Scientists studied technical changes and looked for the larger scientific laws that governed them. Engineers would use scientific principles to improve machines and practices. Scholars applied scientific method to agriculture to increase productivity. By 1800, it was common for manufacturers and farmers to consult scientists. (Broadberry and O'Rourke, I, 39) A scientific community grew that was in regular communication so that news of successful (and failed) experiments could travel quickly. Many think that this is what made the world of wealth and crowding and that technical advance can go on forever so that by the year 2200, the world's GDP will be fifty times larger than it is today. However, careful research shows that many increases in productivity attributed to "technology" are in fact the result of increased energy inputs. (Hall and Klitgaard, 7)

In some ways, science can simply be seen as the standardization of capitalism and its application to other fields. Farmers had long controlled breeding plants and animals for desirable characteristics. The Mesoamerican people created corn from a very unpromising plant. Knowledge of inventions would spread. Now it was done by many people linked by communication in a systematic way. Portuguese and Dutch-style experimentation was applied to medicine, physics, chemistry, astronomy, anatomy, art and so on. A flood of tools for measurement developed: telescope, microscope, precision screw. The pendulum clock and balance spring enabled a more precise measurement of time. (Landes, 204) Science not only created wealth, but as societies in Europe grew wealthier it meant that more people could spend their time thinking, experimenting and creating, rather than having to farm or manufacture for a living. Children could learn to read and write instead of being put out to the field or factory to work.

THE ENLIGHTENMENT

"Enlightenment" refers to a common program of intellectuals in France, the Netherlands, Germany, Italy, Scotland, and elsewhere that lasted from about 1713, the end of a round of European and colonial wars, until 1789, the beginning of the French Revolution. There were many different currents and disagreements, but most Enlightenment writers shared the following ideas: 1) Universal principles exist governing humanity, nature, and society; 2) Human reason, given enough time, will discover all of these principles; 3) A belief in the perfectibility and progress of humanity; 4) A hostility to supernatural revelation.

Physiocrats and Economic Thought

Some writers of the Enlightenment considered economic relations. France was the largest European economy and the center of the Enlightenment, so it pioneered some major economic thinking. Richard Cantillon (d.1730), an associate of John Law's in the Mississippi Bubble, wrote an early French essay on economics. **François Quesnay** was the physician of King Louis XV and his mistress Madame de Pompadour. Quesnay had been born a peasant and retained a fascination with the farm all his life but died a nobleman. (*Cambridge Economic History*, V, 611) An influential group of thinkers called themselves **physiocrats** in honor of Quesnay. He composed the *Tableau économique* in 1758 to show the interrelationship of all economic activities. He then tried to draw up general economic rules in his book *Philosophe rurale* in 1763. In this book, Quesnay argued that agriculture is the most important economic activity and that there are natural economic laws. Economics is an exact science that operates the same way at all times; history is therefore not important. Population growth had led to greater poverty, he said, just look at the cities with jobless and beggars on the roads. Quesnay called for abolishing all internal trade barriers (as England had done long ago) and rationalizing the tax system into one tax on land, paid by all (as England had done in 1694). Internal free trade would encourage more efficient cultivation and larger plots. Grain prices would rise, and farmers would make more money. Quesnay was stunningly wrong about most of this. He was wrong about history, but many others have made the same mistake since. Abolishing internal trade barriers and tariffs would have increased both production and productivity and led to a fall in prices. In any case, there was little response. While the French provinces supported freeing the grain trade, the Paris nobility blocked reform because it still had the feudal right to sell grain first at the highest price. The French crown did abolish some regulations in 1762 and 1774, but when there were bad harvests and prices rose, riots broke out. The focus on the land was perhaps natural when France had such rich and abundant farmland but ignoring trade and industry was a major flaw. The French lifted their ban on calicoes in 1759 as a move to freer trade. (Braudel, II, 180)

The physiocrats denounced government intervention in the grain markets. Since ancient times, governments often forced bread prices lower in time of shortage so people would not riot or starve. The physiocrats opposed this because it reduced the incentive to produce more grain and thus led to a longer crisis. This may be correct from a strict economic standpoint but is politically impossible. The Marquis d'Argenson (d.1757) was the first to promote "laissez-nous faire" ("leave us be") as a principle. (*Cambridge Economic History*, IV, 543) Vincent de **Gournay** was a government official who denounced his own government's regulation, which he claimed reduced trade. His name is associated with the motto "Laissez-faire, laissez-passer" meaning "let them be, let them pass." **Laissez-faire** has come to mean a philosophy that business interests should do whatever they please because they are best suited to create economic growth that will benefit most people in the long run.

Adam Smith

Adam Smith (1723–1790) of Great Britain published *The Wealth of Nations* in 1776. Smith had met with Voltaire, a great French Enlightenment writer, and applied Enlightenment theories to economics: by serving their own self interests and applying reason, people will actually serve the greater good by bringing into effect the "invisible hand" as long as they are properly educated as to their real interests. The government must therefore pay for general education of all boys and girls, a shockingly radical idea for the time. The wealth of a country comes not from its hoard of gold and silver, as the mercantilists would have it. Wealth depends on a nation's productivity. An important step is the division of labor: each person doing one small repetitive task can increase productivity. Production lines were already common in Enlightened Europe. The larger the market, the larger the division of labor could be, and thus all restraints on trade should be lifted. Smith was the founder of the classical liberal economic school focused on free markets and free trade.

Many heads of big corporations who cite Smith with approval want to "get the government off their backs," but Smith also attacked big corporations venomously. "People of the same trade seldom meet together, even for merriment and diversion, but the conversation ends in a conspiracy against the public." (Book One, Chapter X, Part II) If companies get too big, they invariably manipulate and distort the free market so the invisible hand cannot operate properly. Smith advocated government interference of a sort that only communist governments have ever implemented.

With attacks against restraints on trade, Smith set up an economic liberal philosophy that would combine with political liberalism to create one of the most powerful political movements of the nineteenth century.

THE AGRICULTURAL REVOLUTION

Most people in Europe (and the world) in the eighteenth century were farmers and lived out on the countryside. A fundamental change in farming would shake a nation. As seen in Chapter 3, European farming before the modern period had been extremely varied across the map and dependent on laws, customs, family traditions, soil quality, climate, and many other factors. Generally, we may say that there was a rotation of crops usually involving a grain such as wheat, barley, or rye, and protein-rich crops such as broad beans. Animals and their manure were relatively scarce, which meant both fertilizer and meat were far more limited than today. For most farmers in Western Europe, the only choice was to let part of the soil rest and recover its nutrients. The land would lie **fallow**: farmers would plow and remove any weeds that appeared, but they would not plant crops. They left roughly one-third of the farmland fallow, and this has led historians to create a general model called the **three-field system**. The population grew very slowly, and village life remained much the same from generation to generation. There were a few very fertile, densely-populated areas such as the Netherlands and the Po River valley in Italy that used more intensive techniques.

New Foods and Demographic Revolution

The low point of European population in the early modern period was in 1650. It had just suffered terrible wars, bad weather, and crop failures. After that year, population would grow at an accelerating rate for the next three hundred years. The biggest contributor to the growth from 1650 to 1800 was new food. Explorations had brought the Europeans in contact with many unfamiliar foods, but the most significant were

corn (which the Europeans call maize) and the **potato**. The potato is one of the hardiest plants in the world. It is native to the Andes Mountains of South America and almost single-handedly supported the complex society of the Incan Empire of Peru. It is an excellent source of carbohydrates, can be prepared in a variety of ways, and has many uses for human and animal consumption. An acre of potatoes could feed up to five times as many people as an acre of wheat. A farmer could harvest a crop of potatoes in three or four months whereas many grains took ten months to ripen. The planting of potatoes was first mentioned in Ireland in 1606; by 1650, it had become a staple of the Irish diet. (*Cambridge Economic History*, IV, 278, 299) Ireland and the southwest German states became dependent on the potato. That proved to be dangerous. From 1650 to 1800 the population increased in England from five million to nine million, France from twenty-one million to twenty-nine million, the German areas from seventeen million to twenty-nine million, and Russia from seventeen million to thirty-six million.

Improvements in agriculture led to a change in many facets of everyday life. Men and women often lived with their parents until they married. For men, the average age at first marriage was about twenty-five to twenty-seven, for women it was around twenty-one. Then they would move out, having saved up enough money to buy or at least rent enough land for themselves. During early adulthood, children often worked for several years away from home. Social pressures had worked to keep levels of children born to unmarried women very low. The spread of the potato allowed farmers to set up a household more easily because they did not need as much land if they planted potatoes. After 1750, the age of marriage began to drop. Earlier marriage meant more children and a larger population.

Other new foods included increased planting of the turnip, which could be eaten by people in an emergency but was mostly for animals. There was also scientific cultivation of the sugar beet with the aim of increasing its sugar content. In the nineteenth century, sugar from beets increasingly took the place of sugar from cane, which could only be grown in the tropics and, as we have seen, was largely the product of slave labor.

New Tools

The time around 1700 also saw the invention of some simple but ingenious new tools that increased farm productivity. The Englishman **Jethro Tull** (1674–1741) introduced a deeper mold board on the plow. The plow was lighter, and horses could pull it as well as oxen. Plowing would be faster even as it dug more deeply. When one stirs up more soil, it mixes in more oxygen. This means that the microbes that help fertilize soil will increase and work faster making the soil more productive. Tull introduced a new seed-planting method of "seed drilling" in 1701 rather than broadcasting. This meant a family did not have to save as much seed from the previous year's crops and this increased its food supply. It had a modest impact in more advanced Western Europe, but Central and Eastern Europe increased their yield per seed by 24 percent.

Big agricultural machines such as reapers and chemical fertilizer would come only in the nineteenth century. The U.S. wheat yield in 1866 was eleven bushels per acre, about three times medieval Europe's yield. The yield increased to sixteen in 1914, twenty-four in 1960, thirty-six in 1983, and forty in 1998; the growth since 1960 has mainly been because of chemical fertilizer derived from natural gas. The price of wheat in 1919 hit a high of $2.16 per bushel (with inflation, that equals $43.20 in 2007 dollars) as opposed to the current prices of five to eight dollars. What would your life be like if all the prices in the grocery store cost seven times as much? What would you buy and not buy? How much money would be left after you paid for food and rent?

New Means of Cultivation

A number of English spent time in the Netherlands in the seventeenth century and observed the more intensive methods. The scientific revolution inspired some to apply the scientific method to farming. Tull suggested a process of mowing the field while root plants grew. **Charles Townshend** (1674–1738) proposed a scientific model of cultivation based on his experiments on soil fertility. This was known as the **four-crop rotation**: the farmer would plant wheat in the late autumn, it would grow in the winter (thus known as "winter wheat") protected by snow from the cold and then be harvested in early spring. Then the farmer would plant root crops such as potatoes and turnips. The farmer could mow to remove weeds while these grew underground. The farmer would then grow summer grains such as barley and oats that were mainly for animal consumption; autumn would see him plant so-called artificial grasses such as alfalfa and clover or legumes (peas, beans) to fertilize the soil and replenish nourishment. Thus two cycles (wheat and root crops) would take nutrition out while the summer grain and the autumn cycle would replenish nutrition and make the soils ready for winter wheat. Scientific farmers found that on many soils, there would no longer be a need to leave a part fallow, so you could plant the entire area year after year.

Farmers also applied science to animal breeding to create larger animals that were carefully bred for meat or milk or (as with the new sport of thoroughbred horse racing) speed. The ability to feed and keep more horses meant that the average English farmer had up to 67 percent more horsepower to help him than the French farmer in 1800. (Broadberry and O'Rourke, I, 155) **Robert Bakewell** (1725–1795) was a leading breeder. During his lifetime, the average weight of cattle doubled and sheep tripled from twenty-eight to eighty pounds.

Enclosure Acts

There was strong resistance among farmers to the new techniques. For many they seemed to be physically impossible, and the farmers complained that the scientists must have used special soils in special conditions. They would not risk their family's lives on something so uncertain.

The big landlords, however, were eager to increase their profits and turned nasty. They controlled the British Parliament. Only 250,000 men (3 percent of the total population) had the right to vote for the House of Commons. But these were not equally distributed, and by one estimate of the time just 5,723 men (.07% of the population) controlled the House of Commons. After 1700, the Parliament passed large numbers of **Enclosure Acts**. On the one hand, they cut off farm lands owned or traditionally rented by peasants from common land and waste land. The commons and the wastes were areas of lesser fertility that would be used by the village communally for less-demanding plants or pastures for animals or foraging areas. The commons and wastes could make the difference between life and death even though the lands were often owned by a local noble or big landlord. Because the productivity of these lands was low, peasants had used them by custom. Now fences or hedges cut them off with penalties imposed for "poaching." The Enclosure Acts also levied fees for surveying land that many peasants could not afford. The result of enclosure was that many sold or gave up their lands or cooperated with their landlords in converting the land to the new system. From 1761 to 1792, the Parliament enclosed seven times as much land as in the previous thirty years, and the pace accelerated after 1792. By 1800, the nobles or gentry held 80 percent of the land in Britain.

Results of the Agricultural Revolution

From 1700 to 1870, the number of farm workers in England grew by 14 percent, while production of crops grew 181 percent. Labor productivity therefore grew 146 percent. Measured another way, the land productivity of wheat, oats, and legumes doubled. Farmers not only eliminated most fallow land but reclaimed swampy and hilly and infertile land so the total amount of land planted grew 72 percent. Production of potatoes went from 1.31 million bushels to 50.14 million bushels. The population of England and Wales rose from 5.75 million to twenty-five million (335 percent) in this time. England had been a food exporter from 1660 to 1770; now it had to import food. Sixty percent of the English workers had been mainly food producers in 1700; that fell to 22 percent by 1850. (Cameron, 167–9) The increase in population would tend to lead to a rise in food prices, but this was offset by the increase in productivity, which brought prices down. Sara Horrell found that 48 percent of the household budget went to food in the 1787 to 1796 period in Britain, but only 40 percent on average went to food in the 1830 to 1954 period. By another estimate, in 1688 58.5 percent of the British GDP was spent on food, drink, and textiles; that would fall to 16 percent by the 1990s.

The agricultural revolution spread to northern France by 1770. A hundred years later the process was largely complete in that country. From 1780 to 1810, the amount of French land planted with potatoes increased by more than one hundred times. (Broadberry and O'Rourke, I, 154) From there it spread across the rest of western and central Europe. The process was faster than Britain's, and enclosure was rarely used. The new methods resulted because with each new generation, more and more farmers would split up the land until they were left with microplots: farms too small to support a family. (*Cambridge Economic History* V, 113) At that point, families would plant potatoes or introduce the four-crop rotation.

INDUSTRIAL REVOLUTION

Basic Shifts

The Industrial Revolution involved three basic shifts. Firstly, machines replaced and amplified human labor. Secondly, wood burning gave way to coal burning as world coal production grew from ten million tons in 1800 to one billion tons in 1900, a hundredfold increase. This produced about twenty-nine exajoules, roughly half of all the energy produced in the world. One ton of coal produced about the same amount of energy as two tons of dried hardwood, but it would take a long time for another cord of wood to grow while coal seemed limitless. Thirdly, animal or water or wind power gave way to the steam engine. Instead of many separate activities carried out by families across the countryside, unified factories with a central source of power (steam, later electricity) would carry out production with many different machines and either would be centered in cities or new cities would grow up around the factories. (Landes, 186)

Why England?

England had several advantages for industrialization: 1) **Financial**: the Bank of England provided a strong anchor for a credit system to provide financing for projects. Interest rates were lower than in most other European nations. The first English country bank was founded in 1716. The number of banks outside the capital of London grew from twelve in 1750 to four hundred in 1793 and nine hundred in 1815. In 1775, there were still only 150 banks in England and Wales, capitalized at £3.5 million; twenty-five years later, there were four hundred banks capitalized at £5.5 million. (Broadberry and O'Rourke, I, 135) 2) **Geographic**: England, a long and narrow island surrounded by seas, has many navigable waterways, making transportation cheaper. 3) **Economic**: the Agricultural Revolution, pioneered in England, made for lower food prices and thus more disposable income for manufactured goods. Landowners used their agricultural profits to develop many of the coal fields. 4) **Natural resources:** coal and iron were abundant. Even before the Industrial Revolution, Britain was producing about two million tons of coal a year, five times as much as the rest of the world combined. (*Cambridge Economic History*, V, 509) Because the gentry ran the country, there were few regulations on agriculture or industry and landless workers could move where they pleased.

These four factors were necessary to start an industrial revolution. Nearby Ireland had similar geographic advantages and also went through the agricultural revolution. However, Ireland did not industrialize. It did not have a lot of coal and iron. Also, its banking and credit system was underdeveloped.

Ireland suffered as a British colony. Oliver Cromwell had brutally completed the colonization process in the 1650s by taking land away from most Catholics. Although 90 percent of the Irish were Roman Catholics, Protestants owned 86 percent of the land and were often absentee landlords. What wealth Ireland produced was frequently transferred to Britain. Those renting the land had no incentive to improve their land because that would only raise the rent. Ireland's textile industries suffered from British competition, and Ireland actually deindustrialized during the late 1700s: 48 percent of the Irish had been employed in farming in 1775; it was 75 percent in 1845. (Broadberry and O'Rourke, I, 149) After 1699, Britain gained exclusive right to Irish textiles, limiting Irish profit. (*Cambridge Economic History*, V, 511) The Agricultural Revolution brought rapid population growth in Ireland as it did in Britain, but it also brought a dangerous overreliance on the potato. Not only was this the main food for many, but raising potatoes was the main job of many. If anything should happen to the potato crop, the Irish would have nothing to eat and no job to provide money to buy other food. 1,750,000 Irish left for England and America even before the Great Hunger of the 1840s.

New Textile Inventions and Innovations

After agriculture, textile production was the second biggest occupation. Most clothes were made of wool, which comes from sheep. Silk and cotton were very expensive and had to be imported, often from China and India. In the putting-out system, merchants gave wool to peasants to spin into thread, then weave into cloth, and then sew together as clothes. In 1717, Thomas Lombe set up the first true factory, where these functions would be carried out in one central place. In

1733, **John Kay** invented the **flying shuttle**, which sped up the weaving process. This created pressure to speed up the spinning of the thread to meet the weavers' demand. It took ten spinners to meet the need for thread of a single weaver working with the flying shuttle. The problem of thread was solved when **James Hargreaves** invented the **spinning jenny** in 1765. This provided sixteen times the thread as the spinning wheel. (Maddison 2001, 96) Coarser yarn could be turned out faster by the **water frame** of **Richard Arkwright** after 1775. The water frame cut the price of cotton yarn by two-thirds. (Neal and Williamson, I, 497) Finally, **Samuel Crompton's "Mule"** (1779) combined the speed of the water frame with the fine thread of the jenny. The Mule could spin two to three hundred times faster than a hand spinner. However, the Mule required water power, so businessmen built factories near water and cottage spinning declined. The number of hand-weavers kept growing to weave the enormous amounts of spun thread, which grew tenfold from 1770 to 1790. In the 1820s, **Edmund Cartwright's Power Loom** (invented 1785) became dominant in weaving. These inventions all occurred in England. It was not because Englishmen were smarter than men of other nations. These inventors had incentive because credit was cheap, and many of these inventors became very wealthy men. They could borrow money at low interest rates to set up a new business or expand an existing business. Often they borrowed from friends, relatives, or members of their church. Life was harder for businessmen in France and Spain because interest rates were much higher and it was harder to make a profit. They found it easier to put money into land.

The next key problem was the supply of cotton. The North American colonies and India were the main sources of cotton. Production was very slow because cotton seeds had to be picked out by hand, and raw cotton is difficult to work with. A worker could process only six pounds a day. Nevertheless, Britain had tripled its cotton cloth production from the 1740s to the 1770s. In 1793 the American **Eli Whitney** invented the **cotton gin** to pick out seeds automatically. This caused an upsurge in the cotton industry as the gin increased production fiftyfold. Britain imported 2.5 million pounds of cotton in 1760, twenty-two million in 1787, fifty million in 1800, and 366 million in 1837. By 1830, cotton cloth comprised 50 percent of the value of British exports. It also caused the expansion of cotton plantations across the southern U.S. and with it slavery. Before the cotton gin, only the long-staple cotton grown on the American coast had been profitable because short-staple cotton from slightly cooler climates had more seeds. The cotton gin greatly expanded the cotton range. Scientific farmers by 1820 evolved a superior form of cotton of medium staple that could tolerate cooler weather and saltier soil. From 1820 to 1860, the United States exported more than 70 percent of its cotton. (Hugill, 82–3)

The Transportation Revolution

As textile production grew after 1760, it became important to ensure cheap and reliable transportation. Roads were mostly unsuited to wheeled vehicles: a rainstorm turned them into quagmires. Only a few special coaches on the British roads of the 1760s could travel sixty miles a day. France had surfaced most of the main roads with gravel in the time of Louis XIV. (*Cambridge Economic History*, IV, 217) Water transport was cheaper and more efficient. One horse could pull 100,000 pounds loaded onto a water barge, but only 250 pounds on land. After 1760, Britain and France launched many projects to build canals to link rivers and to deepen many waterways. The Erie Canal opened in 1825 and linked Buffalo on Lake

Erie to Albany and the Hudson River. This reduced transport costs by 85 percent. (Neal and Williamson, II, 6) In 1815, engineers led by **John McAdam** built new roads made with crushed stones held together by tar over a solid foundation to accommodate wagons.

The "rail road" had long existed in the mines. The rails were usually made of wood that was joined together. Miners would push carts on grooved wheels loaded with tons of rock. The heavy weights were constantly breaking and splintering the wooden rails, which needed constant replacement. Innovations in iron and steel made better rails possible; mines installed the first iron rail track in 1767. In 1801, the first general railroad was established, pulled by horses to link up canals. The barge would be unloaded onto special carts that sat on iron rails.

Growth in Iron and Steel

The European iron industry had grown steadily from the fifteenth century, when the water-powered blast furnace operated in Italy to increase the production speed of cast iron. Blast furnaces are used to extract the metal from the raw ore. Heating was done with **charcoal**, the result of wood burned in the absence of air to make a smokeless fuel. Britons had cut down many of the forests to make charcoal or to build ships or warm people in their homes. From 1540 to 1640, coal and iron production in Britain increased 800 percent, but limits on mining from water flooding and the nature of coal prevented further expansion.

With the price of wood climbing, especially in Britain, people began to turn to coal for heating. Although very efficient, coal was smoky and could not be used in houses that lacked chimneys. The salt, brick, brewing, dyeing, and glass industries shifted to coal as a source of heat. (*Cambridge*

Economic History, IV, 105) Iron makers could not mix coal with iron because coal had many impurities that made the iron brittle. Another problem was that coal would turn soft and clog the furnaces. **Abraham Darby** borrowed the process of charring coal to remove impurities in coal to create **coke**. The brewing industry had been using coke to dry malt since the 1640s. (*Cambridge Economic History*, V, 474) Darby used it to smelt iron in 1708. British coal production quintupled in the eighteenth century, while iron production rose eightfold from 1740 to 1796. This was an important change because metals are superior materials to wood, brick, and stone. (*Cambridge Economic History*, IV, 144)

The Application of Steam Power

The problem of pumping water from mines still limited coal use. Before 1700, the only sources for the continuous driving of machinery were wind, water, and living muscle. Scientific experiments of the late 1600s in the areas of vacuum and atmospheric pressure had shown the power of steam, pistons, and vacuum power. Thomas Savery built an early steam engine in 1698, but it was **Thomas Newcomen** (1663–1729) who built the first continuous engine in 1712, which pumped 120 gallons of water a minute from the mines. He used steam to create a vacuum which worked a pump at a cycle of twelve strokes a minute. The Newcomen engine produced five horsepower, about the same as an average water mill. By the time of his death, one hundred of his engines were in use, mostly in the coal belt of the British Midlands. The Newcomen engine was still so inefficient that it was not profitable to use it outside of the coal mines. (Landes, 188; Hugill, 67)

In 1763, a small working model of the Newcomen engine was brought to a professor at Glasgow University for repair.

James Watt (1736–1819) recognized the great waste of energy in the engine and worked to improve its efficiency. A problem arose with the Watt engine that the main cylinder had to be snugly contained or steam would escape. Ironmaster **John Wilkinson** had devised in 1774 a new way of boring holes into cannon and the same thing could be done to cylinders and other automatically guided precision tools to within a thousandth of an inch. The first Watt engine set to work pumping water in 1776. A few years later, Watt developed a rotary engine, which was more efficient and could be used to power a variety of machines. (Landes, 198–9) The Watt rotary engine had a thermal efficiency of 4 percent, while Newcomen's had been less than 1 percent. (Hugill, 69) In 1797, Richard Trevithick developed the **high-pressure steam engine**, which was more efficient than Watt's engine and could produce twenty horsepower, four times the power of the Newcomen engine. Trevithick invented a steam locomotive that could haul ten tons at five miles an hour.

Steam power sped up production in industrial areas. Blast furnaces pumped air to speed iron manufacturing. Henry Cort simplified the entire iron production process in the 1780s and produced high-quality iron. Later, steam powered the entire textile process. Factories could be located away from water sources. Canals linked coal fields to the centers of industry. Britain began to export iron in 1797. British iron production was 260,000 tons in 1806. It reached three million in 1844 after the railroad emerged as a major form of transport. (Neal and Williamson, I, 510) By 1852, Britain accounted for half of the world's iron production and was exporting more than a million tons a year. In 1777 Abraham Darby III built the Iron Bridge, the first large work of civil engineering in iron. In 1829, **George and Robert Stephenson**'s locomotive *The Rocket* operated the seventy miles from Liverpool to Manchester at an average of fourteen miles an hour and a maximum speed twice the average. (Hugill, 173)

Transport improvements caused the price of commodities to fall. The first steam-powered railroad line was built in 1830. The railroad expanded horizons of travel and movement, made cheap overland transport possible, and shrank distance for the first time in European history. Steam engines were also placed in boats. At first, they could only travel the calm waters of the rivers. The *Washington* opened the Mississippi watershed to rapid transport with only a few obstacles such as the waterfalls at St. Louis and Louisville. Soon the ships could travel fifteen hundred miles from New Orleans to Pittsburgh in less than five days. Cotton, grown by African-American slaves and processed by the cotton gin, poured out of New Orleans, most of it bound for Britain. In the 1840s, iron hulls, even more efficient steam engines, and marine condensers that avoided using salt water in the engines made faster ocean travel possible. In 1838, the *Great Western* made the trip across the Atlantic in sixteen days; in 1884, the *Etruria* did it in six days. (Hugill, 127–9) With greater efficiency, the cost to cross the ocean as freight or as a passenger plunged, opening a world of greater commerce, travel, and migration.

CONCLUSION

Over about a hundred-year period from 1750 to 1850, Britain became an industrialized economy. This means that more than half of the GDP came from manufacturing and mining and more than half of the workers were employed in industry. The rise in scientific method in the 1600s was both funded by capitalist profits and imitative of the active capitalism of the time. Discoveries brought new crops, and scientific experiments brought new tools and new techniques to the farm.

The resulting increase in farm productivity and the drop in the price of food contributed to Britain's Industrial Revolution, which consisted of three basic shifts: 1) from human labor to machinery; 2) from wood burning to coal burning; 3) from motor power provided by wind, water, or muscle to the steam engine. The textile sector, which had been the second largest employer far behind the farms, industrialized and increased its production and productivity. The tremendous growth in British production led to needed transportation improvements, including canals, more and better roads and bridges, and finally the steam locomotive and steamship.

TIMELINE

1701	Tull introduced seed drilling
1708	Darby used coke in iron smelting
1712	Newcomen engine
1713–89	The Enlightenment in Europe
1733	Kay, flying shuttle
1758	Quesnay, *Tableau Économique*
1765	Hargreaves, spinning jenny
	Watt engine
1776	Smith, *The Wealth of Nations*
1779	Crompton's Mule
1785	Cartwright, power loom
1793	Whitney, cotton gin
1815	macadamized road
1829	Stephenson, *The Rocket*
1838	*Great Western* crossed the Atlantic

KEY TERMS

Energy Returned over Energy Invested (ERoEI)

Physiocrats

Laissez-faire

Adam Smith

four-crop rotation

Enclosure Acts

Flying Shuttle

Spinning Jenny

Water Frame

Crompton's "Mule"

Power loom

Cotton gin

McAdam

Abraham Darby

Thomas Newcomen

The Rocket

Chapter 9

THE EXCHANGES, PAPER MONEY, AND THE MODERN CORPORATION

THE EXCHANGES

Trade has occurred since prehistory. Buying something in advance on an agreed price is a less ancient idea. The Dutch Exchange in Amsterdam dated back at least to 1530, but its real history begins in 1631 when it moved into its new building on the Damplatz across from the Dutch East India Company and the Bank of Amsterdam. Commodity futures trading became lively with the commenda, larger ships, and the law of supply and demand (and the understanding that prices could be manipulated). There was general exhilaration in the 1630s because the Dutch were beating the Spanish and were on their way to independence. The decade saw the value of shares in the Dutch East India Company rise sharply as did the price of large houses. But this spilled over into what Robert Shiller has termed "irrational exuberance." The winter of 1636/7 saw the first trading mania in Amsterdam. The unlikely object was the tulip. Tulips are not native to Europe but were introduced around 1554 and grown regularly in the Netherlands in the 1590s. The supply was limited because it takes seven to twelve years to grow a tulip bulb from a seed. The most prized tulips were rarer still. In 1636, a futures market was established. Tulip bulbs can only be moved after May, so contracts before then would be sold without merchandise changing hands. From November 1636 to March 1637, futures traders began to bid up these contracts. The price reached incredible heights but then collapsed before any deliveries were executed. Very few people lost much money and this was almost a game, but in some ways this was a rehearsal for the serious bubbles in the South Sea and Mississippi companies discussed previously. At this time, shares in the Dutch East India Company were virtually the only ones being traded. Not surprisingly, many saw this as the same as playing cards or dice. John Law was a successful card player, so the regent figured he would be good at modern finance.

We are not sure when an exchange was established in England. Coffee houses became very popular but unofficial places for buyers and sellers to meet. Lloyd's Coffee House became known by 1680 as a place to buy insurance for merchant ships, but other things were exchanged there as well. Eventually, Lloyd's became a famous insurance company. England had exchanges of some kind before 1695 because a law of that year regulated brokers. By 1725, there were fourteen companies trading stocks; by 1740, it was forty companies. England and Holland were far ahead of other countries. In 1815, Paris had only four companies trading stock. In New York City, trading in stocks began with the establishment of the constitutional republic and issuing of the first U.S. government bonds refinancing the revolutionary war debt in 1789 and 1790. In 1792, the New York Stock Exchange was officially established at a coffee house on the corner of Wall and

Water Streets. By 1830, New York had overtaken Philadelphia as the financial center of the United States boosted by the Erie Canal that linked the Great Lakes with the Hudson River and Atlantic Ocean. In 1903, it moved to its current home on Wall Street.

Before 1840, there were very few publicly-traded companies. Business owners were still putting their profits into land. Aside from the chartered companies, there were some family firms that sold shares to the public because the heirs just wanted to collect company profits without running the company.(Kindleberger 1993, 176–82)

PAPER MONEY

The Bank of Sweden issued the first bank notes backed by deposits in Europe in 1661. They did this because much of the coined money in Sweden was made of copper. In the seventeenth century Sweden had nearly a monopoly on copper in Europe. It was very inconvenient to carry many heavy coins with little face value, so paper was suggested. (Kindleberger 1993, 53) However, the bank withdrew them in 1664.

The Bank of England issued paper banknotes from its founding in 1694 but only for large denominations. They were generally held by merchants who signed them over for goods. These notes would be readily exchanged for gold or silver when presented at the Bank. After a few tests calmed anxieties, nobody bothered to redeem them. Other banks such as the Banque Royale inspired no such confidence and people who held their notes would quickly cash them in, often exhausting the bank's store of precious metal. By 1800, the rival English banks had given up, leaving the Bank of England supreme.

The American Love Affair with Paper Money

America was a laboratory for monetary experimentation because mercantilist Britain and France sucked gold and silver out of the continent. In colonial times, residents had used wampum shells (white and black to mark denominations). These were exchangeable for the valuable beaver pelts. When the beaver trade dried up on the east coast, tobacco became a form of currency. Massachusetts Bay colony issued the first American paper money in 1690 to pay soldiers because it lacked coins. French Canada issued playing-card money. Massachusetts, Rhode Island, and South Carolina became notorious for masses of paper money because they were heavily involved in trade. In 1764, Britain outlawed colonial paper money. This was a factor in the American Revolution because had the ban been effective, it would have destroyed the colonies' economies and ruined the merchants who would have had nothing with which to pay. Paper money paid for the American Revolution: the Continental Congress issued $242 million, and the states issued $216 million, while the nations of Europe provided around $7 million in loans. This caused massive price inflation. By 1777, a pair of shoes in Virginia cost $5,000. By 1781, the Congress had devalued this money by 97.5%. It now ordered a "new emission" of paper money which failed. Before the American finances collapsed, the British were unable to secure new loans from the Dutch and when their army surrendered in Virginia, the war was over. Britain had gone to the borrowing well once too often.

Dealing with the paper money was a major challenge for the new American government. For a few years, the only new paper money consisted of notes personally guaranteed by the Philadelphia merchant Robert Morris. Indeed, this was one of the "excesses of democracy" that elites complained about. The Constitution adopted in 1787 barred the states from issuing any more coins, paper money, or bills of credit. Eventually, the remaining bills were exchanged at 1 percent face value for new U.S. government bonds. At that time, the debt had been greatly reduced by effective repudiation: the federal government owed $42 million, the states owed $25 million. With interest, the Americans owed Europe $12 million. Treasury Secretary **Alexander Hamilton** created an English-style financial system with a public/private **Bank of the United States** and a national debt with a sinking fund. A deal was struck to assume the state debts and win the votes of Virginia, Maryland, and Georgia (states that had mainly paid their debts) by placing the new national capital in a district carved from Virginia and Maryland rather than the existing cities of New York or Philadelphia. There was strong opposition to Hamilton's program precisely because it was the English system and some felt that English-style banking and finance was what the new country should avoid. This debate has never gone away. It still exists in the calls by some to abolish central banking, represented today by the Federal Reserve. In the 1790s, 40 percent of the federal government's revenue was going to pay interest on the old debts. It paid off the Spanish and French debts and refinanced the Dutch debts.

In the absence of an American currency, foreign coins, especially Spanish coins, were used by people in everyday commerce. Up to 1857, foreign coins were allowed as legal tender. In 1792, Congress set up a coinage system ranging from copper half-cents to golden eagles (ten-dollar coins). The silver content of a dollar was about one-fifth that of the British pound sterling, fixing an approximate value that would last until the 1930s.

The early American republic abounded in eccentric ideas, such as Thomas Jefferson's that all laws and personal debts should expire every nineteen years. Naturally, Jefferson constantly owed money. State-chartered banks grew from four in 1791 to eighty-seven by 1811. They resented the regulation of the Bank of the United States, especially when it enforced reserve requirements. In 1811, Congress refused to renew the Bank of the United States' charter. The state banks ran wild, printing notes and trying to lure the federal government's deposits. Over two hundred banks had put out $90 million in notes backed by only $17 million in gold and silver. Despite the experience of the Revolutionary War and the strictures of the Constitution, the U.S. still depended on paper money to keep its economy going. The War of 1812 strained the system past the breaking point. Many state banks stopped redeeming notes, and the U.S. government defaulted on its debt in November 1814.

After this catastrophe, Congress established a Second Bank of the United States. Its first action was to curtail the printing presses of the state banks. This cut in credit caused a serious economic downturn in 1819. In 1833, President Andrew Jackson opposed renewing the charter of the Second Bank and then pulled out the federal government's deposits, bringing it down. To make matters worse, the Coinage Act of 1834 undervalued silver, which led to a flow of silver to Europe and the disappearance of silver coins ranging from the dollar to the "half-dime". Since these were the coins that most people did their buying with, it opened the door to over sixteen hundred state banks issuing more than thirty thousand varieties of notes. Jackson, who was devoted to "hard money," actually allowed the biggest flood of paper since the Revolution.

The United States had doubled its wealth and productivity from 1700 to 1820. It was already ranked sixth in the world for wealth and tied in third in life expectancy. Between 1820 and

1870, U.S. GDP grew twice as fast as any European country. Gaps began to open between the North and South. Literacy was higher in the north, even among white men. (Maddison 2001, 30, 90, 187) As the North began to industrialize, 80 percent of the South's workforce remained agricultural. In the 1840s, relative to size, both France and the German states built railroad tracks at a faster pace than did the U.S. The Civil War represented a stark choice: would the United States be a weak, hollowed-out, underdeveloped, and ignorant banana republic or a centralized industrial nation?

The French Experience

France was a rich country. On average, its people had about two-thirds of the wealth of the average English or Dutch resident, but the French were far better off than the people in Spain, China, Mexico, or the Italian lands. (Maddison 2001, 90) Before the Industrial and French Revolutions, the French economy was perhaps one-third or one-half larger than Britain's and was the biggest in Europe. French aid to American colonies during their revolution had put a heavy strain on the French Treasury. French taxes as a percentage of the economy were about one-quarter less in 1788 than they had been when the century started and this caused a chronic budget deficit. (Broadberry and O'Rourke, I, 78) Instead of raising taxes, the Treasury under **Jacques Necker** borrowed a billion *livres* at interest rates as high as 10 percent from 1777 to 1781. By 1787, the monarchy was up against the wall: heavy debts, no way to raise taxes, no way to borrow more money. The finance minister called for a new property tax and the abolition of internal grain tariffs to create free trade. When the nobles resisted, the government called an **Assembly of Notables** to discuss the problems of France. This upper-class group rejected the government's proposal and said that only the **Estates-General** could raise taxes. This was the French equivalent of the British Parliament and had not met in 175 years. The notables demanded that the king give power to the provincial assemblies, which they expected to control, in return for taxes.

The Debt

The government debt was four billion *livres*. The French budget of 1787 would have 475 million *livres* in taxes and borrow 145 million. It spent 50 percent to service the debt, 27 percent on the military, and 6 percent to maintain the king and his palaces. This left only 17 percent for useful spending. France had only half of the equivalent debt of Britain and less than a fifth the per capita debt of the British. Since France had a much larger economy than Britain, there should not have been a problem, but unlike Britain, France did not have a solid banking and credit system.

King Louis XVI called a meeting of the Estates-General, sparking the French Revolution. The upheaval of 1789 did not solve the financial crisis that had started the revolution. The call for "patriotic" loans fell upon deaf ears. Necker announced a budget deficit of 294 million *livres*, worse than ever. The Assembly took the radical step of confiscating all the lands of the Catholic Church and the monasteries in November 1789. This land was to be collateral for 400 million *livres*' worth of **assignats**, a 3 percent bond; by September 1790, another 800 million *livres* in bonds were issued in smaller denominations (fifty *livres*). The value of the land was more than 1,200 million *livres*, but people were hoarding hard money or taking it out of the country. Bad harvests had led to a trade deficit as France tried to buy wheat. When they gained power after

August 1792, the radical Jacobins printed small-money notes, which they would exchange for *assignats*. The government then issued twenty million five-*livre assignats*. This led to a spiral of inflation as the government printed more and more in smaller denominations. At the end of 1791, they were being accepted at 75 percent of face value; four months later, they were at 60 percent. Inflation was in high gear by the spring of 1792 as counterfeit *assignats* circulated and the market was breaking down. From 1790 to 1793, the price of bread rose by 27 percent, beef by 136 percent, and potatoes by 700 percent.

Price Controls

Things went from bad to worse in 1792. There was a vast tax shortfall because of the chaos in the provinces; the government issued more *assignats* and sold the lands that were supposed to be collateral for the *assignats*. The Austrians and Prussians invaded France. Mobs demanded that hoarders of food be killed and called for price controls. The Jacobins now "doubled down" on the Revolution, hoping that a much larger and inspired army could defeat the reactionaries internally and externally. They had no money for trained soldiers so they would have to draft young Frenchmen. Since they would be paid little, the regime had to give these young men a cause: the revolution to make a better future. The government would have to print money and deal with the debts after it gained peace. Printing money caused more price inflation and the Jacobin government's only choice was to freeze prices and wages. To prevent the spread of rebellion or undermining of the war effort, only the harshest of penalties would suffice: death. The government confiscated gold and silver and foreign currency. Resistance and black markets sprang up. Peasants stored or destroyed goods. The government outlawed pastries and white bread, confiscated supplies, and ordered production of items needed for the war. Thus did economic hardship lead to the year-long "Reign of Terror."

After the radicals lost power, the Constitutional Convention abolished price controls in December 1794. Inflation returned: the *assignats* had fallen to 20 percent of face value by the winter of 1794. They would fall to 8 percent by the spring of 1795, and 4 percent by the summer of 1795. Bread prices rose 1,300 percent from March to May 1795. Beef prices rose 500 percent, pork and egg prices rose more than 100 percent. In general, the cost of living rose 900 percent from 1790 to 1795, while wages did not keep pace.

Stabilization

The new government (called the Directory) repaired the damaged economy. It oversaw the rationing of scarce resources and foreign exchange. Metal coinage began to return. It imposed high tariffs to protect industry and reduced spending. The Directory tackled the financial problem in 1799. It repudiated two-thirds of the national debt, including the *assignats*. It established new indirect taxes. This settled the issue of French debt that had hung over the country for so long, but it had come at a heavy cost.

Napoleon Bonaparte seized power at the end of 1799 and finally stabilized the economy. He restored order in the provinces and collected their taxes. His professional tax collectors were much more honest than their royal predecessors, which greatly enhanced tax collection. Napoleon made France's first simple budget. He introduced a sound currency in 1803 by regulating the silver content in the **French franc** and fixed the value of silver to gold. Thanks to the Directory wiping out the *assignats*, the debt was secure. Taxes on consumption, such as salt and tobacco, contributed more and more to the revenue. The Bank of France was established in 1800. It would discount promissory notes, make loans to the treasury, and receive and manage some government assets. It issued thirty thousand shares of one thousand francs each. The biggest two hundred shareholders could elect regents to govern the Bank.

The Bank of England during and after the French Revolution

Britain had not recovered from its heavy debts when it entered war with France in 1793. The government pushed the Bank of England hard for loans. That led to anxiety and bank runs. In 1795, servicing the national debt took three-fourths of Britain's government revenue, far above the level of France in 1789. (Neal and Williamson, I, 367) By 1802, the British national debt was far above the year's Gross Domestic Product. Interest rates were at 6 percent, the highest level in over a hundred years. In 1797, the Bank of England had to suspend convertibility into gold. (Kindleberger 1993, 63) Coins disappeared into hoards as the Bank quickly printed one and two pound notes. Wheat prices trebled from 1797 to 1800. The whole British financial structure seemed on the brink of collapse.

There was a brief period of peace from 1803 to 1805, but when the war with Napoleon resumed, the British borrowed from angry bankers and financiers on the continent. (Broadberry and O'Rourke, I, 194) Napoleon had conquered the Netherlands, but he did not control the Dutch investment funds, which flowed heavily to the British. The interest rates actually fell even as the national debt was more than double that of the GDP. By one estimate, the British transferred a full one-quarter of their GDP to the other powers to enlist them in the war against Napoleon. When they beat him in

1813, confidence grew in the Bank of England's notes. The Bank restored full convertibility to gold in 1821 but four years later, another wave of bubbles from defaulting Latin American bonds led to a humiliating bailout by the Bank of France. (Kindleberger 1993, 65–6; Broadberry and O'Rourke, I, 139, 194) An 1844 law forced the Bank to issue notes only if they were covered by gold and silver in its vault. In other words, the Bank could not engage in fractional reserve banking.

By the 1830s and 1840s, the Bank controlled the flow of gold through interest rates and **open-market operations** with government and commercial bonds. A bank wants to control the flow of funds or in this case precious metal in and out of its national economy. Too much money coming in can increase the money supply and worsen inflation. Too much going out starves the economy of credit and causes the loss of jobs. In this world of the mid-nineteenth century with money moving in considerable volume, the central banks needed to take action. The first part of controlling **liquidity** is to encourage or discourage foreign investment. The simplest way to do this is to raise or lower interest rates. Foreign investment seeks the highest return as long as it is not too risky. A reduced interest rate encourages this investment to go elsewhere. However, it can encourage considerable domestic borrowing, so a central bank also has to consider ways of tightening domestic credit by, for example, requiring banks to reserve more funds. Increasing interest rates will attract foreign investment, but this can dampen domestic credit.

The second part of controlling liquidity is to inject or remove cash from the system. In the 1830s, the Bank of England would inject gold into the system by selling some of its gold in exchange for bonds, which are safe investments. By this time, certain companies were issuing their own bonds, though government bonds still dominated. To reduce liquidity, the Bank would sell its securities for gold, thus removing it from the system. In our world of paper money, how does a central bank get cash into the system? It does not leave cash in paper bags on street corners or drop it from a helicopter. The Bank is the source of printed money in unlimited quantity. It uses that cash to buy or sell commercial bonds. These bonds have a value linked to the real value of the company that issued them. On occasion, central banks have also bought government bonds, bills, and notes with their cash. This can be dangerous because governments are always looking to borrow more money. If they are simply selling debt to the source of unlimited cash, this is simply printing money. This can stimulate the economy but it can also cause inflation. Some imagine that it always causes inflation, but this is not true. From 2008 to 2014, the U.S. Federal Reserve engaged in **Quantitative Easing (QE)** which was a massive injection of trillions of dollars buying government securities, mortgage-backed bonds, and commercial paper. The money supply exploded but inflation remained at a low one to three percent a year. Why? The cash was being "sterilized" as private financial institutions and corporations did not move the cash into the broader economy. They just sat on it or used cash to buy back their own stock to raise the price.

The American Civil War and Greenbacks

In 1861, eleven southern states seceded from the United States and declared themselves to be the independent Confederate States of America because they believed that owning slaves was a basic right. The North had twenty-three million people against six million whites in the Confederacy. The North had better industry and finance. The Confederacy funded its war on almost no financial base. Only 5 or 6 percent of its war spending came from tax revenue. Less than 40 percent came from loans. It paid for most of the war with paper money. By the end of the war in 1865, prices in the Confederacy had risen *ninety-two fold* since 1861. The North blockaded the Confederacy so it could not sell cotton. While the South was gone, the Thirteenth Amendment to the Constitution outlawed slavery. The Congress passed tariffs to protect new industries up to 47 percent of the value of manufactured goods and encouraged settlement of the West in the **Homestead Act**. It granted land to support state agricultural colleges. It subsidized a transcontinental railroad to link California to the rest of the country. This opened in 1869.

The North was more careful in its war financing and started with a more solid structure even though the U.S. lacked a central bank. Taxes only covered 21 percent of spending, but the U.S. was able to sell war bonds. In particular, the skilled bond dealer **Jay Cooke** sold more than a billion dollars' worth of bonds at rather high interest rates. The North only needed to cover 13 percent of the war cost with printed money. Congress authorized the issue of "Greenbacks": money printed on green paper. Inflation set in as prices doubled, but there was not a meltdown like the Confederacy. Congress also regulated state-chartered banks and then at the end of the war abolished all their notes. The federal government finally had control over the U.S. money supply. The year after the Civil War, the Supreme Court ruled that the Greenbacks violated the Constitution's ban on paper money. Slowly, the government used gold and silver to retire the Greenbacks, and in 1879 anyone holding a Greenback could exchange it for gold.

THE MODERN CORPORATION

In the middle of its bubble, the South Sea Company had gotten the British government in 1720 to ban joint-stock companies unless they had special permission. This was to block potential competitors for investment. It was not repealed until 1824. Not until 1844 could companies simply register under the Joint Stock Companies Act of that year. Joint-stock companies began to rise mainly associated with canal building. In 1761, the Duke of Bridgewater oversaw construction of a canal to link the coal fields near Manchester. Shares of stock were sold to the general public. (Baskin and Miranti, 122) Parliament authorized almost two hundred companies, mainly in mining and transport, to issue stock. From 1790 to 1793, the amount of money invested in authorized canal companies tripled, although some never built the canal they were supposed to construct. This became known as "Canal Mania" and showed the growing sophistication of the British financial market. The fall in interest rates of British bonds between the crises of the American and French wars made those bonds less attractive and investors took on greater risk buying canal company stock. This corporate organization had little effect on the Industrial Revolution. Very few textile or iron companies issued shares to the public. They were financed by personal loans, company profit, and bank credit. (Kindleberger 1993, 193)

A company owned by many shareholders could not be governed by them because of the problems of time and distance. The practice started of having indirect ownership where the stockholders chose directors to make the major decisions based on the best interests of the owners and to monitor the company's managers. Thus were ownership and management divorced. Adam Smith in Book V, Chapter 1, Part 3, Article 1 of *Wealth of Nations* denounced this system:

> The Directors of such companies, however, being the managers of other people's money rather than their own it cannot be expected that they should watch over it with the anxious vigilance with which the partners in a private copartnery frequently watch over their own.... Negligence and profusion, therefore, must always prevail, more or less, in the management of the affairs of such a company.

Directors would always have trouble taking care of money that was not their own. Overseas monopolies had only worked because governments helped them. Smith admitted that canal corporations had been quite profitable. But other indirectly-owned firms would just fleece the owners and should be outlawed because they distort the free market. Other problems grew when the managers picked some or all of the directors. The main interest of the managers and directors then becomes lining their own pockets, not safeguarding the long-term profits of the shareholders. The German state of Prussia largely refused joint-stock company requests until 1851. (Kindleberger 1993, 205)

The rise of the railroad companies after the test of Stephenson's *Rocket* changed governance structure. In the 1840s, the British Parliament authorized hundreds of railroad companies. Railroad companies used creative (and sometimes illegal) methods to raise the great amount of investment that a railroad needed. (Kindleberger 1993, 194–6) In 1842, the London merchant bank Baring Brothers marketed French railroad bonds. Companies could borrow money in the same way as governments. This was not entirely new. The Dutch East India Company had issued bonds as early as 1621.

(*Cambridge Economic History*, V, 345) Since corporate bonds were not as safe as government bonds, the interest rate was higher. In the mid-1850s, the Illinois Central railroad raised funds in Amsterdam, beginning the large-scale financing by Europeans of the American railroad construction.(Neal and Williamson, I, 548; Kindleberger 1993, 203)

Investors were reluctant to buy stock because of unlimited liability. This meant that when bankruptcies occurred shareholders had to pay the corporate debt as if it were their personal debt. Few wanted to buy a small share of a company that they had no control over and possibly incur a ruinous debt. In the 1830s, some states in the United States began to **limit liability**. (Baskin and Miranti, 141) This meant that if a company went bankrupt, the stockholder would lose the value of his investment but would not have to pay any of the debts the company had incurred. By the 1850s, some British companies were preferring to incorporate under French or U.S. state commercial laws. The British Parliament passed the **Joint Stock Company Act of 1856** limiting liability and extended it to insurance companies in 1862. Over the next thirty years, company capital doubled as a result of these measures. (Kindleberger 1993, 197–9) France limited liability in 1863. Large corporations were born financed by massive bond or stock issues. The influence of the banks became much greater as they managed these issues. Stock ownership became too diffuse in many cases for owners to exercise real leadership. The British railroads pioneered the issue of **preferred stock** which guarantees a certain dividend payment but can go higher if profit allows. (Baskin and Miranti, 152)

Companies used money from stock and bond issues to expand their plants, build railroad mileage and erect new factories. Large-scale markets and efficient transportation enabled mass production. Before 1800, factories such as the

Venetian arsenal and the French Royal Plate Glass Company employed at most a thousand workers. (*Cambridge Economic History*, V, 427–30) Now companies built much larger factories. In 1870, Krupp's iron works in Essen employed more than seven thousand workers. Companies acquired other companies. **Horizontal integration** is when a company buys similar companies in an attempt to dominate the market and drive out competition. There is also **vertical integration** when a company buys companies involved in supplying materials to the core business or using the products of the core business. This was pioneered by the Swift meat-processing company, which controlled grazing land for animals, the slaughterhouses, and the meat product companies. **Andrew Carnegie** (d.1919) built a leading steel company in the United States. Carnegie bought up coal and iron mines, coking ovens, and the ships and railroads that brought the raw materials to his factories. In 1901, the New York banker **J.P. Morgan** (d.1913) bought out Carnegie for $250 million and merged Carnegie Steel with several other firms to form the **United States Steel Corporation**, which was the first billion-dollar corporation in the world. Integration reduced production costs. Sometimes the savings went into higher wages, other times into lower prices or higher profits.

The rise of the giant corporation meant many changes. Corporations now became powers in their own right. They had control over small towns and cities that became "company towns." Workers not only held their job through the corporation, but often they rented their home and bought their supplies from the company. A worker who angered the company would find no work of any kind in that town. Corporations bought votes and politicians. The sugar island interests had been influential in the eighteenth century, but the giant corporations were far more powerful. In Germany, companies in the same sector often banded together in **cartels**. This was an agreement among independent firms to fix prices, limit output, and divide markets. Firms could maintain high prices thanks to trade protection (after 1879) by the German government while selling at low cost abroad. Britain and the United States banned cartels.

CONCLUSION

Industrialization accelerated trends in finance and corporate organization. Companies grew much larger and financed their growth by issuing shares of stock and corporate bonds. Governments changed stockowner liability law in order to encourage investment by limiting liability. The growth in ownership necessitated a move to the election of representative directors, who were supposed to work for the benefit of the stockowners. Corporations spent the money on new plants and offices as well as acquiring other companies in horizontal and vertical integration. These companies became powers in their own right. Finally, capitalist economies mastered the use of paper money after several failed experiments. Paper money was needed to support the rapid economic growth that industrialization had sparked.

TIMELINE

1631	Dutch Exchange in Amsterdam moved into new building
1636/7	Tulip mania
1661	Bank of Sweden issued first bank notes in Europe backed by deposits
1787	American paper money lost virtually all value
1790–99	*Assignats* in France
1792	New York Stock Exchange established
1800	Napoleon established Bank of France
1825	Erie Canal opened and made New York the American financial center
1842	Baring Brothers marketed corporate French railroad bonds
1856	Britain limited liability
1861–65	U.S. Civil War; successful use of Greenbacks
1863	France limited liability
1901	U.S. Steel, first billion-dollar corporation

KEY TERMS

assignats
open-market operations
Quantitative Easing (QE)
Greenbacks
limited liability
horizontal and vertical integration
J.P. Morgan

Chapter 10

THE IMPACT OF INDUSTRIALISM

THE SPREAD IN EUROPE

Britain

The spread of industrialism was very slow, even in Britain. Between 1811 and 1821, a plurality of economic product and probably employment shifted to industry. As late as 1870, half of total steampower in manufacturing was still in textiles. The great majority of industrial workers in 1851 were still craftsmen in small shops. Britain did not see a massive application of steampower until after 1870. Only in 1883 did British steamships pass sailing ships. British exports grew by 142 percent from 1814 to 1845. British real per capita GDP grew 1.5% per year from 1830 to 1870, an extraordinary increase not seen before. (Broadberry and O'Rourke, I, 204, 220) British firms were mostly financed by their own profits and bank overdrafts that amounted to 20 to 39 percent of the firm's total assets. The British savings rate barely rose from 1770 to 1815; it hit 11 percent in the 1840s after a long stretch of peace. Industry never absorbed more than 10 percent of the available capital in Britain.

The Continent

The wars of the French Revolution and Napoleon from 1792 to 1815 caused continental Europe to fall behind Britain. British goods were very cheap. The technology was hard to understand, and the British tried to prevent the spread of knowledge. Britain forbade skilled mechanics and artisans to leave Britain until 1825 and the export of textile machinery and other equipment until 1843. Capital investment in steam power was very expensive.

Belgium

The treaties of 1713 transferred Belgium from Spanish to Austrian control. Belgium had a long manufacturing tradition and coal and iron resources. The Austrians tried to develop the area into a trading center by setting up a mercantile organization called the Ostend Company, but the British forced the Austrians to shut it down. Belgium was the first area on the continent to install a Newcomen engine in 1720 to pump water from its coal mines. In 1830, Belgium gained full independence. An Englishman named Cockerill slipped out illegally and made a fortune bringing the English iron and steel process in the 1820s. By the 1850s, it had become standard on the continent. Until 1850, despite its small size, Belgium produced more coal than any continental country. It outstripped Britain as a supplier of coal to northern France by using canals and waterways. The cotton industry grew up in Ghent. Power looms and investment banks appeared in the 1830s. Belgium became the second nation to industrialize, with a plurality working in industry by 1900.

France

The French Revolution had swept away the old inefficient trade system, and Napoleon had overseen the creation of a modern financial structure. France followed a completely different path of development from that of England. Robert Allen has argued that France did not adopt the spinning jenny because its labor was much cheaper than Britain's, which would make the use of machines less profitable. (Broadberry and O'Rourke, I, 177) In the nineteenth century, it intensified its previous advantages. The agricultural revolution made French farming even more productive by 1870, and France was a major exporter of produce. It held onto most of its trade position in Europe and the Middle East and continued to market high-value wines, luxury products, and clothes. In the 1820s, the British GDP likely surpassed that of France. Maddison estimates that in 1820 England/Scotland was 75 percent richer than France in per capita GDP. He also states that France's per capita GDP grew faster in the next hundred years. France certainly acted like a considerably wealthier country. France was the first country to stabilize its population. This was a sign of wealth and education. France had very little out-migration. Almost everyone in France was happy to stay in France. It may be that inequality in England was much stronger. France had defaulted on its debt during the French Revolution, thus getting rid of it, while Britain had very high levels of debt and taxes. Less French tax money was going to rich bondholders. So if one considered per capita income after taxes, it may be the median French household's wealth was at least close to that of the British. Finally, most French were living and farming out in the countryside and the rich did not own most of the farmland.

French industrial growth was slow but more diverse than other countries. In the first part of the century, not only did French cotton and coal industries grow (slowly), but so did sugar refineries, chemical, glass, porcelain, and paper. New industries appeared, including gas lighting, matches, photography, and vulcanized rubber. In 1849, the French opened a **joint-stock investment bank**. The bank's capital came from selling stock. This insulated the bank from bank runs or massive defaults. These banks typically looked to invest in profitable ventures, adding another revenue stream. Before Britain's Industrial Revolution took hold, French industrial productivity had actually exceeded that of Britain. (Neal and Williamson, I, 498) Slow population growth and slow industrialization meant that the rate of urbanization was slower in France than elsewhere. France had no filthy slum-ridden industrial cities. French emperor Napoleon III ordered a massive clearing of what slums there were in Paris in the 1860s and moved the lower classes to the outskirts of the city. Even today, the bad parts of Paris are the suburbs. Scarce coal resources meant that France depended more on waterpower. In the early 1860s, water produced twice as much horsepower in France as steam. France did not industrialize until 1954 after the beginning of European integration. By 1968, more French workers were in service sectors than in mining and manufacturing, so France's time as an "industrial" nation was very brief. France proved that a nation could develop and be wealthy without industrialization.

The Expansion of Railroads

France, Belgium, and the German states quickly followed Britain's railroad lead. By 1840 Britain (excluding Ireland) had built 2,390 kilometers of rail, France 410, Germany 469, and Belgium 334. By 1860, the figures were: Britain 14,603, France 9,167, Germany 11,089. One can consider 50 percent of all the rail a country would ever build a benchmark of rail progress. Britain passed this 50 percent mark in 1862 and was the first. Belgium passed it in 1867, Germany in 1876, France in 1877, the United States around 1884, Italy in 1886, and Russia in 1898. Others probably did it after 1900, including Japan around 1920, and China around 1960.

TURKEY AND EGYPT

The Turkish Empire had been declining for more than a hundred years, and Austria and Russia had steadily reduced its territory. The original Ottoman system had depended on constant growth and the ability to reward military leaders with land grants. The core of the Turkish army during the Empire's expansion in the fifteenth and sixteenth centuries had been the Janissaries. Every non-Muslim community had to provide some children for military training and conversion to Islam. The child levy for Janissaries ended around 1650, and Janissary status became hereditary. The Janissaries and officials who came out of that corps had understood Christian Europe and sometimes aided their families. When that ended in the eighteenth century, the Christian part became resentful of Istanbul, the Turkish capital. After 1683, the Ottoman system turned inward: if lords wanted a reward, they had to get it from someone else, and that involved bribing the Sultan who ruled the Empire. The administration was corrupt, and the economy was inefficient. It lost control over Yemen and much of Arabia. Southern Arabia's loss of the coffee monopoly in the eighteenth century was a major blow. The Turks kept power over the port of Jidda and controlled Mecca and Medina during the times of pilgrimage. In 1814, an estimated seventy thousand pilgrims had traveled to Mecca. This provided vital revenues through the governors of Syria and Egypt who assembled the pilgrims and provided protection for them.

The Sultans in the early days of the Empire had gained experience by governing regions. After 1600, they grew up in the palace with little education or practical experience. Large landowners and Muslim religious leaders foiled attempts by the Sultans to reform the government. Jews, Armenians, and others had used the printing press, but there was no press authorized to print in Turkish until 1727. Even so, the press was forbidden anything on religion or law, and produced about a book a year until it was shut down in 1742. The Turkish printing press was not revived until 1784. "Doctors of the law" (*'ulema*) had the right to interpret Islam. Their view of Islam was very rigid, and they were opposed to all western ideas and reforms. Their interests coincided with the Janissaries, who opposed all military reforms and modernization. By 1800, 400,000 claimed Janissary status, but only 20,000 were available to fight. The French ambassador in 1807 said: "To make an alliance with Turkey is the same as putting your arms around a corpse to make it stand up!"

Farmers rented land from landlords who were almost always absent. Local lords pressed the farmers for more than legally required, and Istanbul lacked the power to protect its loyal subjects. There was increasing religious intolerance, and significant numbers of Jews left for Western Europe. The European part suffered constant violence from the Empire's wars with Austria, Russia, and Venice. The Janissaries were supposed to protect the people, but often teamed up with local merchants to fleece the population. The only choice was to look to local strongmen who took the title of *bey* or *dey* rather than the Istanbul-appointed governor (pasha). By 1600, the Janissaries seized power in Tripoli and elected their own *dey* who shared power with the pasha. By 1700, a hereditary family of beys held much of the power in Tunis. Around that time, the *dey* in Algiers won the title of pasha and ruled that area in league with the merchants and the rulers of the grain-producing hinterland. In 1747, a group of Mamluks from Georgia took over Baghdad.

Under the peace treaties of 1699, the Ottomans gave up the right to tax trade, which meant they had to find other revenue or go without. The wealthiest men were non-Muslims and so were cut off from influencing policy or pressing reform. It was impossible that they could force the calling of a Turkish Estates-General as happened in France or collaborate with the government the way the Bank of England directors had with that country. Christians and Jews were not bound by the Muslim ban on usury and so assumed the leading financial role in the Empire. This is what would have happened in Western Europe had Aquinas not provided an ideology for capitalism. In the late eighteenth century, the Ottoman economic position became even more dire. Goods produced in Western Europe or from its colonies in Asia and the Americas competed with Middle Eastern goods such as sugar and coffee in Europe and then in the Middle East itself. The French were selling high-quality textiles to rich and common people alike.

Selim III (ruled 1789–1807) attempted long overdue reforms. He levied new taxes to pay for a new corps of soldiers that would not be linked to the Janissaries. He sent soldiers into southeastern Europe to root out the Janissaries. He attempted to collect fees from the vast majority of Janissaries who were not performing any military duties. He introduced technical training for officers and the first programs for administrative education.

Egypt's Bid to Industrialize

Muhammad Ali was born to a prominent Albanian merchant family in 1769. As a young man, he was a successful tax collector. In 1801 the Sultan asked for military units to take over Egypt after two years of war with an army led by Napoleon. Muhammad Ali arrived as an officer in his cousin's Albanian force, but soon began a rise to power. Ali made a key alliance with Omar Makram, a cleric who had organized resistance against Napoleon. In May 1805, Sultan Selim appointed Ali as pasha of Cairo and he became pasha of all Egypt in October 1806. Ali negotiated a peace that made Egypt a major naval supply post for the British navy. He nationalized all the land in Egypt and reserved a monopoly on trade for the state. Large amounts of revenue flowed into his coffers. Ali used the money to enlarge the army beyond his Albanian mercenaries.

In 1807, the Janissaries rose up and deposed Selim. They got the head of the *'ulema* in Istanbul to declare his reforms as contrary to Islamic law. A reformist force marched on Istanbul, but the conservatives murdered Selim before it arrived. The reformers then installed Selim's brother **Mahmud II** (ruled 1808–1839) to resume the modernization.

Muhammad Ali had continued to build Egyptian power. As the Industrial Revolution grew in Britain, he dedicated large tracts of land to raising cotton. A French expert brought him the highest-quality cotton from Réunion island in the Indian Ocean. In 1826, he imported the first steam-run power looms from Britain, which scornfully allowed the sale because it thought the Egyptians would not know how to run them. In 1836, Egypt produced more than a million bolts of cotton cloth. He built dams and improved irrigation to get more productivity out of the land. He built new canals and hired European engineers to build steam-driven pumps to irrigate fields and allow two crops of cotton each year. He ordered the planting of high-quality cotton cash crops as well as a summer grain in a modified form of the four-crop rotation. He made a sustained attempt to train officers, doctors, engineers, and officials in new schools, and sent them on missions to Europe to learn trades. He initiated a massive program to translate vital European technical works into Arabic. During Muhammad Ali's time in power, the Egyptian population nearly doubled, acreage grew by one-third, revenue grew 300 percent while trade volume increased 900 percent. He increased the size of the army, brought in French officers to train it, built an arms factory in Cairo and a shipyard to Alexandria. Egypt now had a navy to go with its army.

The British demanded that Egypt give up its control of Syria and grabbed the strategic port of Aden. Tensions mounted, British and Turkish troops landed at Beirut, and the Egyptian army fell back. In a treaty of 1841, Ali had to pay a sum to the Ottomans, reduce the size of his army, and give up some land. Ali also had to remove his import barriers and end his monopolies. This would allow the British to flood the Egyptian market with their cheaper goods.

Muhammad Ali was attempting the very difficult feat of industrializing when Britain was still in the middle of the process. Many have attempted to jump-start their economies with "crash" programs of modernization and industrialization. Most have failed. Developmental economics and history are two of the most contentious fields as a result. One path of development clearly does not fit all cases. Could Egypt have succeeded? David Landes says it was impossible. Ali was trying to build an industrial structure, a Muslim merchant class, and a skilled labor force simultaneously. You need the last two before you can get the first. Energy was a critical problem. Without wood or coal, Egypt had to use animals in the fierce desert heat to supply power. Ali used slave labor, and the workers often sabotaged the machines. Finally, he put much of the profit into a powerful military instead of investing in further development. (Landes, 405–7)

Landes' points are well taken. But he goes too far when he says that "Egypt was never a serious competitor." We will discuss the development of Japan later in this chapter, and the key point I will make there is that Japan had developed capitalism before it industrialized. In some ways, the best comparison to Muhammad Ali's Egypt is Stalin's Russia. I will talk about this in detail in a later chapter, but Stalin did succeed in industrializing Russia at a tremendous cost and also built a powerful military. Like Muhammad Ali, Stalin had to do it all at once. One important difference is that Russia had coal, oil, wood, and hydropower. If Muhammad Ali had lived a hundred years later, maybe he could have used the oil resources that were later found in Egypt. He could have harnessed the Nile's water power as the Aswan Dam would in the future. Ali needed military power to fight off the British and their cheap products. Stalin also bound the people together ideologically with Communism. The ordinary men and women made tremendous sacrifices because they believed they were building a better world and a classless society. Perhaps if the Egyptians could have promoted a form of Islam that promised a better world through modernization, it would have created the necessary productivity. Ali also would have had to control population growth. The doubling of Egypt's population swallowed all the productivity gains. In the 1870s, Muhammad Ali's grandson went bankrupt borrowing from the Europeans to pay for the Suez Canal, and the British would take control of Egypt.

THE IMPACT ON INDIA

The British East India Company had established three new ports in the seventeenth century: Madras, Bombay, and Calcutta. As long as the powerful Mughal Empire dominated trade and forced it inland, these ports remained backwaters as far as the larger trade of southern Asia went. However, the Mughal control dissolved after 1700 and the three British ports grew even as Delhi, Agra, and Lahore lost population. Indian merchants flocked to the British centers and essentially ran them while reaping large profits. (Neal and Williamson, I, 179) **Robert Clive** (1725–1774) of the British East India Company had been captured at Madras by the French and saw first-hand how they organized their lands. Clive trained his own force and used the military and bribes to put his favorites into power in the southern Indian principalities. In 1756, the Nawab (ruler) of Bengal overran British Calcutta. He threw sixty-four prisoners into the fort's dungeon, which was only fourteen by eighteen feet large. When the doors were opened twelve hours later, only twenty-one were left alive in the "Black Hole of Calcutta." Clive took Bengal with eight hundred European troops and two thousand natives by bribing the Nawab's generals to desert. The money came from Hindu bankers whom the Nawab had repeatedly fleeced. British warships transported Clive's forces to drive the French out of India. Clive himself became fabulously wealthy. This was a vital shift of territory. In 1730, fully half the value of Dutch Asian imports had come from Bengal.

The Extension of British Control

From 1660 to 1763, the British East India Company had been a power unto itself: it could coin money, hold jurisdiction over English subjects, and make war or peace with non-Christian powers. From 1660 to 1700, it made an average annual profit of 25 percent. Robert Clive used his victories to buy up effective control of company stock. Parliament under King George III tried to unify the British empire by restricting the Company's dividends and imposing a tax. In 1767, the Company failed to pay its annual tax of £400,000 to Britain. Famine and smallpox swept Bengal as about one-third of all residents died, and the Company's finances plunged. Clive was recalled, tried by a Parliamentary committee, and, though acquitted, committed suicide.

The Company named **Warren Hastings** (governed 1772–1785) as the new governor of Bengal. The **Regulating Act** (1773) established a governing council in Calcutta to rule Bengal, Madras, and Bombay, with Hastings as Governor-General, but the council would have three directors named by Parliament and just two named by the Company. To help with finances, the Company would be able to reclaim all taxes paid on tea if it would reexport tea from Britain to America. This had led to the retention of the tea tax and the subsequent Boston Tea Party in America.

Hastings became more engaged in Indian politics, supporting various rulers. The most vigorous challenge to the British came from Mysore, the state centered around Bangalore that dominated most of southern India. A Muslim mercenary named **Haidar Ali Khan** (Sultan 1762–1782), an ally of the French in their British wars, had conquered Mysore in 1762. Khan tried to build a Muslim-Hindu alliance against the British. When the British attacked French outposts in India as part of the American Revolutionary War, Haidar raised an army of eighty-three thousand and inflicted a stinging defeat on the British in 1780. He died in the middle of the war and was succeeded by his son **Tipu**, who forced a peace treaty on the Company. Parliament recalled Hastings and accused him of naked aggression. Like Clive, he was acquitted, but he was the last Company governor.

The **India Act of 1784** put Company directors under Parliamentary supervision. **Lord Charles Cornwallis** (Governor-General 1786–1793) was named to succeed Hastings. The **Cornwallis Code** (1793) was the foundation of British rule in India until independence in 1947. It made a major shift in Bengal landowning policy and effectively gave tax farmers full power over land; this soon created a ruling class loyal to British interests based in the banking centers of Calcutta. It created incentive to bring more land under the plow; this in turn led to rapid population growth in nineteenth-century Bengal. The Code also placed the salt and opium trades under government control. It established a new landlord system where tenant farmers paid rents.

The British were determined to get revenge on Tipu for their humiliation. Tipu attempted to build an Islamic alliance against the British including the Ottoman Empire, the Persian Kingdom, and the Sultanate of Oman. However, none were able to render army or naval assistance. Much later, the French grasped the importance of Tipu, and Napoleon intended for his Egyptian force to reach Mysore and challenge the British in India. Napoleon's defeat left Tipu in a precarious position. In 1799, the British led fifty thousand soldiers in storming Tipu's capital. The "Tiger of Mysore" was killed in battle, and the British took the Malabar coast of southwestern India around Calicut. The British attacked Sri Lanka in 1803 and completed its conquest in 1818. The British reduced the Mughal emperor to puppet status and took over Maratha and the Punjab in countless wars.

The British were surprised that the population did not rebel. People were happy that once they paid taxes to the

British or their allies, they were left in peace for the year, not beleaguered by bandits, wars, or additional requests. In the heyday of the Mughal empire before 1739, the government had taxed perhaps 50 percent of all income. The British taxes were the same or slightly lower. In 1813, the British Parliament extended Britain's sovereignty to all Company possessions and allowed missionaries to go to India. They founded schools to train an Indian elite.

Manufacturing

The English Industrial Revolution affected other countries' manufacturing. From 1813 to 1833, cotton manufacture in Bengal collapsed, throwing millions of Indian men and women out of work. Imports of cotton goods increased by a hundred times from 1814 to 1829, and then sixfold to 1890. British-made cotton goods were cheaper than cotton goods made locally. It cost forty-three pence for Indians to produce a pound of forty-count cotton yarn. In 1802, it cost the British sixty pence. This fell to thirty pence by 1813 and sixteen pence by 1826. (Neal and Williamson, II, 25–6) In an economy where most people had little or no disposable income, this fall in the price of clothing was a miracle. There had never been any incentive to increase productivity; now capitalism destroyed Indian cotton spinning.

The first railroad in India opened in 1853. A Bengal railroad would open the growing cotton fields and help reduce British dependence on American cotton. The telegraph followed. In 1855, a sixteen hundred mile-long railroad linked Calcutta and Bombay. The British extended their idea of a unified postal service to India in 1854, which allowed anybody to send a message anywhere in India for a penny. This not only exerted a unifying force but stimulated literacy as well.

THE IMPACT ON CHINA

China's Problems

China was huge in size and population, and the government was unable to take careful measurements. We are not even sure of the population because some provinces falsified their numbers. Somewhere between 300 million and 350 million people lived in eighteenth-century China, four-fifths of them in the countryside. China has much less fertile land than India or Europe, so most of those people were squeezed along the coast or into the major river valleys. Centuries before, most of the forests had been felled for farmland, depriving China of large-scale wood resources. The farmland was carefully managed with improvements and water control. China added about seven million acres in the eighteenth century. Human labor provided most of the motor power. There were few draft animals, tools, or storage facilities. An eighteenth-century attempt to install a mechanical pump at a well failed when workers refused the water unless it was drawn by hand. Productivity was low and education was concentrated in a bureaucratic class that seldom dealt with agriculture or commerce.

There were many innovations on the farm, but unlike Britain, they did not increase productivity because the population grew so quickly. On sandier soil, the new food of sweet potato served as the poor man's food of southern China. Other new crops included corn, tobacco, and peanuts.

Tea and silk, the major export products, were also the result of large-scale rural labor. There was little credit, and limited currency in copper coin and silver bullion. Paper money was avoided in memory of the disastrous Ming Dynasty experience. China regarded itself as relatively self-sufficient. It did not encourage trade. The empire confined most foreign merchants to live in Gwangzhou (Canton) from 1760 to 1834. The small-scale trade with Portugal went through the isolated port of Macao. Foreigners had to trade with licensed Chinese monopolists (Cohung), who were under the superintendent of Chinese customs at Gwangzhou (called by Europeans "the Hoppo"). Chinese merchant firms (hangs) were licensed to trade between China and East Indies in junks that could carry up to a thousand tons. The government levied an equal amount of tariffs on exports as on imports and so was neither mercantilist nor free trading in policy. The government provided no legal safeguards of trade. There were neither investment markets nor joint-stock companies. According to R. Bin Wong, credit remained underdeveloped as the government tended to run budget surpluses and put the surplus into pawnshops to earn interest. (Wong, 133) Unlike European countries, nationalist competition did not press China: Japan was isolated, Korea and Vietnam were small and weak.

China had no institutionalized science and invention as had developed in seventeenth-century Europe. The government regulated all printing and there were no convenient printing centers over the Chinese borders that could defy the emperor's strict censorship. In the latter part of the century, 150,000 books were burned because they were deemed anti-Manchu in part or in entirety. A census of all works was conducted and a little over half of all the books were recopied by hand and a little under half were destroyed. The government heavily taxed new businesses, which rarely could attract any venture capital. If a new endeavor succeeded, the government could confiscate it for a monopoly. Merchants therefore put their profits into land and/or education for their sons. The severe inequality of income meant there was no substantial domestic market.

Regulation of grain prices made it very difficult for a peasant to make any profit and this discouraged productivity except for the need to feed extra mouths at subsistence level.

From 1775 to 1799, the chief minister **Heshen** plundered the empire for his own benefit and installed relatives and cronies across the land. He deliberately extended military campaigns so as to extort more money. Officials falsified tax receipts and production reports, so it is very difficult for us to get a true sense of Chinese economic and government activity in these years. Heshen's corruption squeezed the peasants, who also suffered under a regressive tax system. Because officials stole the money needed to maintain the dams and canals of the Yellow River, that river flooded catastrophically. In 1799 the Emperor died; the government swiftly charged Heshen with various crimes and allowed him to commit suicide. After his death, authorities found stupendous amounts of wealth and many pawnbrokers under his control. His total assets were estimated at fifteen years of government revenue: the 2013 U.S. equivalent would be $50 trillion! Heshen may be the biggest thief in history. Tellingly, the only imported goods in his fortune were 460 European clocks.

The Opium Wars

Smoking opium came to China after the introduction of tobacco-smoking from America via Manila in the seventeenth century. During the late eighteenth century, China imported an average of sixty-seven tons of opium per year. From 1800 to 1821, this jumped to an average of three hundred tons a year. Prices fell 30 to 50 percent after 1821. By the 1830s, China was importing up to 2,660 tons and 1 percent of the entire population was considered addicted to opium. Population pressure, lower living standards, the increase of corruption, and general demoralization spurred drug addiction. It was not that people had suddenly developed disposable income. Instead they were foregoing necessary food, shelter, and clothing to get opium. The Chinese empire had banned opium smoking and selling in 1729, and banned imports in 1796, but corrupt officials kept bringing it in. British India was dependent on opium for 5 to 10 percent of its revenue. At first, there was competition between British East India Company opium and non-Company opium grown in western India. In the 1830s, the Company got control of ports such as Bombay and was able to tax it.

The British East India Company's monopoly in China decayed as other British traders took jobs as representatives of other European governments. In 1834, Britain replaced the monopoly and sent a superintendent of trade. In 1839, China moved strongly against the opium trade. It had upset the exchange ratio between silver bullion and the copper cash used in everyday transactions. Tensions rose when China detained 350 British merchants and stripped them of their opium and then destroyed it. The British sent steamships with cannon and four thousand soldiers from India against the antiquated junks of China with their primitive cannon. The Chinese military was set up to deal with bandits or rebels; it had no large land or sea units trained together with sufficient striking power. Its naval vessels were much smaller than Chinese trading junks. The British moved up the Pearl River and captured Gwangzhou. Then the squadron moved to the Yangzi and took Shanghai. Seventy ships sailed up the Yangzi to its intersection with the Grand Canal. That was enough.

The **Treaty of Nanjing** (1842) brought an end to the war. China ceded Hong Kong to Britain. The Chinese government was fined $100 million to reimburse the cost of the opium. Other ports, including Shanghai, were opened to British trade.

The British gained the right of **extraterritoriality**, which meant that any Briton accused of a crime in China would be tried by a British court, not a Chinese court. By the 1850s, the opium trade was up to four thousand tons a year, and the Chinese economy was crumbling.

CAPITALISM IN JAPAN

It may be that the sudden opening of gold and silver mines around 1550 gave a vital kick start to Japanese development. At their peak during the next hundred years, production from these mines may have equaled their famous counterparts in the Americas. (*Cambridge Economic History*, V, 256) They helped incite intense political competition and a series of wars. The warlord of Edo (later Tokyo), Tokugawa Ieyasu, seized power in 1603. The Emperor gave Tokugawa the title of **Shogun**, or supreme warlord. In 1615, Tokugawa captured Osaka Castle and cemented his power. The Shogun directly controlled one-quarter of all land. The other warlords controlled the rest under his direction. There was a stratification of the social classes: warrior-bureaucrats, peasants, artisans, and merchants. The Shogun completely dominated the Emperor. In 1637 the government forbade Japanese to leave the country under penalty of death. (Landes, 356) The government expelled the Portuguese in 1639. The Dutch were the only European traders left, and the Shogun confined them to a small island in Nagasaki harbor. The Tsushima islands traded with Korea, and Okinawa with China. Japan exported silver, copper, and later dried fish to China. From 1620 until the 1680s, Europe imported significant amounts of Japanese copper. (*Cambridge Economic History*, V, 246)

The Genesis of Capitalism in Japan

Japan is the one country outside of Europe that generated capitalism on its own. A vital precondition was controlling population growth. The population was 26.1 million in the 1721 census and 26.9 million in the 1846 census. (Macfarlane, 32) Crop production grew 65 percent from 1598 to 1834. The population in those years had grown by 45 percent, so labor productivity grew 14 percent. Land productivity also seemed to grow. Angus Maddison estimates that Japan's per capita GDP grew about as fast from 1700 to 1820 as that of western Europe. (Maddison 2001, 46) The shogun levied a rice tax of 30 to 50 percent that increased pressure on society. Japanese men and women delayed marriage, practiced contraception, and resorted to killing children in hard times. For some reason, Japanese women stopped bearing children in their middle thirties, much sooner than most women around the world. (Macfarlane, 310) The average size of the household fell nearly 20 percent between 1800 and 1870. Japan used comparatively less animal power than many and did not use the wheelbarrow. Farmers, especially women, worked very hard physically, and this may have reduced their fertility. Japanese women breast fed their children twice as long as European mothers. (Macfarlane, 45–8, 320) The Japanese did not fear that family planning might leave them without an heir because there was a system that provided for the adoption of adults as heirs. (362) After Tokugawa defeated his rivals, Japan enjoyed 250 years without a serious war or revolution, though disturbances grew more intense in the last hundred years of the shogunate. Tokugawa had used guns to come to power in 1600 but then strictly forbade them.

There was a clear rise in the living standards, even for peasants. For example, cotton clothing became common.

This helped to create a domestic market, unlike China. The shoguns prevented the great lords (*daimyo*) from piling up wealth by enforcing an "alternate attendance system" where the lords had to live every other year at Edo and leave their families as hostages. (Landes, 365) The rice economy slowly gave way to a money economy, as warlords had to grow money-producing goods in order to maintain residences locally and at Edo, which later approached a population of one million. The mining of gold, silver, and copper increased the money supply, spurred the economy, and improved general living standards. The high road from Kyoto to Edo was crowded with people and inns. This transferred wealth from the lords to the ordinary people and created many jobs. Large estates were broken down into smaller family-sized units. Rich peasants preferred to concentrate on the best land, rent out the rest, and invest profits in the new village industries of *sake* (rice wine), cotton spinning, weaving, and dyeing. Some invested in tobacco or mulberry leaves to raise silk. This was in contrast to the pattern in the rest of the world where prosperity in land or trade usually led to the purchase of more land. Rich peasants challenged merchants and moved into trade by the late eighteenth century. Rice brokers, *sake* merchants, and pawnbrokers became richer than the samurai and the *daimyo*. Edo became an economic and cultural hub. The shogunate lifted the ban on foreign books in 1720.

While foreign merchants were confined to Nagasaki, a single large market was created in Japan. Like Britain, Japan is a series of islands and this aided transport and kept costs down. Sea transport had to grow because the shogunate deliberately destroyed bridges, imposed checkpoints, and banned wheeled transport from the roads to control the populace. Japan used coins and varieties of paper money. The rapid increase of the money supply outpaced the productivity growth and caused price inflation, especially in the first third of the nineteenth century. The volume of money in circulation grew by 80 percent from 1816 to 1841 and another 50 percent from 1841 to the 1880s. Rice markets in Edo and Osaka dealt in commodities futures just like Amsterdam. There was a high literacy rate: in 1850 perhaps 45 percent of men and 15 percent of women could read and write, more than Russia at that time and about the same as the American South. Most merchants lived under the control of the lenient shoguns, not feudal lords. Japanese merchants enjoyed less confiscation or ruinous taxation and controls than most Asian merchants.

The Opening of Japan

These economic changes and social pressures created an irresistible force that would break the immovable object of the shogunate. The old system was deteriorating. Nobles fell increasingly into deep debt to the merchants. In 1814, the first **Shinto** ("the way of the gods") sect was established. Under Shinto, the Emperor, shut away in Kyoto by the shoguns, was the son of heaven. It stressed patriotism and faith-healing. Over time, about half the population of Japan would support Shinto, as it surpassed Buddhism. There was pressure in Japanese society to expand foreign trade. The nobles hoped that it might restore their wealth; lesser lords were willing to enter careers in the army or the civil service. Merchants looking for money wanted to trade abroad. Patriots feared falling behind in military technology. The Japanese authorities were well aware of what had happened in China with the Opium War and its aftermath.

In 1853 and again in 1854, Commodore **Matthew Perry** sailed into Edo harbor with one-quarter of the United States Navy. He demanded that Japan open trade. Two earlier

American negotiators had failed at this. Fishing ships in the North Pacific wanted to have a refueling and repair center. Japan had no navy and its coastal defenses could not withstand an American attack. The Shogun's government (the *bafuku*) signed the **Treaty of Kanagawa** in 1854. This was not as severe as the Chinese Treaty of Nanjing, but it did open two more ports to trade. The European countries now demanded that they receive at least equal treatment as the Americans. In 1858, the American diplomat Townsend Harris got the Shogun's government to sign a new treaty opening more ports and allowing foreign travel in Japan. A crisis opened when the Emperor refused to endorse the treaty. Xenophobia (fear of foreigners) was rising. The powers of Shogun and Emperor were on a collision course. Complicating everything was the problem that the Shogun Iesada was ill and physically weak, then died in 1858. He named Iemochi, a twelve-year-old boy, as his successor over the candidate of the xenophobes.

A number of warlords, especially the lords of Satsuma and Choshu in the southwest, saw the treaties as a way of overthrowing the shogunate if they could charge that the shoguns were weak and betraying Japan. Since the 1830s, Satsuma had grown rich growing sugar cane in another parallel to the European capitalist experience. (Landes, 368) Unlike the Emperor, the Shogun's government had a very precise knowledge of the westerners' military capacities and knew what they had done to China when it resisted. An extremist samurai murdered the head of the *bafuku* council in 1860. In 1863, the Emperor summoned Iemochi to Kyoto (the first summons in 230 years) and issued an order to "drive out the barbarians." Lords launched private wars against westerners. Increased trade had disrupted the monetary system and the ratio of gold to silver. Intense foreign demand for Japanese goods caused their prices to rise and made them unaffordable to some Japanese. The antiforeign reaction that developed in Japan was nationalism instead of Chinese-style disdain. Japan's centralization and homogeneity were key differences from China. The westerners moved warships into Osaka Bay in 1865 and forced the Emperor to sign the trade treaties.

The Meiji Restoration

Provincial lords built new armies from conscripted peasants rather than relying on the samurai. In 1866, the *daimyo* of Choshu illegally bought guns that were surplus from the U.S. Civil War and armed his troops. The new armies were superior to the Shogun's old army. Iemochi died in 1866, and was replaced by Keiki, the candidate of the xenophobes. In January 1867, the Emperor died of smallpox at the age of thirty-six. There was suspicion that Choshu radicals had assassinated him, perhaps with an infected handkerchief, because he and Keiki seemed about to agree on a program to modernize the army on French lines and buy massive amounts of modern weapons from the United States. The new Emperor was **Mutsuhito** (ruled 1868–1912), only fourteen years old. Keiki resigned as Shogun in November 1867 without designating a successor. Keiki may have expected to be named as a Prime Minister, but soldiers from Satsuma and Choshu flooded into Kyoto to block any such move. Reformers, chiefly young samurai from the outlying provinces, declared the emperor restored to full authority. There was a brief war between the Tokugawa supporters and the lords of Satsuma and Choshu, but the latter prevailed.

Mutsuhito presided over the *Meiji* ("Enlightened") era. The imperial capital moved from Kyoto to Edo (renamed Tokyo), and the Emperor took over the Shogun's administration. The Emperor swore that the public would rule and that he would call an assembly. The warlords surrendered their territories and received back other areas to govern. This broke the traditional ties between the lords and their lands. The central government maintained its right to tax and control lands. The Emperor swore to convene deliberative assemblies, have public discussion of issues, allow people to have the occupation of their choice, and base laws on the just laws of Nature. He called for gaining knowledge to strengthen rule. Having used the xenophobes to gain power, the Emperor's supporters dropped all antiforeign policies.

Reforms rapidly transformed the government into a division among legislative, administrative, and judicial functions with a number of ministries. The warlords realized that centralization was necessary to resist the West. The government continued payments to the samurai and warlords to keep them happy. Since they comprised up to 6 percent of the population, this was a considerable expense. Finances were very difficult at first: revenues covered only one-third of the 1868 budget. In 1871, the government introduced a decimal currency of yen throughout Japan. Agricultural taxes would be based on land value, not yields, to encourage productivity. Interest rates were high at 10 percent a year. The government jump-started the modern cotton industry and imported higher-quality fibers. The government ordered universal education in 1872. It developed Hokkaido island to the north. Japan adopted the western calendar in 1873 and accepted religious toleration. In the same year, the rice tax was converted to a money tax, costing 40 to 50 percent of peasant yields. The government abolished the samurai class and removed all peasant dependency on the nobles. The government compensated 1.9 million samurai by giving them bonds. (Neal and Williamson, II, 37) However, rampant inflation in the 1870s cut the real value of paper money in half. This reduced the tax bite on the peasants but ruined many of the samurai who were holding government bonds. The government initiated sharp deflation to bring this under control and established the Bank of Japan in 1882. There is an old saying that the revolution eats its children. This was never truer than in Japan. The samurai and *daimyo* had overthrown the shogun with the aim of taking control. Instead, they had lost their lands, peasants, and wealth. When the samurai plotted a war to loot Korea, the modernizers blocked that scheme because it would divert precious investment. Finally, a Satsuma samurai led a futile revolt that marked the final triumph of the merchants and rich peasants.

Economic Takeoff

The government took the leading role in organizing and encouraging business, especially mining. It introduced the railroad in 1872 and built 1,349 miles of track by 1890. It paid for this by taking a foreign loan. The railroad was critical to development because of Japan's rugged terrain and expensive overland costs. The rickshaw was invented in 1869. It combined western technology with cheap labor and spread throughout Asia. There was a concentrated effort to reclaim land and make it more productive. Land productivity grew by 21 percent in the 1880s alone. Japanese used Western ships and learned Western navigational techniques. Price inflation caused the government to sell many industries at a discount in 1880. Those who were wealthy enough to buy these became captains of industry.

The House of **Mitsui** made the transition from shogun economic leadership to the new regime. It had started by making *sake*, then moved into moneylending and pawnbroking, opened dry goods stores, and finally became the official banker to the shogunate in 1691. A former supervisor of commerce in Nagasaki, **Iwasaki Yataro** (1834–85), set up the **Mitsubishi House.** He brought in foreign experts and French machinery to revamp the silk industry, which became an export along with tea. Before 1900, Japan had become an importer of rice, but had close to a trade surplus. Japan's coal production grew twelve-fold from 1860 to 1900. It also exported cotton cloth, spun and woven mostly by women and girls. By 1913, one-quarter of the world's cotton yarn exports came from Japan. (Landes, 380)

Japan first concentrated on its comparative advantage. It made *sake, miso,* and soy sauce that were immune from foreign competition. (Landes, 378) Because it was a late industrializer, it skipped over much of the steam stage and went directly to electricity. In 1899, Japan revised the western treaties to make them more fair.

CONCLUSION

The impact of British industrialization varied across the world. Belgium prospered by slavishly imitating the British path. France, with its unique strengths, took a completely different road to wealth. Muhammad Ali, under nearly impossible conditions, tried and failed to industrialize Egypt. India and China ignored the trend and found their economies flattened by the British steamroller. Finally, Japan could follow a successful path because it had developed capitalism independently before 1867. Within forty years, Japan had emerged as a global power.

TIMELINE

1775–99	Heshen chief minister of China
1805–49	Muhammad Ali Pasha ruled Egypt
1842	First Opium War and Treaty of Nanjing
1851	Britain industrialized
1853/4	First Indian railroad and telegraph
1854	Perry forced open trade between U.S. and Japan
1868	*Meiji* Restoration in Japan
1900	Belgium industrialized

KEY TERMS

joint-stock investment bank
Muhammad Ali Pasha
Heshen
Opium Wars
Treaty of Nanjing
extraterritoriality
shogun
Matthew Perry
Meiji Restoration
Mitsui
Mitsubishi

Chapter 11

THE LATE NINETEENTH-CENTURY SYSTEM

The last third of the nineteenth century saw even more world-shaking economic developments. For the first time in centuries, China gave up its position as the biggest economy in the world. The United States after the Civil War rapidly industrialized and climbed to a position as the biggest and richest economy in the world. From 1870 to 1913, European per capita GDP grew 1.2% per year, unprecedented for the continent as a whole. (Broadberry and O'Rourke, II, 34) In Europe, the familiar patterns reasserted themselves. British leadership ended as first Germany and then Russia became bigger economies than Britain. The thousand-year pattern of Europe's wealth being in its core returned: the Netherlands to northern Italy connected by a zone a hundred miles on either side of the Rhine River. Some Britons imagine that their country can continue without the rest of Europe. A few even delude themselves that Britain is still a world power.

Despite these momentous changes, many businessmen saw the economic world as stable. Stock and bond issues that were freely traded on exchanges funded the modern corporation. Whether countries used only coins or had banknotes as well, most had valued their money in terms of gold, which in turn froze currency values. Everyone knew that one British pound sterling equaled about four American dollars and eight-seven cents. It had ten years before and would ten years hence, and likely a hundred and a thousand years hence. Clarity in money values encouraged foreign investment around the world, with Britain, France, and Germany as the biggest foreign investors.

World War One shattered this time of certainty.

GOLD STANDARD

The late nineteenth century saw a global system of currency values, with the gold standard at its base. An 1867 international conference in Paris had agreed on a gold standard. England adopted a standard at 113 grains of gold to one pound sterling. The British economy in the last part of the century was perceived as being so strong and London acknowledged by all as the global financial center that the Bank of England only kept a gold backing of 2 to 3 percent of the money in circulation. Other countries set the value of their currencies relative to gold so that the United States set the dollar's value at about twenty-three grains. This fixed the value of the British pound at about $4.87. That was almost the ratio set in 1790 when the U.S. reformed its money at its founding. The long-term effect of the gold standard was to limit the growth of the money supply and depress prices, causing a depression that lasted on and off from 1873 to 1896. California and Australia added as much gold between 1850 and 1913 as the Europeans had mined from 1500 to 1850. In the 1890s new gold supplies were discovered in South Africa, Australia, and Alaska. The world gold supply tripled in this short time but even so could not keep pace with economic growth. Grain prices fell by two-thirds from the 1860s to the 1890s. This deflation forced large numbers of farmers off the land and into the industrial workforce.

URBANIZATION

The railroad made it possible to transport bulky food and fuel into the cities. In 1700, only about 10 percent of West Europeans lived in cities with a population of ten thousand or greater. By 1890, it was 31 percent. Britain became urbanized with more than half of its people living in cities. Furthermore, some had grown to giant-size status. In 1840, only London and Paris had a million people; by 1914, Berlin, Vienna, St. Petersburg, Moscow, Glasgow, New York, Chicago, and Philadelphia had joined them. London had more than seven million persons. The increased population density made distribution of goods more efficient and lowered their price further.

Public transportation in cities also expanded as the size of cities grew beyond walking distance. Traditionally it did not take more than forty-five minutes to walk directly from one side to the other. In the 1870s, many cities authorized private companies to operate horse-drawn streetcars. In 1883, **John Roebling** opened the Brooklyn Bridge, a perfected steel cable suspension bridge. After the 1890s, U.S. cities adopted electric streetcars. European cities followed. Public transportation made it possible to loosen up the city and have less congestion. By 1901, only 9 percent of the urban population lived with more than two persons to a room. A public health movement had grown in the 1840s that cleaned the cities' air and water. Natural gas lighted the streets at night.

Urban planning also came into use. In the past, every scrap of land had been used for maximum effect; unsafe buildings had been crammed together with no air or light. France led the way in demolishing overcrowded Parisian neighborhoods in the 1850s and building massive boulevards. Cities built new houses, neighborhood parks and open spaces. Zoning laws allowed the majority to impose major street or sanitation improvements on a reluctant minority. Cities filled with amenities: schools, libraries, parks and playgrounds. Cities broke the ties of families to the old noble families and church. City-dwellers became avid newspaper readers. By 1900, industrial Europe and Russia had banned child factory labor under the age of twelve and most of Europe had instituted universal primary education. (Broadberry and O'Rourke, II, 114–5)

GERMAN INDUSTRIALIZATION

There was no "Germany" before 1871. During the war against Napoleon, the German nation of Prussia, with its capital in Berlin, took the lead. It abolished serfdom in 1807. The peasants could convert their rented property to private property if they surrendered one-third to the lord. This enriched the great Prussian nobles. Prussia became the first great power of Europe to institute public education around 1810. But Prussia remained mostly agricultural and its trade was handicapped by not having access to the mouths of Elbe, Weser, and Rhine Rivers. Prussia ended internal tolls within the kingdom in 1818. Then in 1834, Prussia led the **Zollverein** (Customs Union) that abolished tariffs in most of Germany. Prussia had established a central bank in 1772 and had a solid financial system, but it was a poor country.

Change began in the 1850s with the exploitation of massive coal and iron reserves in the Ruhr River valley of Rhineland Prussia. By 1860, the German Customs Union became the third largest steel producer and the second largest coal producer in Europe, far behind Britain. In that decade, production of iron, coal, steel, and machines all tripled. The proportion of workers involved in farming fell below 50 percent. In 1850, the German lands had one-fifth of the total horsepower of England; it was one-third in 1860, and five-eighths by 1870.

Belgium had pioneered a new form of financing in the 1830s with the **joint-stock investment bank**. These banks would sell stock to the public like other companies but rarely accepted ordinary deposits or made ordinary loans. Instead they would direct their capital to a few companies with which they kept close relations. They mobilized money from small investors to create huge companies. Four major banks in Germany dominated corporate finance: the Diskontogesellschaft, the Darmstädter Bank, the Deutsche Bank, and the Dresdner Bank. These four became known as the "**D-Banks**" for short because of their names. Britain, France, and Belgium provided much of the capital these banks used to fund corporations. This encouraged the German system of cartels. In 1835, the first German steam railroad opened, running the short distance from Nürnberg to Fürth. By 1850, the German states had 3,750 miles of railroad track, then doubled that in the 1850s. In 1847, steamship service between the German lands and the United States began.

SOCIALISM AS A REACTION TO ECONOMIC CHANGE

The Hungry Forties

With the Industrial Revolution in Britain, many noticed that although national wealth was increasing, many people's conditions became increasingly wretched. Nobles held most positions of leadership and much of the land, which was still the main form of wealth outside Britain. Britain feared that the radicalism of the French Revolution might spread after food riots swept the island in the 1790s. Therefore it raised poor relief until Napoleon was defeated in 1815. (Lindert, I, 48) Britain's 1834 Relief Act cut spending by around 60 percent. (8) The "Hungry Forties" saw peasant revolts break out in Ireland, Wales, Russia, Galicia, and Silesia. While meat had been a main part of the diet in the sixteenth century, the typical peasant meal was now a lot of potatoes with a little milk or cheese and maybe some pork in the autumn months. The people in German cities in the fifteenth century had each consumed about 220 pounds of meat per year, but their nineteenth-century counterparts ate about thirty pounds a year. (*Cambridge Economic History*, IV, 414) An Irish working man of the time typically ate twelve pounds of potatoes a day. In Lille, France, 66 percent of workers were on the relief roll in 1828. Fewer than half could expect to eat meat more than once or twice a year; 30 to 50 percent of their budgets went to buy bread. In the French city of Mulhouse, more than half of the children of workers died before their fourth birthday.

The winters were cold and hungry and hard liquor production skyrocketed as people tried to keep warm. It was common in London for employers to pay workers and craftsmen on Saturday night at the end of the work week from a table in a pub, where many workers would then waste their wages. The pub owner naturally gave a cut to the paymaster. In Antwerp, a survey of the whole population (including children) in 1820 found an average consumption of two bottles of beer a day, one bottle of wine and one bottle of gin every month. Ten percent of all calories came from alcoholic drinks. A later survey of people over the age of fourteen in wine-loving France showed that the average person drank six bottles of wine, two bottles of beer and three shots of hard liquor every week. By the 1820s, Americans on average were drinking five gallons of hard liquor (mostly whiskey) each year. That is about two shots a day. In reaction to the spread of alcoholism, temperance societies sprang up, starting with Ireland in 1818. Because alcoholism often led to violence against women, they took the lead in the movement to restrict or ban alcoholic beverages. Never before or after were things so tough for the common person as in the 1840s.

The Hungry Forties came to a ghastly climax with the Irish potato famine. In August 1845, a fungus ("the blight") destroyed half of the potato crop in Ireland. This was catastrophic because most Irish lived on the potato and made their money growing the potato. Now they had no food to eat and no money to buy other kinds of food. The colonial power of Britain was slow to help. Ireland shipped out wheat and meat even as people starved. At least a million Irish died, and millions fled the country as the blight destroyed the entire crop of 1846 and 1847. Ireland is one of the only places on earth that has fewer people living now than in 1845. Across Europe, the loss of the potatoes caused food prices to skyrocket. In Paris, the price of rye for bread and potatoes doubled. Soup kitchens opened up. In the Prussian capital of Berlin, people fought over scarce potatoes when they appeared. The crisis put a strain on the poor transportation and distribution system. Outside of England there were few railroads in 1848. Revolutionary activity swept many European countries in 1848 and 1849.

The Origins of Socialism

Liberalism mainly appealed to the middle classes. There was very little in the liberal political program for the lower classes. In the generation after Adam Smith, the most significant liberal economic thinker was **David Ricardo** (1772–1823). Ricardo agreed with Malthus that population would always be near its maximum. He devised an **"iron law of wages"** that pay would always be low because there would always be more workers than jobs, therefore pay would not rise above the lowest level necessary for survival. In the 1830s, another political movement called socialism began to take shape. Socialism believes in a fair distribution of property, a fair social order, equal rights, and well-being for the lower classes (usually this means industrial workers and the peasantry). Socialist ideas criticizing private property and inequality had been growing for a while.

The **Count de Saint-Simon** (1760–1825) had fought in the American and French Revolutions. He called on scientific and industrial leaders to reorganize the state based on the brotherhood of man. He considered economic progress to be the driving force of history. Science and technology would solve social problems. Social classes would collaborate guided by an elite of engineers and entrepreneurs. Saint-Simon is often known as the father of modern socialism. His followers called for the abolition of inheritance rights, public control of the means of production, and gradually giving women equal rights as men, including the right to vote.

Louis Blanc (1811–1882), another French socialist, wrote *The Organization of Work* in 1840. This book attacked the competitive system. It is ruinous to common people and to the upper classes since it produces continual crises. Blanc believed that there should be a nationally-planned economy. In a democratic republic, the state would create national workshops in the most important industries. It would regulate production and allocate functions to prevent sudden booms and busts that hurt the workers. Because workers would get fair pay from the state, they would know that they were not being exploited by the owner and would have greater productivity and thus make the nation as a whole richer. Blanc tried to raise seed money in the 1840s to start a few experimental national workshops to prove his ideas, but not surprisingly, few banks or wealthy people were interested.

The Englishman **Robert Owen** (1771–1858) came at socialism from another direction. He was a rich factory owner and tried to build model industrial villages in which he provided education, housing, and insurance facilities for workers. Owen believed that this would make his workers more productive and loyal than workers at other factories. Owen encouraged the formation of the first big labor union in Britain to gain workers' rights. Many other factory owners regarded Owen as a fool and refused to cut into their profits.

There were also writers and leaders who might vaguely endorse socialism, but their main aim was to have a violent Jacobin-style revolution that would overturn the political and economic order. **Auguste Blanqui** (1805–1881) wrote of a "duel to the death between dividends and wages." "Mechanized man" must wage war against a bourgeoisie with whom he shared no common interests. Blanqui supported the most hopeless of conspiracies and spent most of his adult life in jail. His political leaning was probably more anarchist (no government at all should exist) than socialist. Another French writer **Pierre-Joseph Proudhon** (1809–1865) published *What is Property?* in 1840. He answered his own question: Property is theft! Profit is actually money owed to workers because their labor has increased the value of the materials used in the manufacturing process. He promoted the idea that small businesses paying workers fairly could build a network and compete successfully.

Karl Marx (1818–83) and Marxism

Background

Marx was born in the Prussian Rhineland. He attended the University of Berlin in the late 1830s and early 1840s when G.W.F. Hegel's thought was still dominant. There he picked up Hegel's Dialectic: a thesis (idea) meets an antithesis (opposing idea) to form a synthesis (blend). This synthesis is a new thesis, which meets a new antithesis to form a new synthesis, and so on. This was a form of evolutionary theory used in philosophy from the time of Plato and the ancient Greek philosophers more than two thousand years ago. Hegel saw it as leading to higher forms of reason and freedom and suggested that everything is predetermined.

Marx combined Hegel's dialectic with the classical liberal economics of Ricardo and his Iron Law of Wages along with earlier socialist writers. He scorned these earlier socialists such as Saint-Simon, Owen, and Blanc as "Utopian" socialists who believed that socialism could come by gradual change. Marx claimed he was putting socialism on a realistic and scientific basis and that the ruling class would never surrender anything important. A violent revolution was the only thing that would lead to **communism**, which Marx said was true socialism.

Marx saw the dialectic as leading to successively higher economic stages. Everything, including art, science, religion, law and the state, is just a superstructure resting on the mode of production and who controls the means of production. Previously, the means of production had been used to work the land, and feudal lords controlled the land. Now the "feudal" stage is passing, overthrown by the "bourgeoisie" that controls the means of production in factories as the Industrial Revolution spreads. This synthesis is the capitalist stage. When the capitalist stage is complete, there will be only the bourgeoisie and the proletariat (workers). The struggle between classes is the engine that drives history.

Capitalism and Revolution

The first major work was the *Communist Manifesto* published in 1848 by Marx and Frederick Engels (1820–1895). Marx expanded on his views in *Das Kapital* (1867). Engels had already written on the wretched conditions of the English working class. Capitalism exploits workers and does not pay them full value so that the rest of their labor's value becomes the capitalist's profit (Proudhon had first made this point). Only the accumulation of profit made technological and industrial progress possible. This progress throws people out of work. Competition among capitalists drives the weakest ones out and concentrates capital in ever fewer hands showing up in monopolies. Marx sharply disagreed with Adam Smith, who believed that productivity drove economic growth and progress and ultimately created jobs. Marx said that capitalism is marked by recessions caused by overproduction to increase profits or to lessen the buying power of the workers. These recessions cause misery when more people are thrown out of work. Eventually, this will lead to the socialist revolution with a fairer system of distribution. After the revolution will be a period of transition. The capitalists will try to recover their power, and there will have to be a "dictatorship of the proletariat" until the last elements of coercive power, all social classes, and the state itself withered away. Marx was vague on the form of government.

Marx made a number of key errors. He was totally wrong about progress throwing people out of work permanently. Smith has had the better of the argument as productivity gains have meant enough wealth and employment to support more than seven billion people on earth. Marx knew nothing of prehistory or ancient history and little of medieval history, though he tried to construct a grand theory based on history.

Bismarck and Socialism

The Prussian Prime Minister Otto von Bismarck was the driving force in uniting most of the German-speaking states under Prussia's leadership in 1871. The conservative Bismarck became alarmed at the rising popularity of socialism. The coal and steel industries continued to boom. German peasants poured into the cities. Germany enacted an Anti-Socialist Law in 1878 that dissolved socialist organization (though not the Social Democratic political party), and allowed police to break up assemblies and expel speakers. Bismarck followed this with **social insurance programs** designed to win the working class away from socialism. One law provided thirteen weeks of sick pay for many workers. One third of the cost would be paid by employers. Accident Insurance, paid for by employers, would take over after the fourteenth week. In case of full disability, the worker would receive a pension equal to two-thirds of the wages he had been earning. Finally, Bismarck introduced old-age pensions for those who reached age seventy. The government, employers, and employees would share the cost. It should be noted that this transferred very little money from rich to poor and thus did nothing to reduce inequality. (Lindert, I, 172) Age fifty-nine was the average life expectancy at birth in Bismarck's time.

Socialists kept increasing their vote in Germany until they gained 20 percent of the vote in 1890, more than any other party. Bismarck would not budge on laws limiting working hours, female and child labor, strengthening factory inspections or giving unions full freedom. German Emperor William II dismissed Bismarck in 1890 and oversaw the passage of labor arbitration, health and safety regulations in factories, and the end of Sunday work. The government limited the working hours of women and children.

THE RISE OF LABOR

Even as corporations grew in size, the workers had to organize to meet this challenge. Labor unions had grown first in Britain, which tacitly allowed them after 1825, explicitly recognized them after 1871, and allowed them to picket in 1875. French unions were recognized after 1864, suffered for a while after 1870, and gained full legal rights in 1884. The skilled unions organized first; unskilled labor organized after the 1880s. The unions' main interests were higher wages, shorter hours, better benefits, and improved conditions. They did not care about ideology. In 1900, there were two million union members in Britain, 850,000 in Germany, and 250,000 in less-industrialized France. This grew over the following ten years and then from 1910 to 1913, when leftists broke through in a number of countries, union membership boomed 60 percent in Britain, 25 percent in Germany, 20 percent in the U.S., and 12 percent in France. Put another way: in 1913, 5.7% of the British population belonged to unions, 3.7% in

Germany, 3 percent in the U.S., 2.5% in Sweden, 1 percent in France and Austria-Hungary, and 0.08% in Russia. Unions began as carefully nonpartisan organizations, but this changed when the ruling elite used police, sheriffs, mayors, and elected officials to attack the unions. This often included violence and murder. Unions realized that they had to become involved politically and put favored candidates into office, who would at least give them a chance to organize workers. The real wages for British workers doubled from 1850 to 1906.

THE EXPORT OF CAPITAL

Free trade had gradually spread across Europe. Britain had taken the first steps in the 1820s, then in 1846 repealed the Corn Laws. France made a free trade treaty with Britain in 1860, and this opened the way to more treaties. Some nations were hesitant: the United States imposed high tariffs to protect its infant industries during the Civil War and from the 1880s until 1914 it went back and forth on free trade according to the political party holding power. Germany also wavered. From 1830 to 1929, the volume of global trade roughly doubled every twenty years: it was thirty-two times greater in 1929 than it had been in 1830. Trade's percentage of global GDP grew eight times from 1820 to 1913. (Neal and Williamson, II, 7)

In 1854 France and Austria were the first nations to offer their bonds to the general public. Nations had been reluctant after France's disastrous experience with the *assignats*, but the governments kept the denominations high so only wealthy people could buy them and would not use them like paper money.

Steam-powered transportation and the Irish potato famine opened a period of accelerating migration in the 1840s. European capital followed people. Investors bought foreign stocks and bonds. Banks loaned money to foreign banks. Owners took profits and reinvested them in domestic or foreign concerns. Industries opened foreign branches. By 1914 Britain had $20 billion in foreign investment, France $9 billion, and Germany $6 billion. Foreign capital first built railroads in Europe (such as the Baring Brothers' French railroad bonds) and the Americas, then expanded from there. In 1914, American companies owed $4 billion to the Europeans; this was three times the size of the government's national debt. Of their $20 billion in foreign investment, British concerns put about $8 billion into British colonies in Asia, Africa, and Australia. They invested $6.5 billion in the United States and Canada and about $4 billion in Latin America. Foreign investment represented about one-third of all British investment wealth. (Neal and Williamson, II, 11) France used its investment for political purposes. It put nearly $3 billion into Russia and successfully made Russia into a military ally.

A true world market developed as distant areas competed directly for the first time. As early as the 1820s one can find global trade relations affecting the British economy as a whole. This was a very uncertain period of laissez-faire, where governments did not want to intervene. Panics could set in and cause crashes. Boom and bust cycles were violent and unexpected. Changes in faraway industry or agriculture could be ruinous and were little understood by the farmer or worker. The crash of the Vienna market and the "Panic of 1873" when many corporate bonds defaulted opened a long world depression from 1873 to 1896. Governments responded by cutting back on free trade and then Germany led the way in providing more comprehensive social programs. Demands grew for government intervention in the economy, and this increased the popularity of the socialist parties.

BRITAIN'S LOSS OF EUROPEAN DOMINANCE

After 1815, Britain did not have the financial resources for major commitments, and national will would not have supported a prolonged war in China or Russia. The unification of Germany in 1870 marked a major turn. Before it, France and "Germany" were fairly evenly matched. The shift gave the Germans a leading position on the continent. Germany and Russia overtook Britain after 1890. On the eve of World War I, Germany was more dominant than Britain had ever been.

Some of this was due to population change. From 1870 to 1913, more than six million persons left Britain. The collapse of the British farm sector forced many to leave. The United States and Russia became major exporters of wheat at low cost. Russian Emperor Alexander II (ruled 1855–1881) understood that his country had to change to reach the level of the other Great Powers. Firstly, Russia stayed out of European affairs until the middle 1870s. Secondly, Russia expanded its empire in Asia at the expense of China, Persia, and the Ottomans. Thirdly, Russia reformed its farm system. Alexander saw a backward and incredibly inefficient agricultural system. He freed the twenty-two million serfs in 1861, two years before Lincoln's emancipation of the American slaves. The serfs had to pay compensation, and the best land remained with the nobles. Peasant conditions were still wretched, and many landlords also lived in poverty because of inefficiency. With Britain having swung over to free trade after 1846, the imports of cheap Russian wheat undercut the British farmer. In the late 1860s, Britain produced three-quarters of its wool and the food that it consumed. Ten years later, this was down to half. By the 1880s, it was dangerously dependent on trade to supply three-quarters of its grain and 40 percent of its meat. From 1875 to 1885, the land area of wheat farming shrank by 30 percent. The wheat crop fell 6 percent from 1897 to 1912. In 1912, Great Britain spent £260 million on imported food, £100 million more than Germany did. By 1914, it had to import 80 percent of its grain. Britain failed to impose trade barriers, invest in productivity, or move into commercial agriculture. Its response was to expand the Royal Navy, which only sparked an arms race.

The British moved to a careless foreign policy after 1865. It blundered into wars, especially in Asia and Africa, without considering consequences. Just when the British got their national debt down below 100 percent of GDP after fifty years, they got into the Crimean War with Russia in the 1850s. The newer British colonies did not duplicate India's market for British goods. Just about the time Britain paid off the debt from the Crimean War, it got involved in the Boer War, a colonial war in southern Africa that cost more than £200 million. Britain did not match the investments that France and Germany made in education. By 1860, British children were far behind their German counterparts and it got worse from there. The British did not make elementary education free until 1891.

THE SECOND INDUSTRIAL REVOLUTION

Capitalism and industrialism changed in the late 1800s. There had been more improvements in the steam engine, but scientific experiments after 1820 developed electricity. In the 1880s, steam turbines allowed for the mass generation of electricity. It was far more efficient to have a central generating station where all the necessary fuel could be brought rather than many smaller steam engines. Electricity could bring light to people's homes with the nearly simultaneous invention of the light bulb. The big cities could be wired at a handsome profit. Rural areas took decades to be hooked up to the electrical grid. Electrical streetcars and subways could replace the trains that belched soot and scattered coal ash and the horses that left city streets covered in manure. Sweden and Norway, which had started industrializing later, took advantage of their huge hydroelectric potential. Electrical engineering became an important sector in the Scandinavian countries and Sweden developed a process to smelt iron using electricity instead of coal. (Cameron, 257) Electrification spread rapidly but took a long time to become universal, especially in more remote areas. If we take a level of 3.5 million kilocalories of electricity consumed per person as indicating a "modern" level, then the U.S. did not reach that until 1960, Britain until the late 1960s, Germany about 1971, and France, Soviet Russia, and Japan in the 1970s. (Hugill, 92) China in 2010 was about at two-thirds of a modern level, and India at about one-fifth.

Science also propelled the chemical industries with industrial research labs replacing individual inventors. From chemical inventions came artificial fertilizer and high explosives, medicines, dyes, and much else. Gargantuan transportation projects included the Suez Canal that opened in 1869 linking the Mediterranean and Red Seas and taking thousands of miles off the Europe to Asia voyage. The Kiel Canal in 1895 linked the Baltic and North Seas, and the Panama Canal linked the Atlantic to the Pacific in 1914. There were massive tunnels cutting through the Alps. The Bessemer Process (1856) improved steel production. Aluminum and metal alloys changed the urban landscape. Great "skyscraping" buildings rose. In 1889, the Eiffel Tower in Paris surpassed the Great Pyramid in Egypt that had stood unchallenged for forty-four centuries as the tallest manmade structure in the world. Railroads by the 1880s included refrigerated cars to carry fresh meat, fruits, milk, and vegetables long distances.

In the 1820s, the French physicist Louis Ampère had theorized about a telegraph. Samuel Morse learned of these theories in 1832, but did not construct a set of wires and send a message from Baltimore to Washington until 1844. The coded message was based on signals from the long-standing semaphore system. By 1850, most major cities in Europe and America had links. In 1851 came the first successful underwater cable under the English Channel. Europe and America enjoyed nearly instantaneous communication in 1866 with a cable under the North Atlantic ocean. International trade costs fell by one-third from 1870 to 1913 as the steamship and the railroad spread across the world. (Neal and Williamson, II, 15) The telephone was invented by Alexander Graham Bell in 1876. Soon there were too many subscribers to phones to list by name; they had to have numbers. The information age had been born.

For the growing middle class in the thirty years before the World War I in Europe, this was a golden age. As cities became cleaner and lighted by gas and then electricity with Edison's incandescent bulb, and as working hours decreased, new possibilities for leisure and entertainment became possible. The bicycle was perfected around 1865 and "penny-farthing" bicycles with a large front wheel became common: this allowed people more mobility and faster speed than if they rode horses.

CHINA IN FREE FALL

But not every place prospered. For China, the last half of the nineteenth century was a disaster. We have seen the problems for China building for hundreds of years but as late as the 1820s, the Chinese elite could dismiss any talk of problems. The Opium War made it impossible to ignore China's decline. China lost its lead in productivity before 1700 because of the

Europeans' capitalist organization. The Scientific Revolution and the beginnings of scientific farming widened the gap. Around 1888, the United States passed China to become the largest economy in the world.

The Taiping Rebellion

The Treaty of Nanjing was followed by similar treaties with the United States and France in 1844. The French insisted on the toleration of Christianity, which China had prohibited in 1724. Trade boomed in Shanghai. Forty-four foreign ships entered Shanghai in 1844; ten times that number traded in 1855. Foreign residents practically took over the city by the 1860s.

The Chinese administration continued to deteriorate. More people organized secret societies against the Manchus, especially in the south. One of these rebels was Hong Hiuxiu (1814–64), a Hakka peasant who had failed the exam to join the civil service. This was not a surprise since 99 percent failed the test and Hong lacked the funds to bribe the test examiner. He had picked up some Protestant Christian tracts in Quangzhou and became convinced that God had chosen him to conquer and reform China. This was reinforced when he spent two months in 1847 studying under an American missionary. He and his followers attacked Buddhist and Taoist temples and criticized Confucianism. In 1850, the police tried to arrest Hong in Guangxi province but gave up when Hong and his followers overwhelmed them.

This began the **Taiping Rebellion**, so called because Hong proclaimed himself as the founder of a new ruling dynasty, the T'ai P'ing ("Great Peace"). He ordered followers to show their opposition to the Manchus by abandoning the queue hairstyle. Hong denounced opium, tobacco, gambling, alcohol, adultery, prostitution, and the binding of women's feet. He called for equality of the sexes and literacy for the masses. The Qing rulers called them "long-haired bandits." In 1852, the untended Yellow River began a massive shift of hundreds of miles to the north. This was its first major shift since 1194 and caused tremendous destruction. The Grand Canal that linked the Yellow and Yangzi Rivers became blocked in 1855. This suggested to many that the Qing had lost the "Mandate of Heaven" since natural events were supposed to indicate divine approval or disapproval of the regime. The rebellion moved north to the Yangzi River, then came down in boats and captured Nanjing in 1853. The peasants had hoped for land reform when Hong promised egalitarian communities such as his "brother" Jesus had created, but the Taiping plundering seemed to justify the Qing designation of bandit. Seeing little help from the Qing, local scholar-landowners organized their own militias. For the first time under the Qing, Chinese, not Manchus, led armies. The militias defeated the Taipings and reduced them to Nanjing and a few other areas.

The Taiping rebellion touched off other revolts. A secret society in Shanghai attacked the International Settlement in 1853 and held much of the city for over a year. The revolt destroyed the Chinese administration, and the foreigners chose their own inspector who would collect the trade duties on imported goods. There was more unrest as the Taiping rebellion inspired the Muslims in western China to rebel in 1855 and 1862. Bandits controlled much of the northeast in the 1850s and 1860s. The revolts killed millions and destroyed precious capital.

The Second Opium War

Another Chinese-European war broke out in Quangzhou after the Chinese authorities boarded a ship accused of piracy. The

British and French seized Quangzhou, sailed to the Hai River, and then up the river to Tianjin. The Treaty of Tianjin (1858) opened more ports to trade (including several up the Yangzi River), allowed foreigners to travel freely in China, and set up embassies in Beijing. But then the government tried to repudiate this treaty and killed British and French diplomats. In a separate agreement, Russia gained part of the Pacific coast and established its city of Vladivostok. The British and French advanced in wrath on Beijing and burned the Summer Palace. The Emperor fled and left behind his younger brother **Yixin** (or Prince Gong) (d.1898). Yixin signed a new agreement affirming the Treaty of Tianjin, paying damages to the foreigners, and opening Tianjin itself to trade.

European Assistance

The Emperor died in 1861, leaving a five-year-old boy to rule. He had provided for an eight-man regency. However, the former Emperor's widow Ci'an and the young Emperor's mother **Cixi, the Empress Dowager** (1835–1908) plotted with Yixin to overthrow the regents. When the court returned to Beijing, the three formed what amounted to a co-regency. Yixin moved into the estate that had once been Heshen's opulent mansion. The Taipings broke loose from Nanjing and raged down the Yangzi toward Shanghai. The westerners, who had originally sympathized with this "Christian" movement, now agreed that the Taipings were bandits. The merchant community paid for a Chinese force under Western command. This army and the independent militias penned up Hong in Nanjing. In 1864, Hong committed suicide, and the war that had killed perhaps thirty million people was finally over. The northeastern bandits were suppressed by 1868. The Muslim rebels held out until 1878.

The westerners now felt they were part of the Chinese order and should defend it. They helped reorganize accounts and administration. They assisted in building lighthouses, improving harbors and rivers, and setting up a postal service. Telegraph cables linked Vladivostok, Nagasaki, Shanghai, Hong Kong, and Singapore. While westerners benefited from all these things, they were also good for the Chinese economy and society. Yixin set up the first Ministry of Foreign Affairs in 1861, then a College of Foreign Languages in 1862 in Beijing and a school for western science and mathematics in Shanghai in 1863. In 1872, the government sent the first Chinese students to Europe and the United States. Customs revenues from Shanghai paid for this "Self-Strengthening Movement." These programs had mixed success. China established a shipyard and gunpowder plants in the 1860s that were so inefficient that it was cheaper to import ships and weapons.

Conflict

China was so massive in size and so firm in tradition that a Japan-style transformation was almost impossible. Conservatives reasserted themselves after 1860. China did not have the capital reserve of Japan. The government discarded plans to build a modern navy in 1889 in favor of building another big palace. There was little change in the traditional culture, and the government superimposed new institutions on the older pattern. Tension between the two powers of eastern Asia grew in the 1880s over influence in Korea. This broke into a full **Sino-Japanese War** in 1894. Despite China's much bigger size, the modern Japanese army and navy made quick work of the outdated Chinese forces. To its displeasure, Japan found that it had to share influence in Korea with Russia.

The Balance is Broken

The Chinese defeat in 1895 upset the balance of power in eastern Asia. China asked Russia for help and granted concessions to Russia to build its Trans-Siberian railroad. European fleets descended on China and tried to grab ports in so-called ninety-nine-year leases. In 1897, the Germans took Qingdao and the Russians took Port Arthur. In 1898, the French took Kwangchow, and the British made a ninety-nine-year lease of Hong Kong. Establishment of "spheres of influence" was the first step to partition. The American Secretary of State promoted an "Open Door" policy to preserve equality of trade in China and keep the treaty ports open to all nations.

THE BEGINNINGS OF U.S. ECONOMIC LEADERSHIP

From 1865 to 1890, U.S. population and wealth grew. The population increased from about thirty-five million to sixty-three million (80 percent). Steel production went from virtually nothing to 4 million tons a year. Most of the railroad track was built in these years. Millions of migrants arrived from Ireland, Britain, Scandinavia, and Germany already skilled. They just required land and raw materials to employ this productivity. Wealth after the Civil War grew by about 38 percent. Growth in American wealth from 1890 to 1910 was more important than population growth. Per capita GDP grew 46 percent. Electrification and mechanized agriculture greatly boosted U.S. productivity. The American system of education and training transformed lower-productivity immigrants into high-productivity workers. The rise of the modern corporation created a new managerial class working with new information technologies such as the typewriter. (Goldin and Katz, 172)

Britain and Germany had a college attendance rate less than one-tenth that of the U.S. in 1900. (256) Improved medical care and the growth in personal wealth after 1890 created a dramatic improvement in native-born life expectancy at birth.

GERMANY: PROSPERITY AND CRISIS

At the same time that the U.S. was becoming the leading economy in the world, Germany built on its rich mineral deposits, high literacy, and good transportation. Between 1882 and 1895, Germany officially industrialized. By 1910, Germany produced twice as much steel and 50 percent more pig iron than Britain. It was second in shipping tonnage to Britain. Its chemical industry, especially dyes and pharmaceuticals, led the world. Its electrical industry expanded from the 1867 invention of the first dynamo by Werner von Siemens. Germany produced 50 percent of the world's electric equipment with Siemens and AEG founded by the Rathenau family as leading companies.

But after 1900, a number of problems grew. Germany's coinage was not adequate for the rapidly growing economy, and there was hoarding in the panic of 1907, so the government introduced paper money in 1910. There was nothing intrinsically wrong with this and the lowest denomination was still equal to the weekly wage for many, but the public is always wary at the first appearance of paper money. By 1913, only 31 percent of the paper was covered by Germany's gold reserves. The German tax system was also inadequate because it had never been properly unified. Most taxes were collected by the states that had been independent nations before 1871, and they were reluctant to pass on money to the federal government. In 1909, the German parliament refused to pass a package of taxes on brandy, beer, tobacco and inheritance. This in turn hamstrung German foreign policy. It lost an opportunity to aid Russia and win allies in southeastern Europe. Instead, Germany poured ever more funds into its military, including a wholly unnecessary navy. After 1900, the European security system broke down as it divided into two armed camps with southeastern Europe as a point of conflict. Finally, in 1912, the German socialists had their big breakthrough and became the party with the most seats in the Parliament, much to the dismay of Emperor William II. These intertwined monetary, fiscal, international, and domestic crises continued to work on each other and damage Germany for the next twelve years.

In 1914 World War I began. The final crisis began in southeastern Europe with the murder of the heir to the Austro-Hungarian throne. It is not fair to say that Germany alone was responsible for the war, but its entwined problems made it impossible for Germany to prevent the crisis from turning into war. The war shattered the nineteenth-century system.

CONCLUSION

The years just after 1900 saw the maturing of the industrial system. The growth of international investment helped more nations to industrialize. The United States had passed China as the world's largest economy while Germany had passed Britain as Europe's largest economy. The spread of electricity and the start of the use of oil were refinements on the earlier basic shifts of the Industrial Revolution. Urbanization increased economic efficiency and changed social and political life. The gold standard, made possible by an extraordinary boom in gold mining, both defined and confined the global financial system. Trade boomed. The maturing of industrial capitalism also led to the rise of organized labor and socialist theories as responses. A movement began to make society more equal than it ever had been in history.

TIMELINE

1834	German Customs Union (*Zollverein*)
1844	First telegraph message
1845–47	Irish potato famine
1846	Britain abolished grain tariffs
1848	Gold discovered in California
1850–64	Taiping Rebellion in China
1852	Gold discovered in Australia
1865	Perfection of bicycle
1866	Transatlantic cable
1867	Paris conference agreed on gold standard
	Marx, *Das Capital*
1869	Suez Canal opened
1876	Bell, telephone
1883–89	Germany pioneered accident and health insurance and old-age pensions
1883	Brooklyn Bridge opened
1889	Eiffel Tower built
1890s	Gold discovered in Alaska, South Africa
1894/5	Sino-Japanese War
1895	Germany industrialized
1914	World War I began
	Panama Canal opened

KEY TERMS

Zollverein
"D-Banks"
Karl Marx
German social insurance

Chapter 12

THE ECONOMIC IMPACT OF WORLD WAR ONE

In the early twentieth century, the vision of a future society unbelievably rich, leisured, orderly and efficient—a glittering antiseptic world of glass and steel and snow-white concrete—was part of the consciousness of nearly every literate person.

George Orwell, *Nineteen Eighty-Four*

Orwell goes on to explain that short working hours, sufficient food, and a house with bathroom and refrigerator would eliminate the most obvious forms of inequality. If everyone could buy a car or even an airplane for transport, that would threaten the ruling elite. In the last hundred years, wealth has seemed almost limitless and yet many suffer poverty and misery. Even in some rich nations, many experience insecurity about their jobs, health care, house, and even their next meal. The inflation of the 1920s, the Russian Revolution, and the Great Depression of the 1930s destroyed many of the great fortunes that had existed for hundreds of years. By some estimates, Russian Emperor Nicholas II was one of the richest men in the history of the world when the war started in 1914. Five years later, the Communists shot his entire family and dispersed his lands and treasures. In the last hundred years, when there should have been plenty for all thanks to the bounty of energy, ruling classes tried to hang on to their privileges and often hastened the revolutions that destroyed them. Presumably if Nicholas, along with German Emperor William II and Austro-Hungarian Emperor Francis Joseph, could have seen that the War would destroy their empires and exile or kill their families, they would have risked anything for peace, even national humiliation. But as Orwell said: "War is a way of shattering to pieces... materials that might otherwise be used to make the masses too comfortable, and hence, in the long run, too intelligent."

THE ECONOMICS OF THE WAR

Total War

The main fighting in the war ranged across the broad plains of east-central Europe and the concentrated area of the German-Belgian-French border with great destruction. This was the first conflict that fully involved civilians. Their governments taxed them heavily, drafted more soldiers than ever, and put in rationing. The enemy could bomb them or shell them. Germany put in strict limits on consumption because the British blockaded its trade. Other nations imitated Germany and rationed goods. The United States banned the use of scarce materials for making alcoholic beverages and then, partly because German-Americans owned many breweries and partly in response to the temperance movement, passed a constitutional amendment prohibiting all alcoholic beverages. The military draft tended to hit farmhands more than skilled industrial workers who made guns and bombs. Crops rotted in the fields. The German grain harvest of 1917 was only half what it had been in 1913.

Britain, France, and Russia had advantages in industrial and energy production, although Germany and Austria-Hungary combined produced more steel. The Allies could not bring their advantages to bear. British and French colonies in Asia and Africa contributed soldiers but not much else. The German colonies were insignificant; cutting them off made little difference to the German war effort. Germany redeployed its export industries to war. Britain's naval blockade only hampered supplies over the longer term. Britain's huge naval superiority still did not allow it to attack Germany from the sea. The western front stabilized into trenches up to four miles broad, and no army could make a big push. Germany had gained an advantage with its offensive in 1914 that allowed it to fall back to the high ridges, giving it a natural advantage even when the British and French attacked with greater numbers. With good communication and transportation, Germany could shuttle troops between the Eastern and Western Fronts.

German submarines disrupted British trade. Britain had to use many of its merchant ships for the war effort and lost many of them. This permanently crippled British trade around the world. In 1917, Russia left the war and the United States came in. Britain and France had been enjoying the benefits of U.S. credit and goods, but having the full participation of the United States was a big boost.

Economic Regimentation

The socialists had called for government-run economic plans in vain for decades. The war proved the need for big economic and financial plans. The total costs of World War I were about $100 trillion in 2014 dollars. Nations had to eliminate inefficiency. Governments lavishly funded crash research into substitutes for unavailable materials. By December 1916 Germany made employment compulsory for all men aged seventeen to sixty. Millions of women came into the salaried workforce for the first time. By 1917, women were 43 percent of the Russian industrial workforce and about one-third of the German industrial workforce. Sunday rest was disregarded, and the working day was often extended beyond ten hours. "Merchants of death" enjoyed big profits and were hardly taxed. Even conservative governments reached out to labor unions for help. Unions became a vital and accepted part of the economy, and some governments included socialists. In the democracies of Britain and France, labor unions and their workers felt unfairly exploited.

Millions died, and millions more suffered serious wounds. The war had killed up to thirteen million soldiers and ten million civilians. This was less than the Taiping Rebellion in China but a staggering number for Europe. Then a terrible influenza epidemic killed forty million worldwide in 1918 and 1919. Millions of Americans, Germans, and French saw the big cities for the first time and preferred to settle there. Villages were devastated, and many were disillusioned. Almost everyone had seen friends killed or severely wounded. What had sustained them was that the war was so terrible that there could never be war again, thus the World War would be "the war to end all wars." They soon discovered that the war had not ushered in a period of peace and friendship.

THE RISE OF OIL

Many people believed there could not be a large-scale war because it would be too expensive. The Germans kept a gold reserve to pay for war. It was only enough to pay for two days of fighting in World War I. When the war started in August 1914, almost all the nations of the world went off the gold standard, and the New York Stock Exchange closed for four-and-a-half months. As Marx had said in another context, all that seemed solid melted away. Britain and France borrowed heavily from the United States, turning it from the world's biggest debtor nation to the world's biggest creditor. Germany used printed money to pay for the last thirty months of the war after being unable to sell war bonds to its own people. On a global scale, there was a massive growth in credit. There was an increase in the money supply, but except for Germany and a few other places, inflation did not destroy the economy.

Why not? The last hundred years have seen unprecedented increases in credit beyond the astonishing economic growth. In the years before 1914, oil began to make an impact as an energy source. As head of the naval department, Winston Churchill decided to build ships that would run on oil, not coal. Oil is an extraordinary and unique substance. A barrel of oil contains a bit more than six gigajoules of energy. (Hall and Klitgaard, 7) Eighteen thousand people working hard for an hour also produce about six gigajoules. If you paid each person minimum wage, it would cost over a hundred thousand dollars! That is the true worth of a barrel of oil. Over the last ten years, the price of oil has ranged between $30 and $120 a barrel. Oil is cheap. We only consider it expensive because in 1999, oil was $10 per barrel. A ton of oil contains more energy than a ton of high-quality coal and is easier to transport than coal, either in pipelines or in tankers. Oil is usually easier to get out of the ground than coal mining and takes less energy or capital. High-energy concentrates such as gasoline can be extracted. A gallon of gasoline contains 130 megajoules of energy but costs less than a gallon of coffee from Starbucks!

What happens to all that value when the oil is burned? Is that difference between the hundred thousand dollar value and the cost entirely lost? I think not. I believe that much of that value is carried along in the economy. Some of the value that is created is reflected in increased availability of credit. Since the energy is also increasing productivity, it does not carry that much of an inflationary impact.

Commercial exploitation of petroleum began in 1859 with a well in Pennsylvania. Before that, oil had been a curiosity used for some specialized cases of burning and lubrication. The key was the process of "cracking" the petroleum and finding uses for its various distillates: heavy heating oil, kerosene, lubricants. **Standard Oil of Cleveland** headed by **John D. Rockefeller** (1839–1937), emerged as the chief oil company; Rockefeller himself was worth $800 million by 1892. Kerosene to provide lighting was the main product of oil at this time. Rockefeller controlled the refining process at a time when the American oil fields were concentrated near the Great Lakes.

Rockefeller's wealth and power became controversial. To get around the monopoly and cartel laws, Rockefeller had organized a "trust" where Standard Oil oversaw a number of supposedly independent companies. When the state of Ohio won a suit against it as a monopoly, Standard simply reincorporated in New Jersey. By 1904, it produced 91 percent of all crude oil in the United States. In 1909, the U.S. Department of Justice sued Standard. In 1911, the trust was broken into thirty-four successor companies, the most famous one being Exxon.

Just as the government was breaking Standard's monopoly, other developments shook the oil business. By 1911, Standard's share of refining was down to about 65 percent of the market. There had just been massive oil discoveries in California, Oklahoma, and Texas. Many new oil companies sprang up with their refineries far from Standard's reach. U.S. oil production doubled between 1899 and 1904, then doubled again by 1913. It may be that Standard's monopoly delayed oil field development. There was parallel growth overseas. Until 1902, Russia had been the largest oil producer in the world, and oil fields had just been discovered in the Persian Gulf. Since natural gas often occurs in or near oil, engineers began to find new ways of using gas after 1920, especially as electrical lighting replaced oil and gas lighting.

New applications for oil drove these explorations and discoveries. Steam-driven cars had been designed by 1800 but were too complicated. In 1885, the German engineer **Karl Benz** invented a three-wheeled car fueled by the **internal-combustion engine** devised by **Gottlieb Daimler**. By the 1890s, car trips out of the cities were starting. Diesel fuel (named for another German inventor) and gasoline fueled this powerful engine. The small engine allowed for other vehicles. The airplane was invented by a pair of bicycle mechanics from Dayton, **Orville and Wilbur Wright**, in 1903. The airplane and the submarine first showed up as weapons in World War I. The United States, as the richest nation, led the way in auto usage. The growing popularity of the automobile spurred other necessary industries, including rubber tires and road construction as macadamized roads now spread throughout the countryside including secondary routes. The pneumatic tire had been invented in the 1840s, but there was no use for it then, and it was forgotten. The tire was invented again in the

1880s by John Dunlop when the bicycle had created the need for it. The automobile quickly adopted the tire. (Hugill, 210)

In the 1920s, the United States was the leading producer and exporter of crude oil. The biggest problem was how to stop overproduction and a collapse in price that would ruin the drillers. The Texas Railroad Commission took the lead in that state curbing production and maintaining a price. For decades, the price of oil settled at around $1.25 per barrel, which would be about $25 in 2015 money. In the 1920s and 1930s, the United States produced most of the oil in the world. In 1936, it produced three million barrels a day. It exported about 10 percent of that as crude or refined product.

THE LOSERS

Britain

The British national debt was ten times greater than its prewar value. It lost many markets permanently, especially in Latin America (to the United States) and Asia (to Japan). Its unbalanced economy had depended too much on exports. There was no more trade with Russia. Britain had been the first industrial nation, but now it had the oldest industrial plant which had shown signs of decay since 1870. Britain had 38 percent of the world trade market in manufacture in the late 1870s. It still held 25 percent at the start of the War but slipped to 22 percent by 1928. (Aldcroft, 309) A brief postwar boom saw inflation, and an epidemic of strikes hit the country. Most of Ireland left the United Kingdom. The government introduced an eight-hour day to try to boost employment, take care of returning veterans, and raise wages. But Britain had a fatal lack of investment capital since it had lost so much in the

War, and it was no longer bringing in the large trade surpluses. By the end of 1920, two million Britons were unemployed, and unemployment would be a constant problem through 1939. Britain began to retreat from the free trade position it had held since 1846.

France

France lost one-third of its foreign investment, which mostly consisted of its loans to Russia. The French economy balanced prosperous agriculture with a smaller working class than Britain or Germany and a large middle class. Despite the devastation of its industrial northeastern area, France recovered nicely. It had built up Paris as a new industrial center during the War. Aided by reparations and foreign loans, France rebuilt its manufacturing area with the most modern industrial plant. France had a tradition of efficient industrial labor and now that blossomed as aviation, autos, and electrical engineering became bright spots in French development. (Neal and Williamson, I, 516) However, France had heavy debts, and the franc became progressively weaker. The government was afraid to impose an income tax because of reaction and so the lower classes carried much of the burden through excise and sales taxes.

In 1926 the government got new taxes and stabilized the franc without redistribution. France resisted the Depression for the longest period of time. While most nations fell into the Depression in 1929 or 1930, France did not suffer the downturn until late 1931 or early 1932.

Germany

Germany had lost the war. In the peace treaty, it gave up all of its foreign investment and, more importantly, surrendered all of its patent rights. Anyone could copy the things developed by German scientists (such as aspirin, dyes, and electrical equipment) without payment or fear of legal action. German trade was also hurt for a few years after the war as its former enemies were reluctant to trade. Germany responded by intensifying its trade with the other outcast nation, Communist Russia. Germany had been one of the world's largest creditor nations. Now it was one of the largest debtors.

The peace treaty also ordered that Germany must pay "reparations" to repair the war damage it had caused as well as to cover the considerable debts Britain and France owed to the United States. It had long been standard practice to make the losing country pay for the costs of the war. Britain had imposed a 700 million French franc fine in 1815 and Germany had imposed a 5 billion franc fine on France after beating it in 1871. (Kindleberger 1973, 34) The German economy was certainly large enough to pay at a cost of some pain to the German people, which was the point. But the Germans felt they had been treated unfairly, delayed payments, and relied on more borrowing and printing money. The War had increased German national debt from 5 billion Marks to 150 billion Marks, far in excess of its GDP. No longer tied to gold, the paper mark lost some of its value against the U.S. dollar. The end of World War I had come in the middle of a revolution as Germany threw out its emperor and declared a republic. The first few years of the republic were marked by political uncertainty as extremists from the left and right murdered officials and tried to overthrow the government. This caused a loss of investor confidence, and the German Mark lost more of its value as inflation heated up. Rather than accept payment in devalued Marks, the Allies demanded more payments in kind (such as coal and timber) because these would hold their value. When the Allies felt that the Germans were dragging their feet, the French and the Belgians invaded the Ruhr valley, Germany's industrial heartland. Germany declared "passive resistance," urged workers in the French-occupied zones not to work, and paid groups that tried to resist the French. These massive payments set the budget deficit and inflation spiraling out of control. This was the notorious German **hyperinflation**. The economy collapsed as people used wheelbarrows full of paper money to buy a loaf of bread. Some classes benefited, but the middle classes lost their savings, and the resistance and inflation wiped out labor unions' money reserves. At the end of 1923, an obscure former corporal named Adolf Hitler tried to overthrow the government. He was arrested and jailed.

THE WINNERS

The Boom in the U.S.

World War I left the U.S. as the supreme economic power. It produced fifteen times as much oil as Russia in 1920. Even before the war, its GDP was twice that of the second biggest economy in the world, which was Germany since it had also passed China. The U.S. had a higher per capita GDP than any European nation. Only Australia was richer. (Maddison 2001, 185)

The key figure in the 1920s was Secretary of the Treasury **Andrew Mellon** (1921–1932), who was a multimillionaire from banking and aluminum fortunes. He demanded that the Allies repay the massive war debts. He abolished the excess-profits tax and lowered the top income tax rate on the rich from 73 percent to 40 percent. Budget surpluses reduced the national debt to a low of $2.9 billion in 1927. Regulatory agencies were converted into pro-business agencies.

The wealthy became wealthier: the number of millionaires in the U.S. increased from forty-five hundred in 1914 to eleven thousand in 1926. Industrial output doubled from 1921 to 1929 without a major increase in the industrial labor force. Electrification in the U.S. quadrupled on a per person basis from 1910 to 1930 as the U.S. produced as much as the rest of the world combined. (Hugill, 92) Auto sales had quadrupled from 1909 to 1913, then quadrupled again from 1913 to 1919. During this time, the price of a Ford Model T car fell from $950 to $290. (Hall and Ferguson, 18) **Henry Ford** (d.1953) introduced the moving assembly line to his auto plants in 1913; this tripled productivity. (Hugill, 93) He also innovated higher wages of five dollars a day so that employees could afford to buy Ford cars. A Model T cost $290, so fifty-eight days of work could buy a new car outright. Americans bought 3.6 million cars in 1923, and by the end of the decade there were twenty-three million private cars in a population of 124 million. There were 387,000 miles of paved roads in 1921 and 687,000 in 1929. **Frederick Taylor** devised time and motion studies to increase efficiency. By the 1930s, **Alfred Sloan** of **General Motors** had surpassed Ford by introducing flexible mass production and mandating changes in models according to the schedule of when production tools wore out. (Hugill, 216) Sloan's system was more profitable because it created a market among the wealthy who would always want the latest model, even if their car still ran well.

Advertising and easy credit increased American consumer spending. By 1929 U.S. business was spending $1.8 billion on ads. Easy credit and installment plans made expensive items more attractive. By 1929, there was $3 billion in outstanding credit from installment purchases. (Kindleberger 1973, 61) So not only was there considerable wealth in the United States and more equality than in many other advanced nations of the 1920s, but poorer people could afford quality goods and houses based on creative financing. Everyone assumed that he would keep a job at a decent wage. There were other new innovations. Radios became commonplace. The Italian inventor Marconi had sent a radio message across the Atlantic in 1903, but not until after the War were there sufficient radio transmitters built and radio receivers purchased to make radio into an industry. Americans owned ten million radio receivers in 1927. Vacuum cleaners and refrigerators running on electricity made family life easier. Motion pictures joined the top ten industries. The rise of Hitler and Nazi censorship would destroy the German film industry, which was the only serious competition to the Americans. The first feature-length "talky" was *The Jazz Singer* with Al Jolson in 1927.

Japan

Other countries that stayed neutral for most of the war like the United States did well. Denmark, Sweden, and Norway all prospered as did the Netherlands. Japan was nominally involved in the war and took over Germany's colonies on the Chinese coast with hardly a fight. Japan scoffed when China demanded the return of the ports and was not affected by a Chinese boycott. It entered Asian markets that the British had dominated while Britain was tied up in the European war.

In the early twentieth century, Japan's successes continued to grow. There were some problems: population grew rapidly from forty-four million in 1900 to seventy-three million in 1940, and Japan had to import rice. The gap between rich and poor widened. Production tripled and manufacturing production rose 1,100% during Japan's industrial takeoff from 1900 to 1940. Government spending in the economy, mostly for the military, guaranteed a buyer at a time when its heavy industries were not competitive on the global scale. In 1895, 12 percent lived in towns over ten thousand; by the 1930s it was 45 percent. Japan's development had an Achilles heel: it had virtually no oil reserves on its territory and not very much coal. During the 1930s, it had to import considerable amounts of oil from the United States to maintain its industry.

STABILIZATION

The inflation and the War destroyed a certain kind of wealth and a certain kind of wealthy lifestyle. The wealthy class sometimes referred to by the French term *rentier* was badly hurt. These wealthy gained their continued income from rents paid by their tenants or on bonds. As had happened in the sixteenth century, fixed rents did not keep up with inflation and because of the social dislocation and damage from the War, quite a bit of land yielded no rent. Interest paid on bonds also did not match inflation. Russian bonds lost all of their value, German bonds lost most of their value. Before the War, many rich families lived on huge estates with many servants. The War and inflation made it impossible to maintain such a large home except for a handful of superrich families. Domestic service had been so widespread that one was not considered to be a member of the middle class if one did not have at least one servant: a combination of babysitter, housekeeper, and cook. The servants also demanded more pay as many men and women took military or industrial jobs. Governments assumed control of many palaces and great houses and opened them to tourists.

Gustav Stresemann and the Dawes Plan

Just when it seemed hopelessly broken, Germany righted itself in 1923 and 1924. The conservative Gustav Stresemann became Chancellor over a "Grand Coalition" of the left and right. He ended the passive resistance in the Rhineland and Ruhr valley. He balanced the budget. His finance minister Hans Luther introduced a new Reichsmark that equaled a trillion of the old paper marks. Once Germany had taken the first step and put its house in order, the United States supported a "private conference" under its former Budget Director Charles Dawes. The **Dawes Plan** provided a huge loan to Germany in exchange for some international control over the German banks and railroads. The French and Belgians pulled out of the Ruhr and part of the Rhineland. The Dawes Plan not only settled Germany but brought some prosperity to Europe. A system worked for a few years where money came from the U.S. to Germany in loans, went from Germany to the Allies for reparations, and then back to the U.S. for war debt payment. New German elections vastly reduced the votes for extremist Nazis and Communists. In 1925, Germany's coal production surpassed that of Britain. Germany ran a huge budget surplus that year and fell into recession. Luther as Chancellor then executed a stimulus plan of spending and tax cuts to create a budget deficit and get Germans back to work.

CONCLUSION

World War I accelerated the prewar rise of American economic power as Germany, Russia, Britain, and France lost land, patents, money or markets. Japan also consolidated its position as a global power. The War validated state economic power, and governments assumed a role in the economy that they never fully relinquished. Oil became an important resource, especially when used in the internal-combustion engine. Finally, the wartime and postwar inflation destroyed a considerable number of fortunes and promoted equality.

TIMELINE

1859	Oil drilling in Pennsylvania
1885	Three-wheeled car powered by internal-combustion engine
1903	Wright brothers' flight
	Marconi sent first radio message
1911	Standard Oil trust broken up
1913	Ford introduced moving assembly line
1914–18	World War I
1923	German hyperinflation
1924	Dawes Plan

KEY TERMS

John D. Rockefeller
internal-combustion engine
Henry Ford
Dawes Plan

Chapter 13

COMMUNIST ECONOMIC HISTORY

A WORKABLE SOCIALIST ECONOMIC THEORY

How can one construct an economy that is not capitalist without being primitive? Going to barter, tearing down the credit and banking systems, ending joint-stock companies, and returning to the land are not answers. These ultrareactionary policies only lead to massive death and deprivation as in Mao Zedong's China and Pol Pot's Cambodia.

Let us start with two guiding principles. Political socialism, as described in a previous chapter, is based on a fair social order and well being for the lower classes. We are also looking for a system that explicitly rejects the three basic parts of capitalism: individual investment, risk/return, and production for profit. A socialist system would invest both capital and labor from the workers and would then return all profit to the workers. The enterprise could structure pay so that the executives do not receive more than ten times the pay of the average worker. But without profit, how could a business expand or develop? One could ask workers to give to a developmental fund. What happens to morale when some give and some do not? Perhaps the business could withhold pay for the fund on a sliding scale above the pay needed to support a family. Perhaps one could pay the worker in stock shares or options that cannot be cashed in until retirement or some other point. Perhaps the government can tax the business but dedicate the tax to a larger pool of development money. Certain things can exist in both capitalist and socialist systems, including hiring workers based on qualifications and dismissing workers whose production is below expectations.

Certain investments that risk impoverishing the investor would have to be outlawed. How would one get investment for new untried businesses or develop expensive new technology? It could only be the government that could take on this kind of risk. Many of these projects would lose money, perhaps even in fraud. Could a government take this amount of criticism?

What happens when a business becomes obsolete and consumers do not want its products? At signs of trouble, the business could try to diversify or shift into something more popular still using its workers' existing skill sets. The development fund would pay for this transition. What if all is lost: the business exhausts its development fund, or the stock of the workers becomes worthless, or the government declines to devote more money? At that point the government has to do the tough work of closing the plants and offices, finding new jobs for the workers, and likely giving them some kind of recompense for their worthless stock (since after all this was part of their pay).

How would socialist enterprises relate to capitalist enterprises in the same nation? Louis Blanc believed that once socialist businesses got off the ground, they would drive out the capitalists because the socialists would work much more productively. This has not proved to be the case and continues to be a major flaw. Contrary to what Adam Smith thought, even slave labor can work very productively, according to studies. Is it fair to outlaw capitalism and threaten any capitalists with jail and fines? Readers will note that some of the above socialist features do exist, such as Employee Stock Owning Programs. Some are about as successful as capitalist counterparts; to my knowledge, none have ever been spectacularly more successful. Given a choice, many workers would rather have cash in their hands. This degree of force distorts the free market, hurts productivity, and therefore the wealth of all. Is it a fair society if nearly everyone is at subsistence level as opposed to a range of rich people, middle-class people, and some in poverty? Giving this much power to the government (or any large organization) invites corruption and the creation of a new elite and a different kind of inequality that is a betrayal of socialism's promise. But the evidence suggests that if they compete equally, the capitalist business will almost always make more money.

For the system to work at all requires above-average good behavior. The employees have to work hard, go the extra mile, and sacrifice believing that they are making a better life for themselves and their children. The executives must be honest and fair to all. Government officials must be honest and be able to see deeply into the economy and consider both short-term and long-term implications of actions. A workable socialist system does not require angels, but the people have to be superhuman and believe in the higher cause. Given this, most countries today have given in to capitalism tempered by some checks. The United States, peculiarly, seems to have practiced "socialism for the rich" for the last thirty-five years. The rich are hardly taxed for their inheritances or income, but if they lose money, the tax payer bails them out.

STATE CAPITALISM IN RUSSIA

We now see the basic economic puzzle that confronted the Communists when they came to power in revolutions and tried to abolish capitalism. Communists labored under an additional burden because they were Marxists and denied the effects and importance of productivity. Both the capitalist West and the Communists claimed the new system was not capitalistic. Marxist socialism had described a classless society where workers would own the means of production and the state would wither away, but communism in practice has been something quite different. Capitalist rules still hold, but the state runs production and investment and takes the profit with workers on salary. On occasion, Communist Russia and China allowed private businesses to operate within limits set by the state. I suggest that this was not socialism, but rather a form of state capitalism. The Communist elite enforced a class system that was more rigid than anything in the West.

Russia in World War I

The Russian peacetime army was 1.4 million soldiers. During the war, almost fifteen million would serve and by 1917, 36 percent of working age men were in the military. This created a critical shortage of industrial and farm workers in a country where the 51 percent of the prewar labor force had still worked on the farm. (Neal and Williamson, II, 32) Russia responded by using prisoners of war as forced labor and increasing female labor in the factories. By the end of 1916, over half of Russian industrial workers were women. Despite increasing the working hours, industrial productivity plummeted 21 percent. Farm production outside of war-torn western Russia increased, but food shortages appeared because of army demands, the breakdown of railroads, and the unwillingness of peasants to part with their grain. Pre-war governments had skimped on railroad maintenance budgets and now the chickens came home to roost. Food rationing began in the latter part of 1916 and was made general in 1917. Food prices climbed two to four times above the pre-war level. The railroad link between St. Petersburg and ice-free Murmansk was not completed until November 1916.

As with other nations, Russia's war was very costly and mainly funded with borrowed money. Emperor Nicholas II failed to lead. From March 8 to 11, 1917, strikes and riots shook St. Petersburg (then the Russian capital) while Nicholas was away at army headquarters. Nicholas resigned and a Provisional Government took power made up of representatives from the Russian Parliament (Duma). In a few months, the very popular **Alexander Kerensky** took power. Kerensky was the leader of the peasants' party and advocated socialist measures to give land to the peasants. Violence swept the Russian countryside as peasants took the land they regarded as theirs. Kerensky made the critical mistakes of staying in the war, delaying elections until December 1917, and not recognizing the peasant seizures of land.

Lenin's Background

Vladimir Ilyich Ulyanov (1870–1924) had become a revolutionary early in life when the government hanged his older brother in an alleged plot against the Emperor. He took the revolutionary name **Lenin**. The authorities arrested him in December 1895 and sentenced him to five years in Siberia. George Plekhanov was one of the leading Russian Marxists. He believed that Russia was in what Marx had termed the feudal stage. Russia would have to pass through the capitalist stage before socialism. At the 1903 Congress of Social Democrats,

Lenin broke with Plekhanov and the Mensheviks and led the more radical Bolsheviks out of the party. **Bolshevik** means "majority" even though it was not a majority of the Social Democratic party. They had no more than eight thousand members in 1905. When the Bolsheviks took the position that they would not work with Nicholas' government in the War, it arrested all five of their Duma deputies in November 1914 and deported them to Siberia. Lenin went from one place of exile to another. He lived in Switzerland through most of World War I and returned to Russia in April 1917.

Marxism-Leninism

Lenin had to modify Marxist thought considerably because Plekhanov and the Mensheviks had faithfully described Marx's ideas.

1) Lenin believed that Marx's predictions had not happened because of imperialism, something Marx could not have foreseen. In the late nineteenth century, European countries, the U.S., and Japan had conquered lands in Africa and Asia. Lenin saw it as "The Highest Stage of Capitalism" (the title of his 1916 book). An increasing concentration of capital in fewer hands marked this stage. The exchange of goods gives way to a massive export of capital. This was not accurate. The United States and Russia were major beneficiaries of this export of capital and were not colonies. But Lenin needed to draw three conclusions. First, as the imperialists divided up the world, eventually there would be no more free land and the powers would fight among themselves. Thus World War I was an imperialistic conflict. Second, even backward agricultural countries such as Russia could have a proletarian revolution because the capitalistic system had

enmeshed the entire world. Third, capitalists were buying off workers in industrialized countries such as England and Germany with the money from imperialistic exploitation. Colonialism was in fact not particularly profitable, and businesses that made a profit required massive direct or indirect subsidies from governments. Lenin scorned labor unions as an elite that did not represent the worker's true interest and misled the proletariat. This is why there had not been a workers' revolution in the industrialized countries as Marx had predicted.

2) A new type of party. Rather than the mass movements that Marx had worked for in his lifetime, Lenin wanted a very small elite vanguard that would lead the revolution. He took this straight from the anarchist Bakunin (an enemy of Marx) and the Russian terrorist organizations. **Democratic Centralism** would govern the Communist Party. The lower levels of the Party would elect higher ranks. Once decisions are made, everyone must abide by them or leave the party. This was a good way to avoid traitors. Decision-making under Lenin extended to the Communist Party Congress of about nine hundred that met annually. His successors restricted the decisions to smaller bodies.

3) Lenin elevated Marx's phrase of the "Dictatorship of the Proletariat." In the transition period after the revolution, there would still be some capitalists around trying to overthrow the regime. A dictatorship would be necessary for a while to suppress the capitalists before all classes and the government withered away.

Plekhanov denounced Lenin with the book *On the Theses of Lenin, or Why Delirium Is Sometimes Interesting.*

The Communists take Power

Against others' judgment, Lenin persuaded the Bolsheviks that the time had come for revolution before the elections for the Constituent Assembly. The Bolsheviks would certainly win few votes in these elections. The Red Guards of the St. Petersburg Soviet (Council of Workers and Soldiers) surrounded the Winter Palace and seized key points on the night of November 6–7, 1917, while Lenin snuck around the city in disguise to see how things were going. Lenin interfered in the elections but Kerensky's Socialist Revolutionaries were the big winners with 370 out of 707 seats. The Bolsheviks, with all the vote-rigging, got only 170 seats. The Assembly met for one day and elected a Kerensky associate as President. The Red Guards then dissolved the Assembly. This would be the last popular assembly in Russia until the Congress of People's Deputies in 1989.

Lenin dissolved all centers of opposition, demobilized the army, and ousted imperial officers. He recognized the ongoing land reform. Finland, Poland, Lithuania, Latvia, and Estonia declared their independence from Russia. Nationalist movements appeared in Ukraine, Belarus, Azerbaijan, Georgia, Armenia, Russian Asia, and the far north. Lenin announced that he was canceling all debts owed to foreign powers. The Communists signed a controversial treaty ending the war with Germany at great cost to Russia. The Party Congress only ratified the Treaty because Lenin made a great speech. Lenin assured the delegates that the terms did not matter because communism would soon sweep Germany and all national borders would dissolve. Lenin set up a secret (or political) police called the **Cheka**. In the next several years, the Cheka would kill up to fifty thousand people in the "Red Terror."

The Civil War

The canceling of debts angered the Allies, and the British landed a force of forty thousand to prevent ammunition from falling into German hands. Japan landed seventy-two thousand troops in the east to seize key areas. The United States sent eight thousand soldiers to assist the Japanese. The Communists had used the traditional red flag of revolution and were known for short as "Reds." The Allies formed and supplied anti-communist "White" forces made up of those opposing Lenin's regime. These forces varied in their politics from those who wanted to restore the Emperor to Kerensky and his Socialist Revolutionaries. The "Whites" quarreled among themselves. Some would not accept land reform and that cost them peasant support. The various armies would not coordinate their attacks, so the Reds could fight them one by one. By the end of 1920, the war was pretty much over, although the last foreign troops did not leave until 1922. Up to twelve million died in the civil war and the ensuing famine. Another three million left the country. (Suny, 166) The Communists were unable to regain the western end of the Russian empire.

Lenin brought economic control to a new level by ordering "War Communism" to deal with the crisis. The government nationalized industries and made labor compulsory. It imposed general rationing and nationalized land. It forced peasants to give up food so that cities would not face the kind of bread shortages that had sparked the revolutions in the first place. After the Civil War, Lenin had to consider how to repair a land shattered by two terrible wars. The government also had to make concessions to non-Russian nationalities. The Communists put out a constitution that divided the land into a number of "Soviet Socialist Republics." These republics had come together as a Union of Soviet Socialist Republics, and, although the Russians dominated this Union, the nation would be called the USSR or Soviet Union.

The New Economic Policy

In 1921 Lenin and Nicolai Bukharin came up with the New Economic Policy (NEP). This marked a partial return to capitalism. It allowed some private industry for firms with fewer than twenty employees, and a class known as NEPmen rose, especially in the retail trade. The Communist Party kept control of the "commanding heights" of finance, large and medium industry, modern transport, foreign trade, and wholesale commerce. To avoid drains of gold and other assets, the Russian ruble was not freely convertible to gold or any other currency. The NEP allowed peasants to produce privately and trade for profit. The **Kulaks** denoted prosperous peasants, who were allowed to sell their crop surplus at market rates. By 1927, the Soviet economy was returning to 1913 levels. Oil production had returned to its pre-war level. The year 1926 saw a record grain harvest. (Suny, 178) Trade unions regained some independence.

But there were problems. There was a disparity between the high price of manufactured consumer goods and the low price of agricultural goods (the so-called scissors crisis because farmers were not making enough to afford manufactured goods and modern machines). There was not enough of an urban labor force to build industrial power. City dwellers were trying to return to the land and the sources of food while the government had to force peasants into the cities to work. One third of the pre-war factory workforce was gone. Moscow and St. Petersburg lost half their people and the urbanization rate was lower than in 1900. (Suny, 170) History seemed to be moving backwards. Lenin died in 1924 so there was no way to know how he would have reacted to these changes.

Stalin's Economy

Joseph Stalin was the son of a shoemaker who came to rule Russia from 1929 to his death in 1953. He was not a writer and theorist like Lenin. Stalin was convinced that a new war was coming, and this time Russia would have to be ready with a modern military and industrial economy. Productivity was low with many lacking education or good health. Transportation remained poor. In 1928, Stalin outlined his plans for industrialization in the **First Five-Year Plan**. Russia brought in turbines, boilers, generators, machine tools, patents, and engineers from the West. (Gregory, 235) It stressed heavy industry, especially iron and steel that could then in turn be applied to military modernization. Around twelve million people left the villages for industrial jobs. The government exempted only students and mothers of small children from work. (Hanson, 11) Electrical production increased tenfold from 1928 to 1941, coal sevenfold, iron fivefold. Oil production doubled from 1928 to 1931.

Western Europe had financed the first stage of Russian industrialization, but it would not provide new loans as long as the Communists refused to honor the old debts. The USSR would have to rely on its own resources to buy western technology and expertise, and that meant squeezing the peasants and shipping raw materials such as coal and oil abroad to raise money for industrialization. The state paid a low price for crops while charging consumers high prices. As world food prices dropped after 1929, Stalin needed to export more and more crops to finance industrialization. Stalin's government created new sectors of industry from nothing: chemical, automotive, agricultural machinery, aviation, machine tool, and electrical industries. There were over fifteen hundred new factories, including massive complexes in the Ural Mountains and Western Siberia. Stalin outlawed abortion so he would have "healthy Soviet heroes" for his army.

The War against the People

Private plots had been producing 20 percent of all the food in the Soviet Union. Stalin confiscated the private plots and ordered **collectivization** of farm land into giant farms worked by the peasants with what limited machinery there was. The farms did not pay the workers in cash but in work credits which many workers saw as a cheat. (Hanson, 36) The Communists transformed twenty-six million farms into 250,000 collectives. Stalin reduced the price that the government paid for crops. The peasants retaliated by withholding crops. This caused a food shortage in the cities and a shortfall in exports. When Stalin announced that he was taking away private plots, the Kulaks reacted by slaughtering animals and withholding food. Half of all the horses and cattle in the USSR died from 1929 to 1933 along with two-thirds of the sheep and goats, and 42 percent of the hogs. This destroyed tractive power that tractors could not replace. The secret police arrested many peasants and sent them to Siberian labor camps (**GULAGS**). The government shot others. The state used about three million persons as slaves on its construction projects to compensate for the lack of capital. In the 1930s, these slaves built a virtual "landscape by Stalin." New highways and rail track opened, massive hydroelectric dams harnessed the energy of Russia's rivers, a canal connected the White Sea to the Volga River, and Moscow got an entire subway system. Without enough food, starvation and disease ran riot. The richest farm areas were worst hit. There were ten to fifteen million unnatural deaths in the 1930s when famine swept the USSR. In Ukraine, 10 percent of the people disappeared; one million out of four million Kazakhs vanished. As a result, there was little increase in grain production from 1928 to 1938. First food, and then most staples were rationed. Even if you had the money, you could only buy what your ration card allowed. Black markets and barter sprang up to get around government controls.

The Grim Total

Soviet mathematicians trying to estimate demographics came up with the following figures: from 1929 to 1935 fifteen million died unnaturally; from 1936 to 1939 3.5 million; from 1941 to 1945 twenty-eight million (including those killed by Germans); and from 1946 to 1950 four million. That is a total of fifty million unnatural deaths. In February 1990, the Soviet secret police reported that 3,778,234 were sentenced for "counterrevolutionary activity" in the Stalin years and of those 786,098 were executed. Others estimate that the secret police took up to eight million people. The Soviet population slipped down to 165 million.

Yet Stalin succeeded in making the system work. Despite the murder and enslavement, many bought into the system. They believed that Stalin was creating a new world with an equal society of prosperity for their children. The state built schools and ordered children to attend. By 1940, 75 percent of the people could read as opposed to 41 percent in 1926. (Suny, 206) Stalin seemed to be personally honest and the trial and execution of hundreds of thousands of Communists seemed to indicate that Stalin would not tolerate misbehavior even in his associates. He expelled 250,000 Communists for embezzlement. (Gregory, 222) Stakhanov was a mythical worker who performed amazing feats of production. Workers who imitated him were called Stahanovites and honored. A surprising number of workers did far beyond their expected duties. After the Germans invaded the USSR in 1941, the government used patriotism to prod the workers even more. Entire factories were disassembled, moved hundreds of miles out of the war zone, then resumed production. In some cases the factories operated in the winter before the roof was put on, and the workers kept up their labor. Stalin's economy had little to do with a true model of socialism, but it certainly benefited from the ideals and the superhuman commitment of many to the socialist dream.

The Soviet Economy in World War II

Mobilization in 1914 had quickly exhausted armies and industries. The USSR carried many advantages into war: it had a large population and area for both resources and retreat, but it still had a low level of development. Farm workers were still 57 percent of the population even though agricultural productivity was one-third of the non-agricultural sectors. This meant the government had to hold back millions from the army for work in the fields. This was compensated for somewhat by Stalin's militarization during the 1930s: it had allowed for a large army with equipment stocks, established specialized defense industries, and familiarized much of civilian industry with military requirements. By 1940, the government was dedicating 20 percent of the economy to military spending. There was the educational, scientific, engineering, fuel-energy, and transport infrastructure to support production and operations. A centralized planning system would lessen economic shocks. By 1943, 60 percent of the Soviet economy was devoted to the war effort. This was supplemented by American aid equal to 5 percent of the Soviet economy in 1942 and 10 percent in 1943 and 1944. Germany occupied a large part of western Russia, but life was no better under Hitler. He also brought death, enslavement, and brutality, nor did he dissolve the collective farms. (Suny, 232–3)

Success and Failure

Stalin punished officials who did not meet their goals under the Five-Year Plan, so there was falsification all the way down the line. It is likely that no one compiled true economic statistics, so scholars will never be able to make a full assessment of economic change under Stalin. There is no doubt that Stalin greatly boosted the industrial sector. When Stalin died in 1953, the Soviet Union was very close to being industrialized. Stalin had won World War II as opposed to Emperor Nicholas who lost World War I.

The thornier question is: to what degree was there genuine economic growth in the Stalin years or did the economy grow slowly while resources were shifted from farming to industry? The Communists claimed incredible levels of growth during the 1930s when most of the world was mired in the Great Depression. Foreigners received carefully guided tours and marveled at the construction achievements without finding out the human cost of these accomplishments. The destruction of vast lands during World War II complicates things even more. Angus Maddison, who has probably done the most careful global comparisons, estimates that in the borders of the USSR, per capita GDP grew from $1,488 (in 1990$) in 1913 to $2,834 in 1950. If we consider that the USSR did not recover from the first war until 1927 and was probably at a higher level in 1941, that gives us annual growth of over 5 percent a year. That still made it poorer than most of the nations of western Europe. (Maddison 2001, 264) I have used Maddison's numbers in my books but I have big doubts.

Maddison's calculations are largely based on the numbers of the American Central Intelligence Agency from the 1980s, which had a strong political incentive to portray the Soviet Union as more of a power than it really was. Maddison's 1940 number puts the Soviet economy as being 75 percent larger than that of Germany. I think if the gap were that large the USSR would have beaten Germany rather easily in the war. I would reduce the number by a about one-third. That would put the per capita income level at $1,889. That would mean annual growth for the Stalin regime of 2 percent, which I find much more realistic. A very rough estimate of industrial labor productivity states that it grew around 20 percent from 1929 to 1937. (Gregory, 35–6). Let us add another 20 percent for 1937 to 1941. Farm productivity likely did not grow, so this would bring down the total number to about 20 percent over twelve years. That's 1.6% annual growth, and per capita GDP certainly did not more than double productivity growth. At most, the Soviet per capita GDP grew 3 percent a year.

What Stalin built can hardly be called socialism, not even Marxist socialism. Instead of a classless society, he created a class of slaves. The state, not the workers, decided virtually all inputs and outputs. The government did not wither away, it became more powerful than at any time in Russian history. A carefully selected elite class oversaw everything. The government's command, not consumer need nor desire for profit, drove production.

After Stalin

Nikita Khrushchev succeeded Stalin as head of the Soviet Communist Party. He continued the work of industrializing the Soviet Union and rebuilding from the war damage. However, he emptied out the GULAGs and revealed publicly the crimes of the Stalin years. He relaxed some controls on agriculture and attempted to plant crops on unsuitable ground in Central Asia. Farm production did rise 51 percent from 1953 to 1959, but then there were four successive bad harvests, and in 1963, the USSR had to buy half of its wheat from the West. Russia had been a champion grain producer for a hundred years, but Communist policy had so distorted the market that it had to use imports to feed its people. Because price controls meant factories bought materials cheaply, they were wasted and used inefficiently. Factories employed many more workers than they needed since the Communists boasted of full employment. Khrushchev established worker's collectives to provide health and child care as well as consumer goods. He hoped these would provide incentives for more productive work. (Gregory, 259) Many workers sat around doing nothing or got drunk since they knew they would not be fired. The resulting products were usually of poor quality. Khrushchev greatly reduced the military budget, but the army was a reliable employer. Farmers tried when possible to sell at a higher price on the black market. Stores kept goods off the shelves and saved them for favored customers or those who would pay a higher price. Foreign currencies were preferred to the ruble even though this was illegal in most stores. All this meant that stores were always short of goods and people would wait in long lines when goods were expected. Bribery and petty crime started to become a way of life. Khrushchev was the last leader who had been part of the 1917 revolution. He could still promote socialist idealism and have most people believe him.

In 1964, **Leonid Brezhnev** and a group of younger Communists overthrew Khrushchev. Brezhnev's group had come into the Party after the Revolution as a way to gain money and power. They continued to promise that they were leading the way to a classless society and workers' paradise, but nobody believed them. The Brezhnev years were ones of great decline in almost all sectors. Brezhnev's family was notoriously corrupt and millions of rubles disappeared into secret bank accounts, especially the accounts of his son-in-law. The Soviets also diverted more and more money into the military budget, although much Soviet military technology remained backward. At a time when miniaturization and solid-state circuitry were becoming standard in Western equipment, the Soviet Union was still using vacuum tubes. The collapse of agriculture accelerated as the USSR became dependent upon U.S. imports for grain. The leadership grew older and older. For a while, the value of oil and gold masked this. We will discuss the oil situation of the 1970s in depth in chapter 15. From 1945, the USSR had increased its oil production by twentyfold and had become a major producer of natural gas. In the 1970s the oil price shot up from $1.25 per barrel to $20, making the Russian supplies all the more valuable. The market price of gold also rose from about $150 per ounce to $850. This was important because the Soviet Union was a major gold producer and paid its international obligations in gold. The credit of the Soviet Union was now solid as the old Russian bonds were forgotten for the moment. (They were finally paid in the 1990s). This enabled the Communist nations of east-central Europe, especially Poland and Hungary, to borrow enormous sums of cash from European and American banks just to keep their basic economies running. The Soviet per capita GDP was about 40 percent that of the U.S. in 1973 but steady growth since the war and a larger supply of consumer goods satisfied most people.

In the 1980s, the price of oil and gold collapsed. Brezhnev was devoting 15 percent of GDP to an obsolete military and had gotten bogged down in an endless war in Afghanistan. (Maddison 2001, 155) By the time of Brezhnev's death in

1982, the bloc was in bad shape. It was deeply in debt to the West, corruption was rampant, and the economies were in decline. Full employment was supposed to be a strength of communism, but employment as a percentage of the population peaked in Hungary in 1970, Poland in 1978, and the Soviet Union itself in 1984. Communist membership was falling and in Poland the party crumbled and the army took charge. Massive environmental pollution took a toll. Khrushchev's farm disaster had turned most of the Aral Sea into a salty desert. Inefficiency, corruption, and decaying equipment meant it became ever harder to secure raw materials including oil. In 1986, a nuclear power plant at **Chernobyl** malfunctioned and spewed radiation over a large part of Ukraine.

For Brezhnev's successors, it seemed that the only choices were widespread economic reform on the model of Bukharin's New Economic Policy, democratization, or the imposition of a military dictatorship like Poland. **Mikhail Gorbachev** became Communist leader in 1985 and tried an updated version of the NEP. When that failed, the choice was the military or democracy.

STATE CAPITALISM IN CHINA

Communist Revolution

After Xixi died in 1908, a nationalist revolution overthrew the empire and proclaimed a republic. This action opened forty years of war. The Nationalist Party struggled to win control from regional warlords. It also had armed conflict with a Communist Party led by **Mao Zedong** (d.1976). During the Asian part of World War II from 1931 to 1945, the Nationalists and Communists worked together uneasily against Japan.

Mao had taken Lenin a step further by stating that a socialist revolution could occur in an agricultural society like China. At a time when Western science seemed to be the secret of the West's success, many Chinese were attracted to the idea of what claimed to be "scientific socialism." Aided by the Soviet Union, the Chinese Communist Party was set up in 1921. Communism grew among factory workers in port cities working more than eighty hours a week and Chinese students returning from the West eager to free their country from Western domination. During World War II, the Communists stopped confiscating land. Instead they reduced rents for farmers and fostered farm associations to share resources, labor and transportation. This made them very popular. By 1945, the Communists had a million-man army. As soon as Japan surrendered, the Communists and Nationalists fell into a civil war, which the Communists won in 1949. The Nationalists moved their government to the island of Taiwan.

Mao carried out land reform and gave land to 300 million landless peasants. He cracked down on the remaining Nationalists, killing millions of opponents. The government took over the banks. It imposed crushing taxes that brought the budget under control. With the Soviet Union's assistance, it began its own program of crash modernization and industrialization while calling for a "shift to the cities." It expanded and rebuilt railroads and highways and reduced prostitution and drug use. It built up a 2.5 million man army to soak up some manpower. The population grew rapidly. In 1945, it was already the largest in the world, but it had doubled by 1986. (Maddison 1998, 169)

By the late 1950s, the Soviets had become nervous about China getting the atomic bomb and cut off aid. Mao decided to launch a crash industrialization on the Stalin model, which he called the **Great Leap Forward** (1958). Mao's twist was that he wanted to industrialize while preserving China's rural character. The Communists forced teachers, students, officials and other unskilled workers into the fields to help with farmwork. Instead of massive steel factories, peasants were supposed to build small blast furnaces in their back yards. To meet Mao's demands, peasants melted down their pots and pans into useless lumps of metal. The fuel was taken from local trees and when the trees were gone, peasants would steal their neighbor's wooden doors! Labor alone could not make up for shortages in capital and energy. The bureaucracy absurdly lied about huge gains. While China brought more land under cultivation, and built bridges, roads, canals, railways and mines, it wasted much labor and there were colossal errors such as salinizing newly irrigated land. Paying peasants according to their need (thus following Marx's orders) lowered productivity. Mao disregarded all the warnings and advice of scientific farmers and engineers. The demands exhausted people and worked some to death. Some twenty-five million died.

By the time Mao died, the per capita GDP had grown 23 percent from 1949 to 1976. (Maddison 1998, 157) This may sound all right until you realize that the 1950s and 1960s were two decades of the finest growth in human history. As late as 1820, China had controlled about one-third of the world's economy. In Mao's time, it fell to a measly 3.5%. While the Chinese economy more or less stood in place, the structure did change. By Mao's death, China was industrialized. (Maddison 1998, 55)

China after Mao

There was another convulsion in the late 1960s as Mao laid waste to the educational system. When Mao died, a power struggle ensued that was won by **Deng Xiaoping** (1904–97).

Deng had been one of Mao's comrades in the 1930s but had always taken a moderate line. His program emphasized education, including sending Chinese students abroad. The government offered scientific, social scientific, and technical training. People could take courses on television and radio. There were foreign language courses in English and Japanese to break down the isolation of the Mao years. Deng reduced the army to three million soldiers. The government "leased" collective land to the peasants. Peasants could set aside up to 15 percent of the farmland as private plots. Once farmers had met their production quota, they could sell the rest on the open market. With this incentive, farm production doubled. Economic centralization was relaxed. When Deng started, the government provided about 70 percent of the urban economy; the "collective sector" about 25 percent, and the private sector only 5 percent. "Township and village" enterprises more than quadrupled during Deng's rule. By the mid-1980s, industries were allowed to sell their "excess production" on the free market. (Neal and Williamson, II, 44) Relaxation of wage and price controls caused inflation to heat up at the end of the 1980s and into the 1990s. More consumer goods were available. The government set up four Special Economic Zones to foster international trade and commerce. Fourteen ports were especially suited to international trade. Specialized branches of the Bank of China opened to provide credit to particular sectors.

As the population rocketed over the billion-person mark, energy and transportation were huge problems. The government responded with massive hydroelectric projects such as the Three Gorges Dam. It imported oil but relied on mining stupendous amounts of coal. The burning of coal put a thick haze over cities such as Beijing. Modern rail systems were launched to knit together the main areas of China with high-speed rail. The government reinstated the age-old Chinese examination system. Under Deng, the government tried to check population growth by pushing for a national policy of one child per couple. This never succeeded out in the countryside. The hope was that after China modernized, it would pass through the same demographic transition that other nations had and its population would stabilize so that China would not fall into a massive Malthusian trap. Altering the capital/labor ratio, as Japan had two hundred years before, was bound to encourage capitalist development. China passed Russia in 1992 after that country blew apart. By 1993, China had doubled its world economic standing from the Maoist lowpoint. In 1995, it passed Japan to become the second-largest economy in the world. Much of China remains underdeveloped. Even though it is the biggest energy consumer in the world, its per capita level of electricity use is still below what I have defined as "modern."

THE END OF COMMUNISM

Gorbachev was the first Soviet leader not to have risen to power in the Stalin years. He had been put in charge of agriculture in 1978 and somehow survived the usual farm failures. He began a crusade against drunkenness by attacking absenteeism and taxed vodka heavily. This led to a growing budget deficit as people turned to making their own spirits and the government lost vodka tax revenue. Gorbachev also began to speak about *glasnost* (openness) and *perestroika* (restructuring), but it was unclear what he meant. Slowly, there were changes in the military and foreign policy structure. Gorbachev became convinced that the Afghan war was draining the strength of the USSR and was poisoning relations with the West, so he cut his losses and withdrew in 1989. Real change remained scanty.

Gorbachev seemed caught between old conservative leaders and newer, impatient members who wanted to see faster action.

Meanwhile, the Soviet economy continued to crumble. A 1986 law allowed individual and family-based business. The next year, a law gave more authority to factory managers to control production and set prices. Managers took advantage of this law to begin converting control of the factory from the state to private interests. (Suny, 333) None of the reforms seemed to make a difference. Increasingly, his ability to act was constrained by his need for western aid and credit to close the budget deficit. The Soviet Union cut assistance to the communist countries of east-central Europe, lessening their dependence.

In the spring of 1989, Gorbachev ordered a free vote for a new Soviet Congress, the first since 1917. Many Communists lost their seats even though they ran unopposed. Poland's military government resigned in June. The late summer and fall saw the collapse of Soviet clients throughout Europe. This encouraged the non-Russian minorities in the Soviet Union to seek greater rights. Local Communist bosses cut deals, stole assets, and withheld resources from the rest of the USSR. Gorbachev lost his authority when a conservative Communist group tried to overthrow him without having any plan. At the end of 1991, the Soviet Union broke into fifteen independent republics; the largest was the Russian Federation.

Deng Xiaoping and the Chinese Communists were appalled to see the collapse of the senior Communist state. When students demonstrated for democracy and greater rights in Beijing's Tiananmen Square, troops opened fire and killed many. The government now decided to substitute wealth for political freedom. China took advantage of ultra-low fuel costs and cheap transportation to become a major exporter. China built an intimate economic relationship with the United States in the 1990s. Corporations such as Apple built factories filled with what some called slave workers while Wal-Mart stocked its shelves with cheap goods from China.

CONCLUSION

It is theoretically possible to build a modern noncapitalist system that follows socialist principles. It requires careful planning and superhuman commitment. The large communist economies of Russian and China, while professing to follow socialism, actually were closer to state capitalism. Both countries used mass murder and brutality to implement their visions of communism. After Stalin's death in 1953, the Soviet Union abandoned some of the worst aspects of Stalinism but corruption and inefficiency grew. World economic developments (particularly the high prices of oil and gold) disguised this ailment during the Brezhnev years, but the problems overwhelmed Gorbachev and the Soviet Union collapsed. Seeing Russian disarray, the Chinese leader Deng Xiaoping moved its communism in a strongly corporate and private direction. The global economy integrated communist China much more than it ever integrated communist Russia.

TIMELINE

1917	Communist revolution in Russia
1918–20	Civil war in Russia and "War Communism"
1921–29	New Economic Policy (NEP)
1929–34	Stalin's first Five-Year Plan
1944–48	Communism spread across eastern Europe
1949	Communist revolution in China

1950s	Soviet Union industrialized
1958	"Great Leap Forward" in China
1959	Communist revolution in Cuba
1964–82	Brezhnev head of USSR Communist Party
1978–97	Deng Xiaoping ruled in China
1985–91	Gorbachev head of USSR Communist Party
1986	Chernobyl nuclear plant disaster
1989	Revolutions ended communism in east-central Europe
	Chinese crushed protests at Tiananmen Square, Beijing
1991	Collapse of communism in USSR

KEY TERMS

Vladimir Lenin
New Economic Policy
First Five-Year Plan
GULAG
"Great Leap Forward"
Deng Xiaoping

Chapter 14

THE GREAT DEPRESSION

The late nineteenth-century system had many booms and busts, some quite violent. Hans Rosenberg called the period of 1873 to 1896 the First Great Depression. It saw strong deflation and some busts just like the 1930s, but it also had strong periods of boom from productivity growth. Socialists had pushed for government help in these downturns. As we have seen, Germany was the first country to offer comprehensive social insurance. Britain and other European countries followed after 1900. Some tried to consider these downturns as part of a regular business cycle and the free market. Conservatives believed these "depressions" or "slumps" were part of the natural order and that disturbing this order by helping the jobless would only distort things and make things worse. They believed (or pretended to believe) that there really was a free market efficiently distributing goods and making all wealthier as in Adam Smith's ideal.

The Great Depression that began in the late 1920s might have just been another one of these slumps, but it became the most severe crisis of modern times and, for a time, many feared that it would never end. The ordinary crisis was worsened by a conservative desire to return to the gold standard and pretend that World War I had never happened. This distorted financial markets and caused gyrations and finally a financial crash that wiped out many fortunes. Many of the rich who had survived the postwar inflation were ruined by the financial crash. The global economy was further damaged by the policies of the largest economies: the United States, Germany, and the Soviet Union. We have already detailed Stalin's policies. Even if they created robust real growth in the USSR (which is questionable), there is no doubt that Russia ceased to be a major importer of manufactured goods from other countries. Finally, the world engaged in a suicidal trade war. Germany had a political revolution that led directly to the Second World War. The U.S. had a more modest political revolution. The Depression utterly discredited conservative economics for fifty years.

Political Isolation, Financial Engagement

There was a considerable disconnection between U.S. politics and business when it came to international relations. Officially, the U.S. government claimed a policy of isolation. It rejected the negotiated peace treaty with Germany and simply stated that the fighting was over. It withdrew the remaining American soldiers from Europe, paving the way for the disastrous French invasion of the Ruhr and German hyperinflation. It refused to join the League of Nations, the leading international organization of the time. But during the war, American institutions and individuals had extended $9.3 billion in loans to France and Britain and $1.9 billion to Russia and Italy. At the Paris conference, the exact cost of reparations had been postponed. Officially this was so a commission could assess the war damage. Unofficially, the Allies waited to see if the U.S. would forgive or reduce the debts. When it became clear that this would not happen, the Allies fixed the bill in May 1921 at $31.4 billion. It should be noted that the schedule was arranged in such a way to indicate that they never expected a payment of more than $11.9 billion, which almost balanced the war debt amount. American bankers and Treasury Secretary Andrew Mellon asked Congress for the power to vary the repayment of debts so as not to hurt world trade. This would mean some kind of bailout and taxation. The politicians opposed this and set up the World War Foreign Debt Commission which insisted that the Allies set a definite schedule for repayment. This in turn caused the Allies to exert pressure on the Germans. The ensuing hyperinflation cost American investors more than $1 billion in Mark-denominated securities. The Dawes Plan that stabilized the European economy featured a substantial American loan underwritten by the Morgan Bank. Parker Gilbert, a former Undersecretary of the Treasury with ties to Morgan, became the Agent-General for Reparations. His main job was to safeguard American investments. From late 1925 to 1928, long-term U.S. loans poured into Germany; in the 1920s, roughly $18 billion was invested by foreigners into Germany while $10 billion was paid in reparations. The U.S. received $2.6 billion in war debt payments. In December 1932, France and Britain defaulted on their war debt. (Broadberry and O'Rourke, II, 179)

Gold, The Panic of 1907, and the Birth of the Federal Reserve Bank

The United States had tried twice to have a central bank like other advanced nations. Both had failed, mainly due to politics. But during the American era of development, the lack of a central bank led to a troubled relationship with gold. Regardless of natural supplies, some countries had an insatiable need for gold and tended to hoard supplies. As Barry Eichengreen emphasized in his book *Golden Fetters*, the gold standard relied on:

1) **credibility** that the economic powers would protect it by any means necessary. This in turn relied on an elite brand of politics: a government willing to throw millions out of work and depress farm prices just for an abstract idea was not one very sensitive to popularity. The working classes before World War I in the U.S., Britain, France, and Germany were growing in political power but still had little influence on the elite. Debtors, especially farmers in more recently settled areas of the U.S., demanded action. Their calls for government to inflate currency (printing more greenbacks) or adopt bimetallism (using silver as well as gold) went unheeded.

2) **cooperation**. Generally before the War the Bank of England led cooperation, though that was slipping. Banks would support each other, buying and selling gold and currency to maintain parities. The United States had built its industrial revolution on borrowed money and its expansion required enormous sums of gold. Because of its initially small economy and lack of central bank, the U.S. was not involved in international cooperation. (Eichengreen, Chap. 2)

A global gold imbalance caused the **Panic of 1907**. After 1896, the U.S. had become the leading user of gold reserves; it had required 15 percent of global gold reserves in the 1890s; that rose to 25 percent by 1914. Budget surpluses (and a move toward trade surpluses) allowed gold to pile up. In 1906, extensive U.S. borrowing in Britain drained coin and bullion. The Bank of France purchased British treasury bills to get gold to Britain. The crisis seemed to pass, and Britain repaid France. A panic broke out in the U.S. due to speculation on the stock market and federal budget problems. Bankruptcies soared, banks failed, the New York Stock Exchange stocks lost half of their values, people pulled their money out of banks and wanted gold for their cash. The U.S. demand for gold surged and drained Britain again. Of the gold shipped to the U.S. in November and December 1907, 40 percent was newly mined. The Panic only stopped when government officials begged J.P. Morgan to intervene. Morgan, the U.S. Treasury, and John D. Rockefeller coordinated a rescue of two troubled banks. Morgan's U.S. Steel bought stock in the Tennessee Coal, Iron, and Railroad company. The U.S. government waived the Antitrust law even though this purchase gave U.S. Steel a 60 percent market share. The alternative was to close the Exchange for a unknown period to stem the panic. The Bank of England had to raise its discount rate to 7 percent, the highest since 1873, to keep gold in Britain. Both France and Germany kept their rates low so that their gold would flow to Britain. France sold more gold but this time, and balance was not restored until 1910.

The Panic of 1907 revealed a shocking reality: Morgan and Rockefeller controlled the American banking system. People who call for the end of the Federal Reserve should consider this. If there were no central bank, it would not be "the people" who would control American finance, it would be

Chase, Goldman Sachs, and a few other big firms. The shock helped lead to the establishment of the U.S. Federal Reserve system at the end of 1913 as a central bank. "The Fed" would oversee the money supply, including gold flows, and play a role in bank regulation. At the beginning, the key office was not the Board of Governors in Washington, DC, but the Federal Reserve Bank of New York, center of international finance. **Benjamin Strong** (d.1928), a Vice President of Banker's Trust and Morgan's associate, was the first head of the New York Fed.

Gold Again

Winston Churchill became Britain's Chancellor of the Exchequer at the end of 1924. Churchill saw himself as the guardian of Britain's glorious past and foolishly tried to pretend that World War I had not changed global economic and political relations. He not only restored the gold standard but returned the value of the pound to the dollar and gold to pre-war values of $4.87. The one concession was that it was now a **gold/exchange standard**. That meant that currency would be backed by both gold and foreign exchange that was also on gold and presumably would hold its price. Here is the problem: Britain's economy had declined and could no longer export goods with sufficient productivity and thus low prices to compete on the market with (among others) American or Japanese goods. Prices had gone up faster in Britain with the massive war spending than in many nations. The pound floating on the free market between 1920 and 1924 fluctuated between a low of $3.40 and a high of $4.30. (Kindleberger 1973, 44–5) Had Churchill devalued the pound to $4.30 (about 10 percent), exports would have remained fairly strong and the gold supply would be stable. By contrast, France devalued the franc from a prewar value of 5 francs to 1

U.S. dollar down to 25.5 to 1, an 80 percent devaluation. Italy devalued by 72 percent, Portugal by 96 percent, and Greece by 93 percent.

Without devaluation, governments had to rely on interest rate management. Many economists have noted the similarity to problems in the euro currency zone. Nineteen countries (plus six non-EU states as of 2015) use the euro even though they have different prices and different governments. They do not have a separate currency to devalue. There are only two ways to regulate the flow of money. You can have high interest rates on your bonds to attract investors, but that runs the danger of straining your government's budget. There was a consistent pattern in the 1920s: the U.S. had the lowest interest rates, the British somewhat higher, the Germans a little higher than the British. Riskier nations had even higher rates. Whenever nations lowered their rates, gold would gush out.

The other way to regulate the flow of money if your currency is fixed is to lower wages. In the euro zone after 2010, Germany has forced this policy on Spain, Greece, and Ireland. The Greeks have had to cut pay by more than 20 percent. In the 1920s, Britain's remaining export industries had to lower wages to compete because foreign prices of British goods would be so expensive. The British coal industry was especially hurt because oil was beginning to replace coal as the main energy source, the competition from German coal was fierce, and the British coal industry was very inefficient. Mine owners locked out miners to force them to work for less pay. (Hall and Ferguson, 46) The government proposed mine modernization, but mine owners were reluctant to pour money into what they considered a dying industry. Their alternative proposals: the government should abolish the minimum wage, and the miners should work longer hours for less pay. The enraged British unions called a general strike involving one-sixth of all workers in May 1926. The strike failed and the unions had to back down.

The return to gold naturally limited growth opportunities. Interest rate management became increasingly difficult. An attempt by the German central bank to restrict credit led to the crash of the Berlin market in May 1927. Other problems occurred when the French began to redeem their British reserves for gold. The British adamantly refused to raise their rates to protect the overvalued pound. On July 6, 1927, there was a secret bankers' summit on Long Island as Benjamin Strong met with the leaders of the British, French, and German central banks. If the Europeans had raised their rates, it could have led to a recession there. Instead, the U.S. lowered its interest rate from 4 per cent to 3½ percent. From July to September 1927, the Fed engaged in open market operations and injected $200 million into the credit markets (that means it bought that amount in securities with its cash). This easy money set off a wave of domestic speculation in the U.S. (Kindleberger 1973, 69–70)

The Dawes Plan had provided breathing room, but as 1928 loomed with the first full payment of $595 million, the Germans complained again. The **Young Plan** of 1929 (named after Owen Young of General Electric) modified the Dawes Plan, provided another loan, and placed a terminal year of 1988 for payments. The Allies ended their occupation of the Rhineland early in 1930 as a reward for the Germans accepting this. The Saar remained under French control until 1935. Again, had the Americans shared the burden, perhaps the occupation of the Rhineland would have gone on until 1935, which would have been a good thing.

ORIGINS OF THE GREAT DEPRESSION

Charles Kindleberger provided a short summary that accounts for much of the problem of the Depression. Even when it was not Europe's largest economy, Britain had provided leadership in the financial world until 1913. This meant that Britain was willing to sacrifice some of its interests to build a larger system (the gold standard and free trade) that suited Britain. After the war, it refused to do so while the United States, the world's largest economy, would not assert any leadership role in finance until 1936. (Kindleberger 1973, 28)

Warning Signs in the United States

General causes for an economic downturn included deflationary pressures from rapid productivity gains in the U.S. Building on agricultural demand from World War I, wheat production rose 12.3% from 1921 to 1928 while the U.S. farm population fell by 3.7%. From 1910, there was a 44 percent growth in wheat production as the population fell. Inevitably this led to a fall in prices in a significant sector and blighted incomes and caused bankruptcies. The value of farm mortgages in the U.S. had almost tripled from 1910 to 1925. Canadian, Argentinian, Australian, Brazilian, Polish, South African, Romanian, Hungarian, Yugoslavian and German farms also had large debts. The return to gold tended to put downward pressure on raw material prices because it limited the money supply. Many farmers across the western world had borrowed money to buy the new farm equipment running on internal combustion engines. (Kindleberger 1973, 97) Farm prices not only fell from their inflated wartime level, but from 1925 to 1929, prices fell for wheat, corn, oats, wool, hogs, and cotton. (Clingan, 54) Since farmers still made up 22 percent of the American workforce, this had a considerable impact, and the government refused to bail them out. The only feasible response was to increase production, which forced prices still lower. The plight of the farmers became much worse in the 1930s as drought stretched out over many years and dust bowls consumed the more marginal lands that had been farmed profitably since the 1870s. While running for President in 1928, **Herbert Hoover** promised to protect American farmers with tariffs. (Kindleberger 1973, 77)

Since farm products made up almost two-fifths of world trade and employed two-thirds of the world's people, the crash in farm prices spread around the world. (Kindleberger 1973, 86; Aldcroft, 219) By the end of 1927, Australia and the Dutch East Indies were in recession because of falling wheat and sugar prices, respectively. Germany and Brazil joined them in 1928. In the first half of 1929, Argentina, Canada and Poland fell into recession. Farm prices plunged further in 1930 when Soviet Russia dumped twenty-three times more wheat on the world market than in 1929 in response to Stalin's Five-Year Plan. Because of the collapsing prices, the USSR only netted ten times as much money. Stalin doubled the exports of wheat in 1931, but the price of wheat fell by half, leaving the Soviets where they were in 1930. (Kindleberger 1973, 93)

Credit and the Stock Exchange

In 1929, the U.S. was a large creditor nation. The American boom of the 1920s had disguised growing structural problems, especially growing inequality. The Republicans in 1921 had passed a massive tax giveaway to the rich. By 1929, twenty-seven thousand families with the highest annual incomes had as much money as the eleven million families at the bottom. The top 1 percent held 38 percent of all the wealth in the

U.S. (Hall and Ferguson, 21) (In 2010, they had 40 percent of the wealth). The two hundred largest American corporations controlled half of the corporate assets. The top 1 percent of all financial institutions controlled 46 percent of the nation's banking business. This inequality blighted the American consumer market. The National Bureau of Economic Research actually dates the beginning of American economic decline to June 1929, four months before the crash. As dark clouds gathered, the one bright spot seemed to be the New York Stock Exchange, which continued rising in 1929. The Dow Jones Industrial Average, made up of a small number of high-quality firms, doubled in twenty-one months. The low interest rates and the crash of the Berlin stock market in 1927 made New York very attractive. Many people bought stock **on margin**. This means they put down only a fraction of the value to buy stock. The rest is borrowed but if they face a **margin call**, they must put up the rest of the money or sell the stock. In 1929, the Fed tightened credit by pressuring New York banks not to lend, and in September it raised the discount rate. (Kindleberger, 1973, 108–16) This caught investors in a borrowing spiral as they tried to meet stock purchases. Others had to sell more and more stock, and when there were not sufficient buyers, the price of stock fell.

On "**Black Tuesday**," October 29, 1929, the market crashed and would continue to fall for four years. In just two months, it lost half of its value. In nominal terms, the stock market lost 89 percent of its value. Since this was a time of deflation, the loss was 67 percent in real terms. It did not recover its value until 1954. By comparison, the U.S. stock market fell 65 percent from 2000 to 2009, and some indices have still not recovered in real terms as of the end of 2014. Financial companies were especially hard hit with the Shenandoah Corporation, for example, losing 99 percent of its value. In one week, the price of U.S. Steel stock went from $262 to $22 per share. The New York Fed desperately tried to support the market by purchasing hundreds of millions of dollars in securities. (Kindleberger 1973, 118–9)

Hoover cheerfully signed the **Hawley-Smoot Tariff** (1930) which put high tariffs on most manufactured goods. Other nations responded from the time the House of Representatives passed the tariff in May 1929. (Kindleberger 1973, 131) It showed that the United States would not be a responsible economic leader. More than sixty nations retaliated against American products. (Hall and Ferguson, 71) World trade collapsed by 69 percent from April 1929 to February 1933. (Kindleberger 1973, 172) Maldistribution of wealth became a crucial problem when the market crashed. Workers were fired and could not buy goods, thus leading to more layoffs. The U.S. lost 38 percent of its GDP from 1929 to 1932. Thirteen million were unemployed. Treasury Secretary Mellon urged that nothing be done. Hoover made the Depression even worse by insisting on a balanced budget. In bad economic times, with consumers not spending, the government is the only force that can step in to spend money and get the economy rolling again. But in 1931, Hoover ordered massive budget cuts, and in 1932 he ordered major tax increases. (Hall and Ferguson, 105–6) This brutal and mistaken fiscal policy of austerity (repeated in Germany) is what caused the Depression to bite the deepest in the United States and Germany. Hoover gradually decided that government and business should act together, and the government bought up some crops and created a few jobs. But these were drops in an ocean, and Hoover would not unbalance the budget. The President would not allow federal funds to be used for individual relief. The **Reconstruction Finance Corporation** (1932) gave loans to big businesses such as banks, railroads, and insurance companies.

CONTAGION

What made the Depression so bad was what followed the crash. As the big holders of gold, the U.S. and France had more flexibility, but neither contributed to rebalance the gold flows. France had made the opposite mistake of Britain and devalued too much, so that gold was constantly flowing into France. The War and democratization of politics had weakened credibility; now cooperation collapsed. Power at the Fed shifted from New York, desperate to provide credit to the markets, to Washington's Federal Reserve Board of Governors, which opposed monetary expansion. (Kindleberger 1973, 136) Mellon's call for liquidation was matched by the Fed: the Depression should be a cleansing process. The Fed, in an amazing display of incompetence, soaked up desperately needed cash and reduced the money supply. (Hall and Ferguson, 88–9) Then in autumn 1931, the Fed raised the discount rate. The goal was to prevent gold from leaving the U.S. but in a time of deflation, sky-high real interest rates made borrowing very difficult. Today, the Federal Reserve Open Market Committee (FOMC) has replaced that Board of Governors. (101)

The U.S. had loaned $6.4 billion abroad between 1924 and 1929. $3 billion went to Europe, $1.6 billion to Latin America, and $1.2 billion to Canada. (Kindleberger 1973, 56) The pace of U.S. lending lessened by half in 1929 and the U.S. received a surplus of investment. In 1930, the American institutions declined to renew short-term loans to Germany, worsening that country's recession. Both the U.S. and Germany insisted on a deflationary policy to try to build budget surpluses, which took even more money out of the economy. In Germany, the economy collapsed faster than the government could raise taxes, but in the U.S., surplus budgets were run through 1931.

In Soviet Russia, the Five-Year Plan's crash industrialization instituted by Joseph Stalin not only killed millions of people, but caused the value of imports to fall by 60 percent from 1931 to 1932, and another 33 percent from 1932 to 1934. (Kindleberger 1973, 232) Germany was not getting loans and could not gain money through exports to Russia or elsewhere.

The first moves were monetary. Most central banks cut their interest rates. However, because deflation was accelerating, the **real interest rates** in most nations rose. Once a country approaches 0 percent interest rate, monetary policy becomes ineffective. One is "pushing on a string": that means you are offering money for nothing and begging people to spend but if there is no mechanism to put the money into the hands of businesses and (especially) consumers, it will not bring recovery. One by one, nations devalued their currencies and jumped off the gold standard. Britain surprised the world by leaving gold in September 1931 and the pound fell to a level of $3.50, perhaps where it should have been all along. (Kindleberger 1973, 162) The United States under Franklin Roosevelt left gold in March 1933. By 1931, industrial unemployment had reached 25 percent in the U.S., 21 percent in Britain, and 34 percent in Germany. Small wonder that Hitler seemed more attractive and, with the occupation ended, the Allies could do little to restrain him.

Hoover was an internationalist who had gained fame for his relief work in Europe after the War and had been Secretary of Commerce from 1921 to 1929. He tried to take some positive international steps as president, in contrast to his dismal domestic record. Identifying the reparations/war debt problem as the key, he issued the **Hoover Moratorium** (1931) freezing payments. The **Lausanne Treaty** (1932) effectively ended the reparations payments. Of the debtor nations from World War I, only Finland repaid the U.S. in full. In 1934, Germany under Hitler defaulted on the Dawes and Young loans.

Britain

The 1929 election was critical for the British economy. The Liberal Party had been losing ground for years to the mildly socialistic Labour Party. In 1929, the Liberals had an economic plan written by the Cambridge University economist **John Maynard Keynes**. It called for ambitious social spending in order to stimulate the stagnant British economy. Unfortunately, Labour prevailed, and its leader Ramsay MacDonald became Prime Minister. As the Depression hit, Keynes called for spending to stimulate the economy. In 1931, MacDonald resigned but to everyone's surprise, he re-emerged as Prime Minister over a largely Conservative "National Coalition" government. MacDonald's government turned to deflation that was not as severe as Hoover's policy. Britain concluded the **Ottawa Agreements** in the summer of 1932: Commonwealth nations (those that were part of the British empire) won import preferences for their food even as tariff barriers stopped other nations' manufactures. Britain also offered subsidies to its farmers.

The Depression in Germany

Germany had begun an economic downturn in 1928 when American long-term loans dwindled. In 1930, American firms declined to renew their short-term credits, and the Depression hit Germany full blast because the value of short-term loans made up about 60 percent of all foreign loans. (Kindleberger 1973, 138) German unemployment more than doubled from September 1929 to September 1930. The moderate socialist government rejected a budget in February 1930 that would have borrowed money to close the budget deficit. A major problem of socialist politicians was their inability to understand or apply creative financial solutions. They tended to embrace conservative austerity plans while the liberals tended to favor unorthodox solutions. The socialists in Germany, like the Labour Party in Britain, had no idea how to deal with the Depression. When the government rejected borrowing, the conservative parties demanded cuts in unemployment benefits. The socialists refused to enact this and resigned, believing that this would absolve them of responsibility for the Depression.

A conservative government led by **Heinrich Brüning** took power. It ordered a cut in unemployment benefits. When the Parliament rejected the decree, Brüning called for new elections. Unemployment benefits are in fact one of the best ways of fighting depression because they, like food assistance, put money directly into the hands of those most likely to spend it immediately and stimulate the economy. Increasingly desperate German men and women had been watching the antics of the socialists and conservatives and voted in growing numbers for the most radical parties: the Communists who called for a Russian-style system and the Nazis led by Adolf Hitler.

Although the electors had rejected him, Brüning continued to lead the government and proposed to bring the same austerity used by Hoover in the United States. He issued decrees to raise taxes, cut spending, and exalted a balanced budget above everything else. These emergency decrees got people used to authoritarian rule. When the program failed and caused more suffering, it discredited the government and led to more extremism. In June 1931, Brüning announced that Germany would pay no more reparations and issued another austerity decree. This triggered a massive flow of gold out of Germany and a consequent bank crisis. The major banks became insolvent or were nationalized. The number of German unemployed rose another 50 percent between

September 1930 and September 1931, then another 20 percent by September 1932. The Communists and Nazis gained more and more votes. Brüning even rejected a massive French loan offer in 1931 that would have stabilized the economy because he wanted to get rid of reparations.

Hitler

German officials had successfully used deficit spending to pull Germany out of recession in 1926. They had cut taxes and expanded spending programs and urged the government to repeat these moves. Brüning resigned in failure in May 1932. Eight months later, Hitler became Chancellor and began his infamous dictatorship. Hitler and the Nazis had no economic program or expertise beyond a simple demand: put Germans back to work. Freed of Brüning's ideology, the officials found ways to create money and spend it on public works and military projects. Germany stopped paying reparations and repudiated most of its foreign debt. In 1935, the government drafted hundreds of thousands of young men into the army. Germany effectively paid for all this by monetizing national assets, which was far less painful than Stalin's Five-Year Plan. Germany could not have kept this up forever, but in the short run it cured the Depression.

Fascist Economics

Hitler in Germany, the Italian dictator Benito Mussolini (ruled 1922–1943), and others belonged to Fascist political movements. Mussolini wrote that Fascism was for the state and against the individual because "outside the State there can be neither individuals nor groups. . . . Fascism is opposed to socialism, which confines the movement of history within the class struggle and ignores the unity of classes established in one economic and moral reality in the State." Fascism glorified the nation-state and held it supreme to all else. The people of one nation were to dominate all other nations. Their economic views strongly opposed those of Adam Smith and his liberal followers. The free market was not an ideal. The state needed to guide the economy and at times control it. Nazi Germany and Fascist Italy smashed labor unions and forced workers to accept lower pay and benefits. They opposed free trade. They believed that every nation should be self-sufficient in farm produce and in all manufactures. They increased trade barriers and engaged in **import substitution**. This means the government supports domestic industries and keeps out foreign-made goods, even if the domestic industry is very inefficient, expensive, and unproductive. Adam Smith was proved right once again as these policies reduced the standard of living of Italy, which had a head start on Germany. This almost ensured that fascist nations would destroy themselves while communist countries lasted decades despite doubtful economic ideas. Communism also was more aggressive in bringing down wealthy people than fascism. As long as they made certain sacrifices, the fascists would allow the rich to keep most of their property.

The Italian fascist government after 1922 reduced unemployment by starting huge public works and transportation programs and extended social insurance programs. The massive budget deficits weakened the financial structure. The fascist attempt to make Italy self-sufficient in grain simply distorted trade and made bread more expensive. Mussolini wanted a strong currency, but his increasing of the lira's value devastated exports by making Italian goods too expensive on the world market. (Aldcroft, 204) By 1930, Italy's per capita GDP was 15 percent below its level of 1918 and had fallen behind those of Spain and Ireland, traditionally two of the poorest countries in Western Europe. (Maddison 2001, 194, 198) Mussolini did not touch structural problems such as the social and political backwardness of the south, banditry, the Mafia, malaria, and income maldistribution. Mussolini's foreign policy became more aggressive as he tried to distract people from the economic woes.

FRANKLIN ROOSEVELT AND THE NEW DEAL

By 1932, the American economy had hit bottom. Cities were going bankrupt. Homeless families built "Hoovervilles" of boxes and rusty sheet metal. Thousands of tramps roamed the countryside. In July 1932, twenty thousand unemployed veterans marched on Washington. They demanded war bonuses promised by the government. Washington had intended to pay these bonuses from the proceeds of war debt repayments. Two thousand veterans refused to leave and built Hoovervilles. Hoover sent in the army under General Douglas MacArthur to break them up.

The Democrats nominated New York Governor **Franklin D. Roosevelt** (FDR) for President in 1932. FDR had sponsored relief measures in New York, but his campaign was short of specifics and indeed called for maintaining the balanced budget. To many he was too eager to please everyone. Roosevelt called for a **New Deal**, which would consist of "bold, persistent experimentation." FDR was elected overwhelmingly, and Democrats swept into control of Congress.

Between the November election and the March inauguration, the American banking system crumbled. The Fed districts in the farm belt — Chicago, Minneapolis, Kansas City, and St. Louis — led the way in bank failures. (Kindleberger 1973, 96) By March 4, 1933, 80 percent of states had suspended banking operations. 45 percent of all the banks had failed. (Hall and Ferguson, 83) FDR called Congress into special session, declared a bank holiday, and forbade the export of gold. Congress gave the President the power to issue new greenbacks unbacked by gold and to fix the price of gold by proclamation. (Kindleberger 1973, 202) FDR set it at $35 per ounce, 69 percent higher than the pre-New Deal level. Congress passed an emergency bank law reopening banks under Treasury Department licenses. The **Federal Deposit Insurance Corporation (FDIC)** would guarantee deposits of the ordinary saver. The **Home Owners Loan Corporation** would refinance mortgages and prevent foreclosures. The **Securities and Exchange Commission (SEC)** forced full disclosure of all stock issues. In April, the U.S. abandoned the gold standard.

FDR and Congress also dealt with unemployment: the National Recovery Act set minimum wages and maximum hours. Workers gained the right to bargain collectively. Business codes outlawed child labor. The Works Progress Administration set up public works and work relief. The New Deal was enormously popular even if it did not end the Depression right away: Democrats picked up seats in the midterm elections. Repudiating Hawley-Smoot, Roosevelt committed the U.S. to freer trade and concluded a number of agreements with Latin American nations. (Kindleberger 1973, 236–7)

The farm problem was especially difficult. The government gave agricultural subsidies while limiting production. This saved thousands of farmers. Droughts in 1934 and 1936 created **dust bowl** conditions in much of the American Midwest. The wind blew the soil away. Farmers abandoned marginal lands such as eastern Montana that had experienced unusual rainfall from the 1890s to 1920. Bad farming practices had worsened the dust bowl conditions. Terrifying dust storms created blackout conditions. The U.S. actually had to import corn from Argentina because drought destroyed so much of the crop. (Kindleberger 1973, 96) The government used the hydroelectric dam and nitrate plants of the Tennessee River Valley, one of poorest regions, to develop, reforest, and industrialize the area.

The U.S. per capita GDP grew by 7 percent in 1934 and 1935, but it remained 20 percent below the 1929 peak. Roosevelt moved to more aggressive actions in 1935, including old-age pensions and unemployment insurance to be paid by payroll tax. Still fearing an unbalanced budget, the government raised taxes on the rich. The Wagner Act of 1935 established the National Labor Relations Board to restrain employers from unfair labor practices. The U.S. established a minimum wage at forty cents an hour. The U.S. per capita GDP grew by 13.5% in 1936. (Maddison 2001, 196) Commercial loans became more available, and the government injected money into the economy when it finally paid its veterans their promised bonuses. Gross industrial production passed the 1929 level. (Kindleberger 1973, 262) The massive oil discoveries in East Texas boosted production. It seemed that the U.S. was about to come out of the Depression. FDR had campaigned on the balanced budget and in 1933 cut federal salaries and veterans benefits. (202) In 1937, the Fed raised bank reserve requirements in order to reduce credit. The federal budget deficit was cut in half, and Roosevelt planned to end deficit spending by 1939. (266–74)

Republicans gleefully denounced the resulting "Roosevelt recession." Keynes had published his key book in 1936 showing how budget deficit spending can stimulate a depressed economy. It had some influence on Roosevelt's advisers at the Fed and in the Treasury Department and they set up a single disastrous meeting between the President and the British economist. Finally, in 1938, FDR proposed a relaxing of credit reserves and a massive public works and spending program financed by borrowed money. It would triple the federal budget deficit. At the end of 1939, per capita GDP passed the 1929 level. The Depression in the U.S. was over. It is sometimes said erroneously by right-wingers that World War II, not the New Deal and deficit spending, ended the Depression. Unemployment is always a lagging indicator, and there were still many Americans out of work even in 1941 who were absorbed by the rapid increase in the military, but they would have been employed in a peacetime economy.

LATIN AMERICA

The Great Depression had a catastrophic effect on Latin America as the demand for raw materials from industrial nations plummeted and world prices collapsed. The total value of exports fell by half from 1929 to 1934. The Depression discredited the political elites. Fascist economic ideas had an impact here, particularly before 1943 when Germany and Italy seemed to be advancing. Economies became more self-sufficient and integrated and provided jobs for working-class men. Industrialization in Argentina, Brazil, and Mexico created a new class of factory workers. Much of this industrialization was in military goods. The farm depression caused a massive loss of gold in Argentina from 1929 to 1933. Argentina abandoned the gold standard in December 1929. (Kindleberger 1973, 101–2) In 1930, army officers took over in Argentina and Brazil. As part of a move to inflate prices and win votes in silver-mining states, Roosevelt instituted massive purchasing of silver. This disrupted the Mexican currency, which was on a silver standard. (235) Lazaro Cardenas in Mexico organized a strong government, carried out land reform to break up the big estates, and set up the Mexican Revolutionary Party (PRM) based on four sectors: peasants, labor, military, and the middle class. Cardenas' one-party state borrowed aspects of Italian fascism and expropriated foreign oil holdings.

JAPAN

After World War I, Japan had introduced more democracy, including universal male suffrage in 1925. From 1924 to 1932 the parliamentary majority ruled and passed pro-labor legislation, national health insurance, and labor disputes mediation. The military share of the budget shrank from 42 percent in 1922 to 28 percent in 1927.

After 1926, criticism grew of governments that were influenced by Mitsui or Mitsubishi. The Depression hurt Japanese exports terribly: they lost 50 percent of their value, and Japanese wages fell by 31 percent. The collapse in farm prices impoverished rural Japan. Farmers blamed this on the political parties working hand-in-hand with the big corporations. In January 1930, the worst possible time, Japan returned to the gold standard using prewar parity, precisely the same mistake Britain had made in 1925. (Kindleberger 1973, 23) A year later, Japan left the gold standard and some recovery began. It used both monetary and fiscal policy to revive the economy. **Korekiyo Takahashi** became Finance Minister at the end of 1931 and massively expanded government spending in 1932, 1933 and 1934. With the yen off gold, Japanese exports became cheaper and Japan was able to expand its markets, especially in East Asia. (167) Japan flooded its empire (Taiwan, Korea, Manchuria, and Kwantung) with exports. (282) Takahashi controlled foreign exchange to prevent gold from flowing out of Japan and oversaw a reduction in interest rates even as the Bank of Japan increased the money supply eightfold.

In 1931, the Japanese military attacked Manchuria without authorization because it feared that the Nationalists were revitalizing the Chinese government. An ultranationalist murdered the last of the Japanese party prime ministers because the Premier had opposed the Manchurian war. After that came "cabinets of national unity" that included military officers. Takahashi increased spending by 70 percent, and by 1936, Japan reached full employment because of this strong monetary and fiscal stimulus. He tried to cut military spending at that point. This would aid Japan's economy, because military spending tends to be the least efficient and stimulative aspect of government spending. Increasing military spending tends to reduce GDP over time. A soldier then murdered Takahashi. From 1932 to 1935, the Japanese government systematically purged left-wing elements because they had criticized the emperor, who some regarded as a god-like figure. The religious interpretation of the Japanese state became official. The end of German democracy also made a big impression.

After a coup attempt, the cabinet was mostly made of military officers and bloated the military spending. In December 1936, Japan signed an anti-Soviet Pact with Germany. Japanese voters soundly rejected the government: in 1937 the pro-government party won only nineteen seats out of 466, but the government ignored the voters.

THE SCANDINAVIAN RESPONSE AND THE "WELFARE STATE"

The Great Depression hit Scandinavia hard. Unemployment reached 31.5% in Sweden, 42.5% in Norway, and 42.8% in

Denmark. Class conflicts worsened as companies tried to employ strike-breakers. Scandinavian Nazis founded parties in the 1930s. In 1933, the Social Democrats in Denmark and Sweden made alliances with the agrarian parties to gain support in exchange for farm subsidies, lower farm taxes, and a currency devaluation to stimulate farm exports. The Swedes put in a modest program of public works financed by increased inheritance taxes. Only Sweden and Japan increased the value of their exports more than industrial production. (Kindleberger 1973, 182–3)

Cooperative movements had long dominated agriculture and large-scale democratic Folk Schools had fostered a similar culture which brought classes together. Laws banned strike-breaking and enacted national paid holidays in the 1930s. Danish taxes rose 30 percent and Swedish taxes 50 percent to pay for an extensive program of social insurance, including unemployment insurance, old-age pensions, public works to put the unemployed to work, and payments to farmers and fishermen. The Norwegian government guaranteed every schoolchild in Oslo a free breakfast. Sweden's and Norway's GNP grew by 50 percent in the 1930s, while the rest of the continent, except for Germany and the Soviet Union, was mired in Depression.

The Scandinavian countries pioneered the use of controlled deficit spending on the Keynesian model. They also led the way in deliberate redistribution of income that lessened inequality and stimulated consumer spending. Before the Depression, only Britain during the Napoleonic Wars had engaged in significant redistribution. That peaked at 2.7% of GDP in 1820/1 and fell thereafter. (Lindert, I, 7) The rise of democracy at the end of the nineteenth century gave the lower classes some political power. Longer life expectancies created a demand for old-age pensions. (21) The Soviet model of aggressive redistribution was also an influence to some degree. The Soviet Union, though poor, devoted considerable resources to child care, public housing, education, and pensions. (213)

In the eighty years since the Scandinavians set up the "welfare state," it has been proved that higher taxes and transfer do not harm productivity or economic growth. This is because the governments give generously to general education and work training that increase the value of their human capital. Early pensions remove less productive employees from the workplace. (227–8) Inequality by itself worsens health which in turn reduces productivity. (259) After World War II, the Scandinavian countries kept building on their success and had some of the fastest growth rates in Europe. Today, they are among the richest nations with the longest life expectancies and lowest infant mortalities.

THE ECONOMICS OF THE SECOND WORLD WAR

In the late 1930s, more nations imitated Germany, the Soviet Union, and Japan and increased their military budgets paid for by borrowing. This is sometimes called "military Keynesianism." Britain was bouncing back from the Depression three years before rearmament boosted its economy.

The war itself had diverse impacts on economies. In the early years, Japan and Germany extended their economic gains by doing more of the same. They profited off of plunder from their conquered lands. But this dependence on plunder meant that when expansion stopped, as symbolized by the losses at Midway in June 1942 and Stalingrad in January 1943, their economies suffered greatly. At that point, they had been diverting resources from productive purposes to the military for ten years, and their economies were strained. Even if the Axis powers could have negotiated a peace in 1943, I suspect they would have collapsed economically within several years. The war drew out Britain's last reserves. It harnessed its aged industrial equipment one last time to hold off Germany's onslaught. But even before Pearl Harbor, Britain became the financial ward of the United States. This led to later complaints that Britain had "lost" the war and the fantasy that somehow there could have been a permanent understanding with Germany that would have allowed Britain to modernize itself.

The war had both strong positive and negative impacts upon the Soviet Union. The German invasion seemed to justify Stalin's harsh policies. It necessitated the building of new industrial centers in the Urals. Raw material production boomed in the war years. The USSR also got to plunder occupied areas of central and eastern Europe, although the harvest from these "bloodlands" was rather less than what the Germans had reaped. The USSR ended the war as the second-largest economy in the world and used this to gain some benefits in the postwar economic world. The negative side was appalling. The staggering loss of life and the destruction in the most developed areas of the Soviet Union took years to repair.

In contrast, the war was an almost unalloyed blessing for the United States. By 1939, American per hour productivity vastly exceeded all other nations. If something happened to create full employment, both the total and per capita numbers would surge as the economy absorbed the unemployed. This is precisely what happened when the war served as the catalyst. The country achieved full employment while having its territory virtually undamaged by enemy attacks. The damage to its economic rivals allowed the U.S. to shape the postwar world to its liking.

CONCLUSION

The era of the Depression and World War II fundamentally transformed the economic world. Wealthy elites, hurt by the inflation of the 1920s, saw their power broken by the collapse of the banking and financial sectors. The political will of the masses could triumph at last, and the elites feared that the alternative was communism. The ideas of a balanced budget and austerity for their own sakes were discredited. Governments borrowed more money, put people to work, and then put money in their pockets so they could boost consumer spending. Keynes provided the intellectual justification for these actions. The Depression brought in militaristic regimes in Germany and Japan, and they started a new war. The military consumed much of the new spending, and the spread of World War II accelerated all the trends. Nearly all adults contributed to the war effort as soldiers or workers. Taxing, borrowing, spending, and planning all reached new heights with governments learning the lessons from the First World War. Losses offset gains in the war-torn areas of Europe and Asia, but the United States emerged in 1945 as the supreme economy with the Soviet Union a distant second.

TIMELINE

1907	Financial panic
1913	U.S. Federal Reserve Bank established
1925	Churchill returned U.K. to gold at wrong rate
1927	Recession began to spread across world
1929	New York stock market crash
1930–32	Brüning austerity policy in Germany
1930	Hawley-Smoot Tariff

1931	Britain left gold standard
	World War II began in Asia
1931/2	Military seized power in Japan
1933	Hitler seized power in Germany
	Roosevelt became U.S. President
1939–45	World War II in Europe
1941	U.S. entered World War II
1945	War ended: Germany, Italy, Japan defeated

KEY TERMS

Panic of 1907
on margin
"Black Tuesday"
Hawley-Smoot Tariff
Heinrich Brüning
New Deal
Federal Deposit Insurance Corporation
Securities and Exchange Commission

Chapter 15

THE MODERN ECONOMIC STRUCTURE SINCE 1945

THE AGE OF KEYNES

John Maynard Keynes, Adam Smith, and Karl Marx are the most influential economic thinkers of the modern age. Keynes grew up in an upper middle class household, the son of an economist in late nineteenth-century England, and enjoyed a comfortable life. As a young man, he was attracted to the artistic and philosophical life but received a degree in mathematics. Unlike Smith or Marx, he was a government policymaker. When the British government declined to accept his advice on postwar reparations, he resigned and returned to Cambridge University as a professor. Keynes' politics were liberal at a time when Britons increasingly voted for the Conservative or Labour Party. He called Marx's work "not only scientifically erroneous but without interest or application to the modern world." Keynes largely invented the branch of economics called **macroeconomics** that studies total spending, investment, and employment. He published the summation of his work in *The General Theory of Employment, Interest, and*

Money (1936). Previous economists had focused on small-scale economic relationships and prices. This led them to a belief that economies adjusted themselves just as prices should in theory adjust to changes in supply and demand. If you add consumer spending, business investment, and government spending, you get **aggregate demand**. Falling spending can feed on itself without ever adjusting. Growing numbers of people lose their jobs and consumer spending collapses, which throws more people out of work. Frightened investors will delay or cancel investment, costing even more jobs. Thus, if consumer spending and/or business investment declines, the government must step in to keep up the demand until the other spending recovers. At that point, the government should gradually reduce its spending or it will risk price inflation. **Fiscal policy** refers to deliberate government decisions to run a budget surplus or deficit. It can cut or raise taxes or cut or raise spending in order to maintain a proper level of aggregate demand. Just as falling spending feeds upon itself, the injection of money acts as a multiplier because it encourages consumer spending and business investment. Macroeconomic study over the last seventy years has figured out how large multipliers are. The most effective spending is putting cash into the hands of those with none, such as food stamps or unemployment insurance. Recipients immediately spend the money and send it into other parts of the economy.

Keynes' work built on governments' experience in modern finance. There had been "public works" back to the days of most ancient history. Germany in the 1920s and 1930s made effective use of fiscal policy. Japan also used a broad stimulus program before Keynes' theories were widely known. With his 1936 book, Keynes' explanation of why fiscal policy works became widely influential, especially among younger economists in the United States. Keynes was also successful investing the funds of Cambridge University and his own money and died a very rich man. Keynes' reputation rose steadily in the 1930s as he was proved right on every matter. He had criticized reparations, he had warned against the gold standard, he had said deflation must be avoided at all costs, and he had urged international cooperation.

SETTING UP A NEW STRUCTURE

As World War II expanded after 1939 and damaged or destroyed other leading economies, the position of the United States became ever more powerful. The financial part of the U.S. government was dominated by Keynesians and others determined to avoid the mistakes of the 1920s and 1930s. Austerity never created prosperity, and the trade wars and lack of cooperation had worsened the Depression. Economic problems had encouraged the extremist movements of fascism and communism, so economic growth was vitally necessary.

By 1941, only Britain and the United States were left as the big liberal democracies. But they hardly had an equal relationship. The U.S. economy was three times larger than that of Britain, and the latter desperately needed help against Germany. In August 1941, even before the United States came into World War II, it issued the **Atlantic Charter** with Britain which called for lowering trade barriers, promoting global cooperation, and reducing inequality by relieving people around the world of fear and want. These were the goals of Roosevelt's Democratic administration, not Churchill's Conservative party. Starting in February 1942, the Americans concluded a series of **Lend-Lease Agreements**. Britain, the Soviet Union, and other nations accepted up to $50 billion in assistance to fight the Axis of Germany, Japan, and Italy. The U.S. did not want a repeat of the war debt debacle. Under

Article VII of the Agreement, repayment would consist of cooperation in achieving the goals of the Atlantic Charter. In a taste of things to come, the U.S. Treasury forced a British rayon manufacturer to sell its American subsidiary. (Kindleberger 1993, 414) Keynes, negotiating for the British, bitterly objected to the trade provisions of Article VII, but the British had no choice.

Bretton Woods

Keynes traveled to the United States in July 1944 for the United Nations Monetary and Financial Conference, held in Bretton Woods, New Hampshire. The British government sent Keynes because he had the best chance of influencing American officials to create a financial structure that would guarantee postwar assistance to Britain. Bretton Woods established the **International Monetary Fund (IMF)** and capitalized it at $8.8 billion. The IMF would be a pool of capital that the developed nations could draw upon. Its main job was to balance flows of capital among countries. If a country ran a persistent outflow, the IMF would step in to prevent a crisis and would impose reforms in exchange for aid. This would prevent a repeat of the flow problems of the late 1920s where Germany and Britain lost gold while the United States and France accumulated gold. The United States was given virtual veto power over IMF grants. The conference also established the International Bank for Reconstruction and Development (today known as the **World Bank**) at $10 billion. This bank helped nations rebuild war damage and provided money to less developed countries. It started operating in the summer 1946.

Bretton Woods ratified the abandonment of the gold standard. The U.S. had fixed the value of gold at $35 per ounce, but since 1934 ownership of gold bullion was only permissible by license of the Treasury Department for export or industrial purposes. Other countries put in similar provisions. Under Bretton Woods, foreign countries could turn in their dollars for gold bullion at the official rate. The dollar would then be the standard against which all other currencies would be measured. Currencies (except for that of the USSR) would be freely convertible and were fixed against the dollar, but there were provisions by which the value could be changed so there would not be a repeat of Britain's mistaken valuation of 1925. In 1958, Western European nations were allowed greater flexibility to move their currencies up and down where needed so that minute adjustments could be made when economic relations changed. Britain's financial leadership was gone for good.

Finally, Bretton Woods called for the establishment of an International Trade Organization. This body would function like an international court by arbitrating trade disputes so they would not degenerate into the destructive trade wars as in the past.

Postwar Pressure

Japan's surrender in August 1945 brought an end to World War II. The U.S. suddenly terminated Lend-Lease assistance at the end of the month, much to the displeasure of Britain and the Soviet Union. The U.S. forgave $20 billion of British assistance but insisted on $650 million, payable with interest over the next fifty years. The USSR asked for a $10 billion loan, but the U.S. only offered a $1 billion loan from the Export-Import Bank. When the Soviets applied, the Director first claimed that the application had been "lost." The British sent Keynes across the ocean again, hoping for a blanket forgiveness of all Lend-Lease help and additional grants.

To Keynes' shock, the Americans only offered a $4 billion loan at interest, conditional on Britain making its currency convertible within a year and ending trade discrimination against American-made goods by 1956. (Kindleberger 1993, 419) Having no choice, Keynes agreed. Within a few months, the century's greatest economist was dead from heart failure. The French also had to come to Washington to beg for a $550 million loan from the Export-Import Bank. They had to promise to limit nationalization measures and open access to American goods. There was no doubt that the U.S. was going to play hardball to get its way. The Soviet Union had sent delegates to Bretton Woods, secured the third-largest quota of votes and exemption from currency convertibility, but declined to ratify the agreement in December 1945.

Trade

Despite the loan, the British financial position became desperate. As promised in the loan agreement, Britain restored currency convertibility in July 1947, but so much capital flowed out of Britain that it suspended that provision seven weeks later. Though the war had been over for two years, Britain was still rationing food and other key materials. France in 1947 had food rationing more severe than the worst point in the war. Western Europe was producing only 91 percent of its food level of the mid-1930s. (Milward, 17) There were follow-up meetings on Bretton Woods' International Trade Organization in Geneva and London. Oddly, the Soviet Union was invited but never responded positively or negatively. In March 1948, fifty-three nations signed the ITO Charter in Havana. Following Keynes' recommendation, the goal was to keep trade balanced with no nation running a persistent trade surplus or deficit. (Kindleberger 1993, 419) The agreement would protect the rights of workers while committing all parties to a full-employment policy. American corporations opposed this, and the U.S. Senate refused even to schedule a vote on the ITO, so it died.

While the ITO was being negotiated, there were also discussions about a provisional treaty. Twenty-three nations signed the **General Agreement on Tariffs and Trade (GATT)** in 1947. It committed nations to lower trade barriers. This was followed by a series of "rounds" of negotiations that culminated in new treaties as ever more nations around the world signed. The last successful round (called the "Uruguay round") culminated in 1995 with the formation of the **World Trade Organization (WTO)** which carried out many of the functions of the stillborn ITO. Neither GATT nor WTO said anything about workers' rights or full employment.

Marshall Plan

More than ever, reserves were flowing out of Asia and Europe and into the United States. In 1947, West Europe lost one-third of its gold reserves. (Milward, 45) A country that removed barriers on the movement of capital, as Britain did for seven weeks, risked losing massive amounts of precious reserves. The U.S. recognized that this risked a replay of 1930/31 unless it forced funds out. Interest rate policies and open-market operations could not balance the flow. The Truman Administration also decided that as political conflicts grew with the USSR, the western German economy had to be revived and reindustrialized. In June 1947, American Secretary of State George Marshall announced a plan for European recovery. The U.S. had contributed to a United Nations recovery fund in 1945 but was frustrated by its inability to direct or control the spending. The **Marshall Plan** (officially "the European

Recovery Plan" or ERP) was ordered by American rules. The Soviet Union and the communist countries refused to accept the money as long as those rules were attached.

When it took effect in mid-1948, France received 60 percent of interim ERP aid, giving it a lift. This ensured that France raised no objections to the trade negotiations or the Americans' political reordering of western Germany. Britain received the next largest share of aid. Some $13 billion of aid was sent by the U.S. to Europe on top of a previous $13 billion. This helped to balance the outflow. The U.S. was a safe haven and a good economic investment. In 1948, Germany issued yet another new currency, the deutschmark. In September 1949, Britain devalued the pound sterling from $4.02 to $2.80. The pound was not fully convertible against the dollar until 1958. (Kindleberger 1993, 434) This marked a 31 percent devaluation and finally solved the British currency problem. France followed by devaluing the franc by 22 percent, West Germany devalued the deutschmark by 21 percent, and Italy devalued the lira by 8 percent. Devaluation solved the problem for the moment.

International Development

The final piece of the economic structure erected by the United States after 1945 was a commitment to develop the poorer nations. In the fourth point of his Presidential inaugural speech of 1949, Harry Truman promised to provide American scientific expertise in industry and farming. This would lead to the **Agency for International Development (AID)** within the U.S. State Department. This was a different approach than the Marshall Plan, which was designed to reverse capital flows and operated on the premise that the European countries simply needed money to develop. The AID assumed that some nations were underproductive because they lacked knowledge. It showed a stunning lack of understanding of ecology, culture, and real economic development. The AID helped in a few cases, but most nations still hold the same relative position of wealth that they did in 1949 (excepting those damaged by World War II).

The Soviet Position

Where did all this leave the USSR? On the surface at least, it was isolated from the integrated economy led by the United States. It was not part of the IMF or GATT. The ruble was not convertible into other currencies. Nations under Soviet control had to withdraw from the IMF and refuse Marshall Plan money. Of course, this meant that their capital could not flow out to the western countries nor were they under U.S. influence. For the first few years after 1945, the USSR relied on plundering the occupied and ruined areas of east-central Europe. With the American Marshall Plan, however, the Soviets accepted that they had to provide assistance to coordinate the communist economies of Eastern Europe and so formed COMECON. Parts of eastern Germany remained in damaged condition down to the revolution of 1989. Things changed in the later 1950s. Stalin was dead, and the western European nations had recovered prosperity and restored currency convertibility. Around 1957, the USSR expanded its participation in European banks, especially those in London and Switzerland. The Europeans conducted many transactions in dollars and this interested the Soviets because they had quite a large store of dollars that had come to them in one way or another. It would be most embarrassing to both the USSR and the U.S. for the Soviets to cash in their dollars for gold on a regular basis. The Soviet State Bank could open dollar-denominated accounts in western European banks (so-called **Eurodollars**). The Soviets conducted much of their foreign trade in dollars and gold. There was also a dollar-denominated Eurobond market. In 1991, 31 percent of international bonds in Europe were issued in dollars. (Kindleberger 1993, 439–41) As seen in chapter 13, the Soviets bought large amounts of grain from Canada and then the U.S. itself by the 1970s. The communist nations also openly borrowed large sums from European (mostly German) banks. In 1958, the Moscow Narodny Bank, a London-based Soviet bank, asked whether the State Bank of the USSR could join the Bank for International Settlements in Basel, a relic of the 1930s that coordinated European central bank actions. In 1962, a Paris-based Soviet bank made a similar inquiry. The BIS refused this request but between 1962 and 1965 bought 830 tons of gold from the Soviets. To what degree the communist banks were participating in the 1960s is murky, but in 1976, the BIS began to have bi-annual meetings with Eastern European central bank governors. (Toniolo, 348–9, 582)

THE THIRTY GLORIOUS YEARS

General Comments

From 1945 to 1975, the western world grew at a pace never seen in human history. The accelerating production of energy, especially oil and natural gas, fueled it. World energy consumption roughly quadrupled during this time. The world population somewhat less than doubled, so that meant energy consumption on a per person basis doubled. Not only did the economies grow, governed by Keynesian principles, but equality grew as well. No one confiscated the fortunes of the rich, although the Republican administration of Dwight Eisenhower in the 1950s did tax people making more than $200,000 a year 90 percent of their marginal income (that would be about $4 million in 2014 value). Through generous union contracts, government programs, and overall productivity growth, working-class families enjoyed prosperous lives. Education and training spread within nations and among nations. Poverty did not end, but it seemed to be shrinking into identifiable pockets such as those suffering from racism or the elderly who lacked pensions and health care. Free trade and judicious regulation helped increase wealth while preventing corporations from distorting the market. It seemed that both Adam Smith and John Maynard Keynes had proved victorious.

West Germany's Economic Miracle

By 1949, Germany was already well on the way to economic recovery following the currency reform. Despite all the war damage, Germany still had a lot of well-educated and productive people. West Germany took a share of the Marshall Plan, and this spurred the economy further. West Germany was already close to its 1936 level of industrial production. In January 1950, the government lifted the last rationing restrictions, years before the British. Industrialists agreed to the labor unions' demands for **Co-Determination**, which put union leaders on boards of directors, gave unions a big say in the governance of industry, allowed union leaders to look at the real accounting books, and gave workers a stake in the factories. Exports spurred tremendous growth in the 1950s. East Germany grew much more slowly under the heavy hand of Soviet domination but still did better than the other communist satellites in east-central Europe. Middle-class Germans continued to flee the East and brought their training and education.

France

During the Nazi occupation of France, a number of young technocrats emerged. They used the dictatorial regime to enforce the will of a technical elite to make France modern and more efficient. They reorganized industry to favor the largest and most efficient firms. They outlawed strikes. The fall of the Nazis brought a return of democracy. The economist **Jean Monnet** (1888–1979), who had been active in international organizations in the 1920s and an advisor to Roosevelt and Free French leader Charles de Gaulle during the War, drew up a comprehensive plan for economic reform. He worked to make industry more efficient, update farming methods, and guide the Marshall Plan aid to key industries. Monnet's plan nationalized some major banks, the insurance industry, gas and electric networks, and Paris public transit. France led the way in national economic planning by a democracy. The plan emphasized heavy industry so that France became an industrial country for first time. By 1956, French industrial production was 50 percent above its pre-Depression high. The plan transformed agriculture as the holdings of the small farmers became more profitable. Population, which had been stable from 1840 to 1940, now climbed by 12 percent while national income rose 85 percent. The republic reformed society as unions returned, and factory committees with worker representatives were re-established. The government broadened social security.

Britain

A 1945 election brought the Labour party to power. This was the socialist left that remained after MacDonald joined the Conservatives. Prime Minister **Clement Attlee** (1945–1951) had to cope with continued austerity because so much money had gone into the war effort even though Britain had not been occupied. Britain's economic decline had continued as its trade lost even more markets. In 1946, the government had to re-impose food rationing which lasted until 1954. Britain was overextended with its military and colonies. The Attlee government provided wider benefits for health, old age, and unemployment; it gave free medical care to all registered British subjects. It nationalized the coal industry, communications, and the Bank of England in the hope that this would make the British economy more efficient. Finally, despite sharp opposition, it nationalized the iron and steel industries. It gave compensation in all cases. The elections of 1950 gave Labour a very narrow advantage. Another election in 1951 returned the Conservatives under Churchill. He had run on a platform of rolling back Labour programs and resisting de-colonization. He broke both promises.

Japan after the War

From 1950 to 1970, Japan's growth averaged more than 10 percent a year for a total of 528 percent. For the thirty glorious years, Japanese per capita GDP grew 747 percent. Like Germany, Japan had the advantage of rebuilding its industry with the latest equipment. The government scrapped its antitrust policy, and large monopoly organizations grew with government encouragement. New industrial giants appeared such as Sony, Toshiba, and Matsuhita. The workforce was literate, hard-working, and technically skilled. Agricultural productivity grew, but food remained expensive because of a system of subsidies and tariffs. Japan made a virtue out of necessity by introducing the "just-in-time" inventory system in the 1950s. Instead of keeping a large reserve of all parts and materials, Japanese factories only had enough for a few hours of work and trusted that nothing would interrupt the flow of supplies. (Hugill, 217)

Exports made up 12 percent of the economy by 1975; the biggest trade partner was the U.S. followed by other Asian nations. Unions were organized on the basis of companies, not trades; union members were 46 percent of the labor force in 1950, but fell to 29 percent by 1985. While paid less, Japanese industrial workers had prestige. Factories promoted individual worker responsibility. Any auto worker had the right to stop the production line if he spotted a problem. (Hugill, 216) This helped Japanese cars have better quality than American cars. The Bank of Japan financed business with loans, so there were fewer stock offerings. The Finance Ministry and the Ministry of International Trade and Industry (**MITI**) worked through the Economic Planning Agency. They targeted growth industries, set production goals, and estimated foreign markets. For their favored industries, they provided high depreciation allowances, cheap loans, subsidies, and light taxes.

Bucking the trend of free trade, Japan had a protectionist system: it allowed competition only where foreign companies could not compete or where it planned no production. It used tariffs, quotas, currency controls, foreign investment controls, and bureaucratic red tape. By the early 1970s, Japan had to liberalize markets in order to prevent trade wars, but by that time, other countries found it difficult to compete with Japanese-made goods. Nevertheless, private companies chafed at regulations and engaged in cutthroat competition with one another. MITI was not perfect in its forecasting. For example, it tried to discourage auto production believing that Japanese cars could never compete in the world market.

From the mid-1980s to the mid-1990s, Japan was the second-largest economy in the world and some thought it might pass the United States someday.

The New Technologies

The period after 1945 saw technology playing an ever greater role in the everyday life of people around the world, but especially among the middle and upper classes of the industrialized world. The technologies transformed both work and play. World War II had spurred the development of smaller, more powerful motors, especially in war planes. After the war, these motors could be used in refrigerators, vacuum cleaners, clothes washers and dryers, and dishwashers. This reduced or eliminated the need for domestic servants and freed the upper or middle-class woman to enjoy more leisure time or enter the salaried work force. (Hugill, 97) Not all technology was "new" in terms of being invented after 1945. Electrical generators had been devised before 1900, but electrification was a slow process, especially in rural areas. By 1950, most houses had electricity in the U.S., Canada, and Europe. Colonial areas had also had electrical lines built, but after independence many areas had problems keeping generators going. Blackouts were common. As households added more and more electrical devices, the need grew for more and more power, with oil generating most of that energy. After the oil crises of the 1970s, natural gas and nuclear power began to play more of a role. Air conditioning played a big role in the development of the U.S. It allowed a mass migration to hot southern states. It was much less important in underdeveloped countries and in Europe, which is generally cooler.

The airplane also existed before 1945, but air travel became increasingly common and cheaper after the war. In 1957, air passengers flying over the Atlantic exceeded ship passengers. (Hugill, 283) Railroads grew more decrepit and less used. After 1970, governments introduced faster, cleaner railroads to save energy and help the environment. Tourists, especially from the U.S., Japan, and Germany, were seen all over the globe. The world became closer.

The radio was another old piece of technology that flourished. The introduction of FM radio (invented in 1933) gave a cleaner sound with less static. It became a natural home for music stations. It also provided for the spread of culture, especially American culture and music, to all parts of the world. The development of the transistor in 1948 led to miniaturization and smaller radios that could be carried around.

Television had been invented before the war but was not introduced until afterwards. TVs were very small and expensive at first. In the prosperity of the 1950s, more and more people owned televisions. Networks controlled by private corporations or governments provided news and entertainment. People stayed in more and (probably) stayed up later. Movies felt stiff competition from TV and tried to do things to attract people. The problem grew worse for the movies with the introduction of color televisions in the mid-1960s. By the late 1960s, censorship codes in the movies had given way to a rating system so that people would have some idea of the content of violence, nudity, and sex. In the 1980s, cable channels grew, and the domination of the networks in the U.S. fell. Bigger corporations bought all the U.S. networks. New press lords such as the Australian Rupert Murdoch of Fox Broadcasting gained in wealth and power.

The use of rockets had taken a big step forward during World War II, especially ballistic missiles that went high into the atmosphere. The military continued to develop rockets. By the late

1950s, the U.S. and USSR had Intercontinental Ballistic Missiles (ICBMs). In 1957, the Soviet Union fired a rocket into space carrying the satellite Sputnik. The U.S. feared an attack from above, and the "space race" was on. The Americans put their first satellite into space in 1958. Satellites would help communication. Better mapping of weather made for superior forecasting. In 1961, the USSR again beat the U.S. in the race to put the first man into space. President John F. Kennedy announced his determination to put a man on the moon, and in 1969, astronauts planted the U.S. flag there. By that year, détente was on between the United States and Soviet Union, and the space race eased. Exploratory vehicles brought interesting discoveries, but many doubted that the costs were worth the trouble. Japan and Western Europe kept only modest space programs.

The discovery of the structure of DNA in 1954 was part of a flurry of medical advances. Scientists developed vaccines against polio. By 1975, the world had eradicated smallpox. Plastics made possible various devices for transplant, and organ transplants became common. Operations to prolong life caused life expectancy to grow in many countries, but the new medicine was very expensive.

The copying machine (usually identified with the Xerox Corporation) made multiple copies of any document possible. It eliminated laborious retyping and the use of carbon copies. It also made secrecy more difficult and publishing easier as people no longer needed a printing press to express themselves, just a typewriter and a copying machine. Improvements in transistors and semiconductors allowed computers to become more common. Cumbersome computer tape and punchcards were replaced by disks, then by internal platters, then flash memory. Communication among computers improved, culminating in the Internet. By 1980, families could buy affordable computers.

WESTERN EUROPEAN INTEGRATION

Beginnings

Under the Marshall Plan, the participating nations had to form an Organization for European Economic Cooperation (1948). The countries' representatives also met in a Congress of Europe to discuss a union. By 1949, there were already agreements for full economic union between France and Italy and among Belgium, the Netherlands, and Luxemburg (Benelux).

Once the allies had agreed on a more liberal policy towards Germany, the question arose of how to discourage it from rebuilding armaments. How could Germany's mineral wealth in iron and coal be used for the common benefit of all? France had become convinced that its hard line towards Germany was self-defeating. French Foreign Minister Robert Schuman and Jean Monnet drew up the **Schuman Plan** (1950) for coal and steel cooperation. Monnet saw this as the first real step towards European economic integration. Under the plan, all French and German coal and steel production would be put under a single high authority, and there would be an open market between the two countries in these products. It encouraged modernization and planning without nationalization. Britain foolishly refused to join in such a plan, but the other governments were in agreement. France, West Germany, Italy, Netherlands, Belgium, and Luxemburg set up the **European Coal and Steel Community** in 1951. Monnet became president of its high authority. The iron and steel businesses opposed this bitterly, out of a reflex against government regulation and leadership, but the Community hugely increased their profits. (Milward, 419)

The Common Market

In 1957, European organizations in atomic and space research were established. The **Treaty of Rome** (1957) set up a **European Economic Community (EEC or Common Market)**, starting with the six members of the Coal and Steel Community. The Treaty's goal was to abolish customs barriers among the six states, permit free movement of labor and capital, as well as equalize wages and the social insurance programs. It would work in stages and have its headquarters in Brussels, Belgium. In 1968, the EEC abolished customs and agreed to a common tariff with non-member states. There has been endless debate over the French policy of paying farmers to sell at a lower price so that French goods can remain competitive on the global market.

Britain finally applied for EEC membership in 1963 but was blocked by French President De Gaulle. He feared British economic power, disliked Britain personally, and opposed Britain's expansive social welfare programs. After De Gaulle's retirement, Britain was admitted to the Common Market, effective in 1973.

THE ECONOMIC BALANCE OF POWER

By the late 1960s, an important shift was clearly taking place in the economic balance of power. The world of the Cold War had been built on the fact that two great powers, the U.S. and USSR, stood victorious. Britain was badly damaged, Germany and Japan were flattened, and France had been occupied. The colonial powers controlled much of the rest of the world. China was big but in the throes of a civil war. By 1970, this balance had changed considerably. The U.S. and USSR were still reckoned as the two leading powers of the world, although we may question the size of the Soviet economy. Germany and Japan had rebuilt themselves and had emerged as major economic powers.

Britain and France remained considerable forces, and Italy was emerging as an economic power. The European Community had come together in Western Europe and was a growing power. The Communists had united China, even if its progress was uncertain. China and India were able to feed themselves, and China had nuclear weapons. Other nations such as Canada, Australia, and Brazil were at least minor or regional powers. Most of Africa and Asia had been decolonized. Europe and Japan as well as the U.S. were conducting major research work.

By the 1960s, this diffusion of power made itself clearer. The U.S. had increasing difficulty maintaining the world's financial system and controlling the prices of gold (at $35 an ounce versus market rates of $150) and silver (at $1.25 an ounce) and limited convertibility. Because of the growing expense of silver, the U.S. stopped minting silver coins for general use in 1964. De Gaulle of France took special delight in tweaking the U.S. He would exchange dollars for gold at the official rate of $35 an ounce and then sell it at the world market rate, draining gold from the U.S. Canada sold great amounts of wheat to the USSR and China in the 1960s and reduced its military contribution to NATO. The Iron Curtain dividing the West from the communists was rusting away.

THE END OF THE BRETTON WOODS MONETARY SYSTEM

As the old diplomatic system transformed, the U.S. acknowledged the relative weakening of its economic position. Pressure built on the U.S. gold supply, maintained at $35 per ounce while the market price continued to climb. Inflation was also seen as a growing problem in the U.S. as Presidents Johnson and Nixon declined to raise taxes to pay for the

Vietnam War. In 1971, Western European steel production surpassed that of the U.S. European and Japanese car imports were beginning to take a major share of the U.S. market. By 1970, the U.S. trade deficit with Western Europe was $10 billion a year. The Europeans had $50 billion in dollar reserves that exceeded the U.S. gold supply valued at the official rate.

The administration of Richard Nixon made a number of moves. It raised the official price of gold by a small amount. It also imposed a surtax on imports to try to correct the trade balance. (Kindleberger 1993, 453) On August 15, 1971, with no prior warning, Nixon suspended convertibility in gold and allowed the dollar to "float" to its true level. From this point on, the price of gold reached the market level. Currencies would be revalued each day as they floated. The Japanese yen, Deutschmark, and Swiss Franc became major currencies along with the dollar. The Western European countries established a Monetary System to keep their values roughly in line with periodic adjustments. Over the years, the dollar's value in other currencies has fluctuated considerably. The cutting of the last ties to gold ended a drag on the economy but encouraged inflation as the Federal Reserve Bank and consumers' decisions determined the American money supply.

THE FIRST AND SECOND ENERGY CRISES

As economies grew in Western Europe, the U.S., and Japan, they became increasingly dependent on oil supplies. The **Organization of Petroleum Exporting Countries (OPEC)** had been formed in 1960 but had little effect until after 1969. The 1969 world oil price was 65 percent below the 1947 level in real terms. Even in nominal terms, the price had dropped 6 percent from 1950 to 1970 as a barrel of crude oil cost $2.88 and a gallon of gasoline (including taxes) cost thirty-five cents.

Between 1950 and 1973, demand for oil increased fivefold, while reserves grew eightfold. There had just been major oil discoveries in the North Sea, Mexico, and the North Slope of Alaska. But between 1969 and 1979, the price increased from $1.20 per barrel to $41. How did this happen?

In 1970, U.S. production peaked at 3.5 billion barrels, which represented 21 percent of global production. Had not Interior Secretary Walter Hickel badly bungled oil production in Alaska and offshore California, this peak could have been delayed and occurred at a higher level. (Anderson, 52–74) This opened a 1.5 million barrel a day gap that had to be filled by Middle Eastern oil. This danger had long been projected and remedies prescribed (including import quotas to force a rise in the domestic price) to avoid it, but the politicians would not endorse any solution. (85) Through a series of blunders by Nixon's administration, the Alaska Pipeline was delayed a full five years. Nixon also did not act in 1969 when a small band under Muammar Qadaffi took over in Libya. Nixon actually wanted oil prices to rise, so that Iran could afford to buy weapons to fulfill its regional defense role. When the oil companies tried to prevent Qadaffi from raising prices, Nixon threatened antitrust action.

This all came to a head in 1973. Demand for oil grew rapidly with the Clean Air Act, which discouraged companies from burning coal. Nixon had imposed wage and price controls in 1971 in order to postpone inflation until after the 1972 election. The decision to allow the dollar to float pushed the price in dollars higher. By 1973, after the controls were lifted, oil was up to $5 a barrel. The Arab countries declared an embargo on selling oil to the West in 1973 after Egypt and Syria lost a war to Israel. The total available oil only dropped 7 percent, but panic and poor distribution made for shortages. On the open market, oil briefly reached $17.40 a barrel. OPEC decided in December 1974 to raise the official price to $12 a barrel. When Nixon was inaugurated in

1969, the U.S. imported 13 percent of its oil, two-thirds of which came from the Americas. In 1973, it imported 26 percent. Of that 42 percent came from the Americas, and 33 percent came from Muslim nations of the Mediterranean and Middle East.

In 1979 came a second oil shock. An Islamic revolution overthrew the Shah of Iran in February 1979 and the "spot" price of oil rose. Panic and mismanagement (and perhaps some oil company greed) led to regional oil shortages and the price began to rise again by the summer of 1979. The market peaked at $41 a barrel. This touched off another round of inflation, which had partly subsided in the mid-1970s during a recession. President Jimmy Carter's conservation projects and Alaskan, Mexican, and North Sea production would sap the power of OPEC by the 1980s as the oil price steadily fell.

The thirty glorious years were over.

STAGFLATION IN THE LATE 1970S

The oil shocks, the final end of the gold link, and structural issues caused a problem which many economists had thought impossible. They believed that there was a tradeoff between inflation and unemployment, but in the 1970s, there was both stagnation (which led to growing joblessness) and inflation. Inflation had become locked into the economic structure as large corporations wanted guaranteed profit and workers were reluctant to take cuts in pay. Government programs included cost-of-living adjustments (COLAs). Inflation was identified as the biggest problem by wealthy investors because their bonds were losing value. In reality, the late 1970s actually saw quite robust economic growth, but the oil shock of 1979 and a new bout of inflation led many to conclude that strong action was needed. The Fed and other central banks hiked interest rates high above the inflation rate and caused a lesser version of the Depression. Companies then used widespread unemployment to force the unions to give up gains or smash the unions entirely. Structural inflation was broken and the surge in oil production from Alaska, the North Sea, and Mexico brought those prices down. Corporations proclaimed the 1980s a good time, and they were. . . for corporations. They pocketed the productivity gains as profit and gave little back to the workers. Inequality began to rise again.

CONCLUSION

The Second World War left the United States as the leading economy, and it pressed this advantage by shaping the postwar economic structure as it pleased. The U.S. dollar became the world's standard. The IMF would balance flows of capital among nations. The World Bank and AID would provide funds to develop countries on the American model. GATT brought down trade barriers among a growing number of nations so American companies could sell their goods. The Marshall Plan rebuilt Western Europe in exchange for acquiescence to American policies.

This structure and ever-cheaper energy supplies led to the thirty glorious years from 1945 to 1975. Not only did GDP grow, but the poverty ended in some places and the life of the poor improved. Inequality diminished. Business and labor worked together. Some developed countries such as France and Japan used a high degree of economic planning. The European Economic Community brought together former enemies as partners in economic progress.

The 1970s marked a turning point. American oil production peaked and the wages of U.S. workers stagnated. The days of cheap oil came to an end. The new multipolar world with many strong economies and an emerging China and India existed uneasily with the American-built structure.

Energy prices fell in the 1980s, but the good times did not return. Inequality began to grow across the world as productivity gains were reaped by the rich.

TIMELINE

1936	Keynes, *The General Theory of Employment, Interest, and Money*
1944	Bretton Woods conference
1947	General Agreement on Tariffs and Trade (GATT)
	Marshall Plan
1948	West German currency reform
1951	European Coal and Steel Community
1957	Treaty of Rome established European Economic Community (EEC)
1970	U.S. oil production peaked
1969–74	First oil shock and consequent "stagflation"
1979	Second oil shock

KEY TERMS

John Maynard Keynes
Bretton Woods Conference
International Monetary Fund (IMF)
World Bank
General Agreement on Tariffs and Trade (GATT)
Marshall Plan
Co-Determination
Jean Monnet
Ministry of International Trade and Industry (MITI)
Organization of Petroleum Exporting Countries (OPEC)

Chapter 16

THE "LONG EMERGENCY" BEGINS

We come to the final chapter of the book. This is the economic history of our current time. It does not have an ending. The reader knows that as of this writing (2015) that economic times are hard. If the reader has not personally experienced economic hardship, he surely has friends and relatives who have. It is the worst crisis since the Great Depression and gets called variously "the lesser Depression" or "the Great Recession." Most analysts, who do not know economic history, do not understand the causes of the crisis or the reasons for its duration. In the United States, stagnation in real average hourly wages dates back to 1970 and in household income to the end of 2000. No one mentions what happened in these years. On the household level, this crisis has already outlasted the Great Depression, which had a ten-year duration in the U.S. and rather less in most other nations.

From 1960 to 2004, global energy use tripled. This was mainly driven by oil as the vast fields of Southwest Asia and

North Africa joined the rich American and Russian fields. (Koppelaar) Then drilling tapped the new supergiant oil fields discovered in Alaska, Mexico, and the North Sea. As oil production expanded, so did that of natural gas. The 1970s and 1980s saw the blooming of nuclear power as some nations including France and Japan invested heavily in fission reactors. A temporary "energy crisis" in the 1970s caused by political miscalculation and greed more than resource shortage had the benefit of making people more energy aware and efficient in their use. This energy boom powered a new phase of global economic development, especially in developing economies such as South Korea, China, and India. Mature economies such as those in West Europe came to new levels of prosperity even for the poorer members of society.

It is highly unlikely that energy production will triple again from 2005 to 2050. From 2005 through 2013, global oil production only increased by a sum total of 3 percent (**not** 3 percent a year). This was misleadingly called an "oil boom." The price of oil quadrupled, hit all-time real highs, and caused a global financial seizure. Nuclear power development certainly looks stalled. Lower energy density sources such as coal and natural gas have taken up some of the slack, but neither has the versatility of oil. Many wonder when things will return to "normal" and are puzzled why economies remain slack. Not least are young people who are not enjoying the job opportunities or pay that young people did forty years ago. How this came about and why it is not likely to change is this chapter's subject. The author hopes that understanding will give the reader an advantage in career and life. In 2005, James Howard Kunstler published *The Long Emergency* describing a problem that will last decades, not years. That book inspires the title of this chapter.

Cuba and Russia

Existing capital must be maintained and collapse occurs when production can no longer maintain that capital. At that point capital *loses* value, practically a reversal of history as we have seen it. A preview of the long emergency occurred in Russia and Cuba in the 1990s after the collapse of the Soviet Union. Communists took power in Cuba in 1959, and the United States imposed a trade embargo that has lasted through 2014. Cuba was very dependent on the Soviet Union, especially for its oil. At the beginning of 1990, Cuba lost its grain supplies from eastern Europe and had to cut its bread ration. The Soviets cut their oil supply to Cuba by 20 percent. The Cuban government had to compensate for the loss of energy by sending city workers out into the fields for the planting season. From 1989 to 1991, aid and goods were cut by more than 60 percent. As the USSR collapsed, Cuba faced a cutoff in oil. By the start of 1992, food supplies were reduced and the government imposed electricity conservation measures. Oil consumption fell from 225,000 barrels a day to 175,000. By December 1992, eight-hour blackouts each day were regular occurrences in the cities. Hoping to destroy the Communist government, the U.S. tightened its embargo further with the Torricelli Law. Cuba's exports, mainly sugar, also were reduced by 60 percent so it had less ability to buy goods on the world market. Without chemical fertilizer or fuel to run farm equipment, the sugar production in 1994 fell to the lowest level since the 1940s. It had defaulted on its debt in 1986, so it could only borrow at very high interest rates. It sold oil exploration rights to companies from Brazil and Europe. By some estimates, the Cuban economy contracted by a third between 1989 and 1993. (Maddison 2001, 285) In 1995, it borrowed $100 million from European banks at 14 percent interest to buy fertilizer, herbicide, fuel, and spare parts for machinery.

The *New York Times* felt confident enough to run a cover story in its magazine of March 14, 1993, entitled "The Last Days of Castro." But twenty years later, the Castros were still in charge. How did Cuba survive what seemed like certain doomsday? For a population of eleven million people, Cuba brought 1.2 million bicycles from China for transport in 1992 and made another 500,000 itself. In 1993, Australian agricultural experts came in to teach sustainable farming techniques that did not require pesticides and chemical fertilizers. The government allowed city-dwellers to own up to one-third of an acre as a private farm lot on the periphery of the cities. Enough Cubans still had experience or at least family with farm skills to take advantage of this. On top of that, Cubans used patios, rooftops, and abandoned parking lots as urban gardens. Eating meat and dairy became much rarer since stock-raising consumes more resources. In 2000, buying food took two-thirds of the average household budget. In 2012, Cuba imported much less oil than it did in 1989, and most of it came from special deals worked out with Venezuela. Nevertheless, electricity production passed the 1989 peak in 2007 and Cuba has tripled its own oil production. Cuba is not prospering, but it survived without 10 percent of its population dying as happened in famine Ireland, Stalin's Soviet Union, and elsewhere.

Collapse in Russia brought dire predictions. There were some hard winters, and significant numbers of men between the ages of forty-five and fifty-five effectively drank themselves to death. Government-run health care ended and many diseases went untreated. (Orlov, 90) But the impact was not as harsh as the Great Depression had been on the Americans or Germans. The process was relatively slow. Communism had been declining over decades. Even in the 1980s and early 1990s, the government was reluctant to dismiss people from work, so that gave them a long lead time to think about what their lives would be like when they lost their jobs. (69) They had fallback plans ready when the Soviet Union dissolved at the end of 1991 and the Russian Federation began "shock therapy" in the 1990s. State factories, which had corruptly hoarded resources for many years, did not shut immediately when their supply was cut off. The redundancies and inefficiencies now cushioned the decline.

Most Russians lived in government housing. When the government collapsed, people kept living where they always had because there was no mechanism to throw them out. The houses were not pretty but were functional and insulated against the cold Russian winter. Hot water came from neighborhood boilers, and neighborhoods carried out their own services, which had been centralized and efficient. (63) The apartments were crammed full of people often from three generations. Grandparents provided child care while the parents worked. Each apartment building also had the kitchen gardens for food needed during the communist era. In the communist times, people needed to fend for themselves, and they simply continued to do so. The Soviet Union had built a very efficient, extensive, and affordable public transportation system. About one-third of the USSR's rail system was electrified. (Hugill, 201) As long as generators kept pumping out electricity, the system continued even after the government fell. In the U.S. in 2010, about 1 percent of the track system is electrified, and most of that is Amtrak's northeast corridor and New York City's subway and commuter rail systems. Low costs meant that Russians could keep traveling to their jobs (if they still had jobs) or elsewhere. (Orlov, 66–7) Relatively few people had cars. Industrial and refinery breakdowns led to gasoline shortages but the decline in car use did not mean a significant fall in transportation, just emptier and cleaner streets. Money already had limited value in Communist Russia, and barter for goods and services made up a significant part of the economy, even if it was a crime. When inflation made that money worthless, it did not have the kind of jolt that it did in Germany (twice). (Orlov, 76–7) The state-owned industries were given away to politically-connected operators who became known as "the oligarchs." Lower levels of crime also flourished.

Then Russia turned it around. Russia produced enough oil to support itself and was no longer sending oil to Cuba, the Soviet republics, or the satellites of Eastern Europe. It could get a market value for the oil. As it modernized oil facilities, long-declining production rose again. Russia returned to great power status after 1999, when the prices of oil and gold skyrocketed.

China and India

In the late 1990s, China and India took advantage of cheap energy costs and modern transportation and communication systems to expand rapidly. China copied Japan's example and used cheap labor and efficient production to take a large share of basic manufacturing such as steel and textiles. By the mid-2000s, it had built plants to construct sophisticated electronics for Apple and other companies. From 1980 to 2011, its coal production quintupled, so that China now accounts for half of the world's coal consumption. Starting in 2009, China became a coal importer. In 1993, China went from an oil exporter to an oil importer. By 2012, it was importing six million barrels a day. It consumed ten million barrels of oil a day that year but has built refining capacity in anticipation of consuming thirteen million barrels a day. From 2001 to 2010, China's overall energy consumption doubled and the portion of energy it needed to import went from 2 percent to 10 percent. In 2013, China became the largest energy producer and consumer in the world. It would seem that China's economy has either passed that of the U.S. or is about to pass it. If so, China will reclaim the title it held for centuries until 1888. History wins again.

India mainly produced at first for its vast domestic market. From 1950, it only doubled its per capita GDP by 1988, a growth rate under 2 percent a year. But the next doubling took place in only seventeen years for a growth rate over 4 percent. Despite its huge population, India consumes about one-quarter the energy that China does. From 1980 to 1985, it more than tripled its energy production, jump-starting the economy. Through the 1990s, India imported about a quarter of its energy; now it imports a third of its needs. Oil imports grew tenfold from 1985 to 2012.

Oil

American oil production peaked in 1970, and even the advent of production in Alaska could not surpass that peak. The U.S. produced 9.77 million barrels a day in 1970. It produced somewhat less than that for about seventeen years, then there was a sharp fall to about 60 percent of the peak. Not coincidentally, 1970 also marks the peak in American real wages and individual median income. Household income was able to rise modestly because of second incomes.

Crude oil hit a low of $10.72 per barrel on December 10, 1998. The cost of oil as a percentage of the economy had fallen back to the levels before Nixon's presidency. It was bad news for Russia and the other oil producers but good news for many others. Wal-Mart became a giant on this model of low-cost energy. It could buy manufactured goods dirt cheap in China and transport them for little cost. It built stores in rural areas or far outside cities where land was cheap and customers could drive there frequently because gasoline only cost $1.50 per gallon. Wal-Mart made huge profits by employing the opposite strategy from that of Henry Ford. It paid its workers so little that many remained eligible for welfare and food stamps, and those workers could only afford to shop at Wal-Mart. The demand from China and India caused the price of oil to rise to $35 by September 2000. From 2000 to 2003, global oil production rose 900,000 barrels a day and China and India took almost all of it. After the price of oil rose in 2000, there was strong incentive to produce more. From 2000 to 2005, global production rose 9 percent as one would expect with rising prices and increasing incentive to bring marginal sources of oil on line. In 2005, global oil production rose 2.5% as Chinese demand skyrocketed. Then the system broke as oil production peaked. This was more serious because some of the largest exporters such as Saudi Arabia and Russia consumed more oil for their own needs. In addition, former exporters such as Britain and Indonesia have become net importers. The pool of exportable oil and oil-like liquids contracted. To continue trend growth required oil production and export growth that simply did not happen. Finally, the Chinese were able to use their enormous trade surplus accounts to buy up all the oil they needed, leaving shortages for other nations. To a lesser degree India also used its current account surpluses. By 2011, the export oil market had shrunk while the share taken by China and India had risen from 7 percent to 19 percent. Petroleum remains the biggest single contributor of energy to the American economy with almost 40 percent of the total. Most of that is used in transportation.

The peak of 2005 and the move to a bumpy plateau constituted a second shock wave after the U.S. peak of 1970. The American economy came under increasing strain and the weakest parts—the housing market and the financial system—broke when the oil price doubled again. The U.S. financial system had been weak since December 2000 when George Bush seized power despite losing the presidential election. Foreigners sold more of their U.S. treasury bills and bonds than in the whole history of the country. Investors, mainly from Europe, sold their American stocks. By April 2003, there was a cumulative loss of $285 billion in potential investment. Small wonder that the American stock market crashed. This was misleadingly conflated as the "bursting of the tech bubble," although one can find many major companies unrelated to technology, telecommunications, or dot-com companies whose stocks lost over half their value in this time. (For example from December 2000 to March 2003: Albertson's -60%, Phillip Morris -57%, American Electric Power -70%, American Express -57%, Aquila -86%, Bank of New York -66%, Bristol Myers Squibb -73%, Citigroup -57%, Fleet Financial -60%, General Motors -56%, Lincoln National Bank -53%, May Department Stores -56%, Merck -59%, Merrill Lynch -64%, Morgan Stanley -52%, PNC Bank -57%, Schering-Plough -73%, Sears -69%, and Wal-Mart -57%.)

Massive corporate frauds also weakened U.S. finance. Most companies reported profits to the tax offices much lower than their announced profits. The Enron Corporation, a pipeline company that was one of the largest companies in the United States, lied about tens of billions of dollars of debt and went bankrupt. Its chief executive, a close ally of George Bush, was convicted of fraud and died suddenly. Enron's accounting company, Arthur Andersen, was convicted of destroying documents and dissolved. In 2002, investigators found that the large telecom company WorldCom had fraudulently reported its assets to boost its stock price.

Even when the S&P 500 recovered from 2003 to 2007, its growth lagged every other country's stock index, with the exceptions of Trinidad, Jamaica, Ecuador, and Costa Rica. Also after 2000, a shadow banking system grew up without any regulation or monitor. The Bush regime ignored warnings and blocked states from regulating these risky financial gambits. In March 2008, the dollar hit an all-time low against other currencies. American health indicators plunged and native-born Americans are shorter in height than the natives of western and northern Europe.

The American love affair with the automobile ended. The total miles driven by Americans peaked in November 2007 and only recovered in January 2015. If we account for the growth of population and so look at the per capita miles driven, the effect is more stark. The peak here is June 2005 and we have steadily fallen back to the level of 1994, a 7 percent drop. This relates to the housing crisis because of tighter credit but also because families had bought houses that were long drives from their jobs and their shopping. High gasoline prices made this lifestyle unsustainable for some. 7.3 million Americans lost their homes with the largest group of foreclosures occurring in 2010. The worst-hit areas in this crisis have been suburbs and even more the so-called exurbs. As developments emptied, their very emptiness deterred potential buyers and accelerated their slide into "shruburbs" (named in dishonor of George "Shrub" Bush to recall Hoovervilles) haunted by squatters and thieves stripping houses of valuable pipes and wires. The California counties with the highest foreclosure rates were those that had become exurbs of San Francisco and Los Angeles. In 2011, the population grew more in Bronx County than in Nassau County, New York. When is the last time that happened?

With these problems in health and education and transportation, it is no surprise that per hour productivity stagnated. Despite the falling dollar, the trade deficit got steadily worse and American exports became steadily less competitive. In 2004, Germany passed the U.S. in international volume of exports. The U.S. fell to third place in 2007, despite the euro's appreciation. In 2009, China took over the lead in world exports. Bush weakened America's position even more with his prolonged wars in Iraq and Afghanistan.

There was another controversial election in 2004 when the European election monitors were barred from the polling places in the close states of Colorado and Florida. Exit polls indicated Bush's defeat, but reported vote totals were at wild variance in twenty-one states, all in favor of Bush. Monitors compared the American system unfavorably to Venezuela, Kazakhstan, and the Republic of Georgia. The Federal Reserve did not want a repeat of the 2000 run on the dollar so it hiked interest rates to protect the currency while using open-market operations to flood the credit system. Many used the easy credit to get home or commercial building mortgages.

So by 2007, the financial system was blighted, there was a real estate bubble, and energy problems had become critical. The world had left the gold standard after 1930 when it was too confining to economic growth. The world had substituted a kind of oil standard, even if treaties did not fix values as the gold standard did. For eighty years, the growth in oil production allowed for stupendous growth in credit and unprecedented economic and population growth.

The crisis of 2008 was concentrated in the larger banks, especially those that did not take advantage of the repeal of the Glass-Steagall Act of 1933 and remained mostly commercial- or investment-based. Let us be clear: Glass-Steagall would not have saved Bear, Stearns, Glass-Steagall would not have saved Wachovia, Glass-Steagall would not have saved Merrill Lynch, Glass-Steagall would not have saved Washington Mutual, Glass-Steagall would not have saved Lehman Brothers. These banks made a growing percentage of their profits from collateralizing debt obligations (CDOs). A financial institution would bundle loans (most notoriously mortgages) and sell bonds equal to the value of the bundle. In theory, the bundle would contain enough high-quality loans to compensate for any loans that defaulted as long as housing prices kept rising. These bonds could be sold to other institutions or themselves be collateralized in another bundle. The true value of these bundles was thus obscured and a value put on them dictated either by a model that always assumed a rising value of real estate ("mark-to-model") or by established market prices for similar bundles ("mark-to-market"). Like any security, its value is only what someone is willing to pay for it, not any underlying value.

The year 2008 opened with Bank of America (BOA) taking over Countrywide Financial, a company that had been very aggressive in creating mortgages of dubious value. BOA thought it was getting a bargain because it was buying Countrywide at one-third of its stated net worth. Some observers suspected that the Fed had brokered this deal after Moody's downgraded many of Countrywide's CDOs. The Fed steadily announced new swap programs with larger amounts and easier terms of collateral. The investment bank Bear, Stearns failed and was taken over by Chase. The Fed openly brokered this deal and assumed $29 billion in troubled assets. Over the summer, anxiety grew. A list of "zombie banks" circulated on the Internet: all of those banks are today gone or taken over. In July, William Poole, the retired head of the

St. Louis Federal Reserve, said that the government-sponsored housing enterprises Freddie Mac and Fannie Mae were insolvent. The turning point, though few realized it, came on July 29, 2008. Merrill Lynch, desperate to raise capital, announced that it was selling "U.S. super senior Asset-Backed Security Collateralized Debt Obligations." These had a "gross notional value" of $31 billion, but Merrill had valued them at $11 billion, that is thirty-six cents on the dollar. Their rating was AAA, the highest possible. Merrill sold these bonds to an affiliate of Lone Star Funds for $7 billion, that is twenty-two cents on the dollar. However, analysts scrutinizing the deal quickly realized that Merrill was sending cash along with the bonds so that the bonds were actually valued at 5.5 cents on the dollar. This sent shock waves along Wall Street. As long as virtually no bundles were being sold, the banks could cling to the fantasy of "mark to model" and claim them at eighty cents or sixty cents or thirty-six cents. Now there was a sale made, a real market had been established, and all firms would be compelled to follow the market by accounting rules. Revaluing all the AAA troubled assets at 5.5 cents to the dollar would make most if not all of the major banks insolvent.

September 2008 was the climax. The government put Fannie and Freddie into "conservatorship." The Fed massively expanded its programs and brokered another deal for Bank of America to take over Merrill Lynch. Lehman Brothers filed for bankruptcy. The Fed invoked emergency powers to provide the insurer AIG with $85 billion. Chase took Washington Mutual bank in another brokered deal. The Treasury Department guaranteed $3.5 trillion in money market deposits. Mitsubishi UFJ bought 21 percent of Morgan Stanley. The credit market almost entirely froze until Congress passed the Troubled Assets Relief Program (TARP) which committed $700 billion to the Treasury Department. The Fed over the next year swapped for $624 billion of mortgage-backed securities at face value while increasing its overall balance by more than a trillion dollars. The financial institutions had little interest in selling their troubled assets to the Treasury at what could be deep discounts.

The shock caused a massive rise in joblessness. In the first stage of the Long Emergency, Iceland, Ireland, and the United States saw massive layoffs from the crisis of the shadow banking system. The second stage was caused by foolish austerity policies in Greece, Spain, and Ireland (again). Many had forgotten or ignored the lessons of the Great Depression. The ghosts of Hoover and Brüning would have cheered as millions lost their jobs in the fantasy that this would create prosperity. The United States only carried out mild austerity. Barack Obama became president in 2009 and enacted a jobs program that stopped the economic free fall. However, hundreds of thousands of government employees lost their jobs, especially in the states. Having stopped the worst, Obama focused on cutting the federal budget deficit by three-quarters and failed to keep people in their homes. The high price of oil enabled the exploitation of "tight oil" reserves locked in rocks in North Dakota and Texas. This gave the U.S. a short-term boost and allowed it to import less oil.

Conclusion

Oil, credit, and the shifting balance of power will influence each other in changing and unpredictable ways. It seems likely that China will soon fall back. Rapid economic expansion brings a host of social and economic problems that a nation must accommodate. China's crony capitalism, environmental degradation, economic controls, and local overdevelopment, and political opacity are all dangerous conditions. Its very success can contain the seeds of recession. As oil grows more expensive, the American consumer cannot buy as many goods from China. Many of these goods are discretionary. Oil also increases the transport costs. These trends have already led to a modest revival of American manufacturing. The Chinese trade surplus has diminished and in some months disappeared entirely. This in turn means that China has a lower cash reserve to buy oil. This causes the price of oil to fall, which creates more American desire to buy Chinese discretionary goods. That increases the Chinese trade surplus and allows them to bid up the price of oil. We have gone through several of these cycles of oil prices booming and busting.

Since the long emergency began we have rationed gasoline and electricity, not by government order, but by price. Oil use has fallen by 10 percent, mostly in transportation. OPEC has estimated that 2015 global oil consumption will be the lowest since 2002. The percentage of the American population holding a job has barely recovered since 2008 and real wages are stuck at the 1970 level. What recovery there has been has been concentrated overwhelmingly in the richer classes. Millions of Americans have been pushed out of the labor force and lost their homes. No wonder so many people are angry.

The great New York Yankee catcher Yogi Berra is supposed to have said "Predictions are always difficult, especially about the future." So how long will the Long Emergency last? At a guess, somewhere until about 2060. We will have to get past the effective end of the oil export market somewhere around 2040. By that time, we may be having issues with finding natural gas and high-quality coal. The world will change its focus to maintenance and sustainability. Another tripling of the global energy consumption is highly unlikely.

Money and credit still exist for the United States. Japan's national debt as a ratio of the economy is twice that of the

United States and its interest rates are low. That suggests that the U.S. could fund a dozen programs of the size of the 2009 Obama jobs act. One needs to focus spending on making a fair and orderly transition to a new energy regime using less oil more efficiently. A peacetime military budget would correct debt and trade problems. There must be focus on increasing productivity by modernizing transportation, improving education, and bringing American health care results to the level of other developed nations. Increased productivity can compensate for a stagnating energy supply to provide a measure of growth. Complacency is the biggest enemy. As long as we understand we are in a long emergency and we know our economic history and don't do anything stupid, we'll be all right.

FURTHER READING

Aldcroft, Derek H., *From Versailles to Wall Street, 1919–1929* (Berkeley, CA, 1977).

Anderson, Jack, with James Boyd, *Fiasco* (New York, 1983).

Baskin, Jonathan Barron, and Paul J. Miranti, Jr., *A History of Corporate Finance* (Cambridge, 1997).

Becker, Gary, *The Economic Approach to Human Behavior* (Chicago, 1976).

Bivens, Josh, "Inequality, Exhibit A," <http://www.epi.org/blog/inquality-exhibit-wal-mart-wealth-american>, posted July 12, 2012, accessed August 30, 2014.

Braudel, Fernand, *Civilization and Capitalism 15th–18th Century*, 3 vols. (New York, 1986).

Brewer, John, *The Sinews of Power: War, Money, and the English State, 1688-1783* (New York, 1989).

Broadberry, Stephen, and Kevin H. O'Rourke, eds., *The Cambridge Economic History of Modern Europe*, 2 vols. (Cambridge, 2010).

The Cambridge Economic History of Europe, vol. III: Economic Organization and Policies in the Middle Ages, ed. by M.M. Postan, E.E. Rich, and Edward Miller (Cambridge, 1963).

The Cambridge Economic History of Europe, vol. IV: The Economy of Expanding Europe in the 16th and 17th Centuries, ed by E.E. Rich and C.H. Wilson (Cambridge, 1967).

The Cambridge Economic History of Europe, vol. V: The Economic Organization of Early Modern Europe, ed. by E.E. Rich and C.H. Wilson (Cambridge, 1977).

Cameron, Rondo, *An Economic History of the World: From Paleolithic Times to the Present*, 2nd edition (Oxford, 1993).

Cipolla, Carlo, *Before the Industrial Revolution: European Society and Economy, 1000–1700*, 3rd edition (New York, 1993).

Clingan, Edmund, *Twilight's Last Gleaming: American Hegemony and Dominance in the Modern World* (Lanham, MD, 2013).

Crosby, Alfred W., *Ecological Imperialism: The Biological Expansion of Europe, 900-1900* (Cambridge, 1986).

de Vries, Jan and Ad van der Woude, *The First Modern Economy: Success, Failure, and Perseverance of the Dutch Economy, 1500-1815* (Cambridge, 1997) .

Diamond, Jared, *Guns, Germs, and Steel: The Fates of Human Societies* (New York, 1997).

Eichengreen, Barry, *Golden Fetters: The Gold Standard and the Great Depression* (Oxford, 1992).

Fischer, David Hackett, *The Great Wave: Price Revolutions and the Rhythm of History* (Oxford, 1996).

Galbraith, John Kenneth, *The Age of Uncertainty: A History of Economic Ideas and their Consequences* (Boston, 1977).

Goldin, Claudia, and Lawrence F. Katz, *The Race between Education and Technology* (Cambridge, MA, 2008).

Gregory, Paul R., *The Political Economy of Stalinism: Evidence from the Secret Soviet Archives* (Cambridge, 2004).

Hall, Charles A.S., and Kent A. Klitgaard, *Energy and the Wealth of Nations: Understanding the Biophysical Economy* (New York, 2012).

Hall, Thomas E., and J. David Ferguson, *The Great Depression: An International Disaster of Perverse Economic Policies* (Ann Arbor, MI, 1998).

Hanson, Philip, *The Rise and Fall of the Soviet Economy: An Economic History of the USSR from 1945* (London, 2003).

Hugill, Peter J., *World Trade since 1431: Geography, Technology, and Capitalism* (Baltimore, 1993).

Kindleberger, Charles P., *A Financial History of Western Europe*, 2nd edition (Oxford, 1993).

___, *The World in Depression, 1929–1939* (Berkeley, CA, 1973).

Klein, Herbert S., *The Atlantic Slave Trade* (Cambridge, 1999).

Koppelaar, Rembrandt, "World Energy Consumption–Beyond 500 Exajoules," <http://www.oildrum.com/node/8936>, posted February 16, 2012, accessed April 8, 2015.

Landes, David, *The Wealth and Poverty of Nations: Why Some are so Rich and Some so Poor* (New York, 1998).

Langley, Lester D., *The Americas in the Age of Revolution, 1750–1850* (New Haven, 1996).

Lindert, Peter, *Growing Public: Social Spending and Economic Growth since the Eighteenth Century*, 2 vols. (Cambridge, 2004).

Lopez, Robert S., *The Commercial Revolution of the Middle Ages, 950-1350* (Cambridge, 1976).

Lopez, Robert S., and Irving W. Raymond, eds., *Medieval Trade in the Mediterranean World* (New York, 1955).

Macfarlane, Alan, *The Savage Wars of Peace: England, Japan, and the Malthusian Trap* (New York, 2003).

Maddison, Angus, *Chinese Economic Performance in the Long Run* (Paris, 1998)., *The World Economy: A Millennial Perspective* (Paris, 2001).

McEvedy, Colin and Richard Jones, *Atlas of World Population* (New York, 1978).

McNeill, William, "The Eccentricity of Wheels or Eurasian Transportation in Historical Perspective," *American Historical Review* 92, #5 (Dec. 1987), 1111–26.

Milward, Alan S., *The Reconstruction of Western Europe, 1945–51* (Berkeley, CA, 1984).

Neal, Larry and Jeffrey Williamson, *The Cambridge History of Capitalism*, 2 vols. (Cambridge, 2014).

Nef, John U., *The Conquest of the Material World* (Chicago, 1964).

Orlov, Dmitry, *Reinventing Collapse: The Soviet Example and American Prospects* (Gabriola I., BC, 2008).

Parry, J.H., *The Age of Reconnaissance: Discovery, Exploration, and Settlement, 1450-1650* (London, 1963).

Raymond, Robert, *Out of the Fiery Furnace: The Impact of Metals on the History of Mankind* (University Park, PA, 1984).

Samuelson, Paul A., *Economics*, Tenth Edition (New York, 1976).

Scheidel, Walter, Ian Morris, and Richard Saller, eds., *The Cambridge Economic History of the Greco-Roman World* (Cambridge, 2007).

Scheidel, Walter and Sitta von Reden, eds., *The Ancient Economy* (New York, 2002).

Suny, Ronald Gregor, ed., *The Cambridge History of Russia*, vol. III: The Twentieth Century (Cambridge, 2006).

Toniolo, Gianni, with the assistance of Piet Clement, *Central Bank Cooperation at the Bank for International Settlements, 1930–1973* (Cambridge, 2005).

Williams, Jonathan, ed., *Money: A History* (New York, 1997).

Wong, R. Bin, *China Transformed: Historical Change and the Limits of European Expansion* (Ithaca, NY, 1997).

Printed in the United States
By Bookmasters